westermann

CAMDEN TOWN

Oberstufe

Arbeitsheft zu den
Pflichtmaterialien

Erarbeitet von

Svenja Alpen-Kühne
Anne-Kathrin Böker
Svenja Kelly
Ilka Kratz

Abkürzungen:

AE	American English	*infml.*	informal
BE	British English	*pl.*	plural
e.g.	exempli gratia (Latin) = for example	*sb*	somebody
i.e.	id est (Latin) = that is	*sth*	something

Webcodes
Auf manchen Seiten findest du Webcodes, die dich zu zusätzlichen Materialien im Internet führen. Gib dazu einfach den Code auf www.westermann.de/webcode ins Suchfeld ein.

Filmauszüge
Je nach Abspielgerät und verwendeter Software kann es vorkommen, dass die Zeitangaben zu den Filmauszügen nicht exakt mit den im Kapitel angegebenen übereinstimmen.

Behold the Dreamers
Die Verweise zu *Behold the Dreamers* beziehen sich auf die Ausgabe: Imbolo Mbue, *Behold the Dreamers*, Westermann 2024, ISBN: 978-3-425-73073-8.

seven methods of killing kylie jenner
Die Verweise zu *seven methods of killing kylie jenner* beziehen sich auf diese Ausgabe, die bei Westermann erhältlich ist: Jasmine Lee-Jones, *seven methods of killing kylie jenner*, ISBN: 978-3-425-73070-7. Kostenlose Annotationen finden sich auf www.westermann.de.

Verweise auf *Skills pages* und *Workshops*
Die Verweise auf *Skills pages* und *Workshops* beziehen sich auf das Schulbuch *Camden Town Oberstufe Qualifikationsphase Niedersachsen*, ISBN: 978-3-425-73642-6.

© 2024 Westermann Bildungsmedien Verlag GmbH, Georg-Westermann-Allee 66, 38104 Braunschweig
www.westermann.de

Das Werk und seine Teile sind urheberrechtlich geschützt. Jede Nutzung in anderen als den gesetzlich zugelassenen bzw. vertraglich zugestandenen Fällen bedarf der vorherigen schriftlichen Einwilligung des Verlages.
Nähere Informationen zur vertraglich gestatteten Anzahl von Kopien finden Sie auf www.schulbuchkopie.de.
Für Verweise (Links) auf Internet-Adressen gilt folgender Haftungshinweis: Trotz sorgfältiger inhaltlicher Kontrolle wird die Haftung für die Inhalte der externen Seiten ausgeschlossen. Für den Inhalt dieser externen Seiten sind ausschließlich deren Betreiber verantwortlich. Sollten Sie daher auf kostenpflichtige, illegale oder anstößige Inhalte treffen, so bedauern wir dies ausdrücklich und bitten Sie, uns umgehend per E-Mail davon in Kenntnis zu setzen, damit beim Nachdruck der Verweis gelöscht wird.

Druck A[1] / Jahr 2024
Alle Drucke der Serie A sind im Unterricht parallel verwendbar.

Redaktion: Isabel Klein, Schönau
Umschlaggestaltung: Gingco.Net Werbeagentur GmbH & Co. KG, Braunschweig
Layout: Visuelle Lebensfreude, Hannover; thom bahr GRAFIK, Mainz
Druck und Bindung: Westermann Druck GmbH, Georg-Westermann-Allee 66, 38104 Braunschweig

ISBN 978-3-425-**73698**-3

Contents

			Abiturvorgaben / Themen
Part 1	**Short stories**		
6	Short stories	Pre-reading While reading Post-reading	Kurzgeschichte: Charlotte Perkins Gilman, "The Yellow Wallpaper" (1892)
18		Pre-reading While reading Post-reading	Kurzgeschichte: Kate Chopin, "The Story of an Hour" (1894)
21		Pre-reading While reading Post-reading	Kurzgeschichte: Fay Weldon, "Weekend" (1978)
32		Pre-reading While reading Post-reading	Kurzgeschichte: Bernardine Evaristo, "The First Feminists" (2020)
36	Post-reading	The short stories	The individual and society Questions of identity Gender issues
38	Topic	**The individual and society** Questions of identity – Ambitions and obstacles Questions of identity – Conformity vs. individualism Chances and challenges for society – Gender issues	The individual and society Questions of identity: ambitions and obstacles, conformity vs. individualism Chances and challenges for society: gender issues
45		**The individual and society – Questions of identity and gender issues in the short stories**	
Part 2	**Behold the Dreamers**		
46	Novel	Pre-reading	Roman: Imbolo Mbue, *Behold the Dreamers* (2016)
47		While reading	
54		Post-reading	
60	Topic	**The American Dream: Freedom, equality and the pursuit of happiness**	Politics, culture, society – between tradition and change (USA) From past to present: American ideals and realities – freedom, equality and the pursuit of happiness
63		**Freedom, equality and the pursuit of happiness in *Behold the Dreamers***	
64		**Questions of identity**	Politics, culture, society – between tradition and change (USA) Current issues: questions of identity
64		**Identity in *Behold the Dreamers***	
64		**The financial crisis**	Politics, culture, society – between tradition and change (USA) Current issues: political, cultural and social developments
67		**The financial crisis in *Behold the Dreamers***	
67		**Political, cultural and social developments**	Politics, culture, society – between tradition and change (USA) Current issues: political, cultural and social developments
73		**Political, cultural and social issues in *Behold the Dreamers***	

Contents

			Abiturvorgaben / Themen
Part 3		**seven methods of killing kylie jenner**	
74	Play	Pre-reading	Kurzdrama: Jasmine Lee-Jones, *seven methods of killing kylie jenner* (2019, Neubearbeitung 2021)
77		While reading	
83		Post-reading: Relationships Characterization Illustrations and graphic layout of the play's script Putting the play on stage VIPs Body images Elements and structure of a play Identities Stating your opinion Reviews	
89	Topic	The changing media landscape: traditional and modern media	The media The changing media landscape: traditional and modern media
90		The impact of the media on the individual and society Stereotypes and images of black female identity Looking back at the play	The media The impact of the media on the individual and society: information, entertainment, manipulation
Part 4		**A Midsummer Night's Dream**	
97	Play	Pre-reading	Shakespeare: The world that made him Drama: Auszüge aus: William Shakespeare, *A Midsummer Night's Dream* (ca. 1595 / 1596)
100		While reading: Act I	
111		While reading: Act II	
121		While reading: Act III	
130		While reading: Act IV	
135		While reading: Act V	
141		Post-reading	
142	Film	Pre-viewing While viewing Post-viewing	Film: Michael Hoffman (Regie), *A Midsummer Night's Dream* (1999) Shakespeare: Modern adaptations
146	Topic	Questions of identity Ambitions and obstacles, conformity vs. individualism	The individual and society Questions of identity: ambitions and obstacles, conformity vs. individualism
149		Questions of identity in *A Midsummer Night's Dream*	
152		Chances and challenges for society: gender issues	The individual and society Chances and challenges for society: gender issues
154		Gender issues in *A Midsummer Night's Dream*	

Introduction

Liebe Schülerin, lieber Schüler,
mit diesem Arbeitsheft kannst du dich ideal auf das Abitur vorbereiten. Du beschäftigst dich mit allen Texten und dem Film, die für das Abitur vorgeschrieben sind, und außerdem mit weiteren abiturrelevanten Themen.

Für das schriftliche Abitur 2026 müssen die folgenden Materialien unter den genannten inhaltlichen Gesichtspunkten behandelt werden:

Kurzprosa:
Charlotte Perkins Gilman, "The Yellow Wallpaper" (1892)
Kate Chopin, "The Story of an Hour" (1894)
Fay Weldon, "Weekend" (1978)
Bernardine Evaristo, "The First Feminists" (2020)
→ Themenfeldbezug: The individual and society
- Questions of identity: ambitions and obstacles, conformity vs. individualism
- Chances and challenges for society: gender issues

Roman:
Imbolo Mbue, *Behold the Dreamers* (2016)
→ Themenfeldbezug: Politics, culture, society – between tradition and change (Bezugskultur: USA)
- From past to present: American ideals and realities – freedom, equality and the pursuit of happiness
- Current issues: questions of identity, political, cultural and social developments

Kurzdrama:
Jasmine Lee-Jones, *seven methods of killing kylie jenner* (2019, Neubearbeitung 2021)
→ Themenfeldbezug: The media
- The changing media landscape: traditional and modern media
- The impact of the media on the individual and society: information, entertainment, manipulation

Drama:
Auszüge aus: William Shakespeare, *A Midsummer Night's Dream* (ca. 1595/1596)
Film:
Michael Hoffman (Regie), *A Midsummer Night's Dream* (1999)
→ Themenfeldbezug: The individual and society
- Questions of identity: ambitions and obstacles, conformity vs. individualism
- Chances and challenges for society: gender issues

Aufbau des Arbeitsheftes

In jedem Kapitel erfolgt zunächst eine inhaltliche Sicherung und allgemeine Bearbeitung der jeweiligen Materialien. Auf speziell ausgewiesenen *Topic*-Seiten werden die Themenfeldbezüge generell eingeführt, bevor sie im Kontext der jeweiligen Materialien noch einmal vertieft werden. Wo es sich anbietet, werden auch weitere Themen aus dem Lehrplan (Kerncurriculum) aufgegriffen.

An vielen Stellen findest du Verweise auf *Skills pages* und *Workshops* im Schulbuch *Camden Town Oberstufe Qualifikationsphase* (ISBN: 978-3-425-73642-6). Die *Skills pages* geben dir Hilfestellungen zu wichtigen Aufgabenformaten. In den *Workshops* werden bestimmte Kompetenzen intensiv trainiert. Im Schulbuch werden außerdem weitere Aspekte der Themen dieses Arbeitsheftes behandelt.

Short stories — The Yellow Wallpaper

The Yellow Wallpaper – A short story (1892)

PRE-READING

1
Research information about the author Charlotte Perkins Gilman on the Internet.

2
a) Look at the painting below. Try to make predictions and speculate about the content of the short story. Consider the information you found about the author.

Edvard Munch: *The Girl by the Window* (1893)

_____

_____

_____

_____

_____

_____

b) **Pair work** Exchange your ideas with a partner.
c) Present your ideas to the class.

The Yellow Wallpaper

by Charlotte Perkins Gilman

It is very seldom that mere ordinary people like John and myself secure ancestral[1] halls for the summer.

A colonial mansion, a hereditary estate, I would say a haunted house, and reach the height of romantic felicity[2] – but that would be asking too much of fate!

Still I will proudly declare that there is something queer[3] about it.

Else, why should it be let so cheaply? And why have stood so long untenanted[4]?

John laughs at me, of course, but one expects that in marriage.

John is practical in the extreme. He has no patience with faith, an intense horror of superstition, and he scoffs[5] openly at any talk of things not to be felt and seen and put down in figures.

John is a physician, and *perhaps* – (I would not say it to a living soul, of course, but this is dead paper and a great relief to my mind) – *perhaps* that is one reason I do not get well faster.

You see he does not believe I am sick!

And what can one do?

If a physician of high standing, and one's own husband, assures friends and relatives that there is really nothing the matter with one but temporary nervous depression – a slight hysterical tendency – what is one to do?

My brother is also a physician, and also of high standing, and he says the same thing.

So I take phosphates or phosphites – whichever it is, and tonics[6], and journeys, and air, and exercise, and am absolutely forbidden to "work" until I am well again.

Personally, I disagree with their ideas.

Personally, I believe that congenial[7] work, with excitement and change, would do me good.

But what is one to do?

I did write for a while in spite of them; but it *does* exhaust me a good deal – having to be so sly[8] about it, or else meet with heavy opposition.

I sometimes fancy that in my condition if I had less opposition and more society and stimulus – but John says the very worst thing I can do is to think about my condition, and I confess it always makes me feel bad.

So I will let it alone and talk about the house.

The most beautiful place! It is quite alone, standing well back from the road, quite three miles from the village. It makes me think of English places that you read about, for there are hedges and walls and gates that lock, and lots of separate little houses for the gardeners and people.

There is a *delicious* garden! I never saw such a garden – large and shady, full of box[9]-bordered paths, and lined with long grape[10]-covered arbors[11] with seats under them.

There were greenhouses, too, but they are all broken now.

There was some legal trouble, I believe, something about the heirs and co-heirs; anyhow, the place has been empty for years.

That spoils my ghostliness[12], I am afraid, but I don't care – there is something strange about the house – I can feel it.

I even said so to John one moonlight evening, but he said what I felt was a *draught*[13], and shut the window.

I get unreasonably angry with John sometimes. I'm sure I never used to be so sensitive. I think it is due to this nervous condition.

But John says if I feel so, I shall neglect proper self-control; so I take pains to control myself – before him, at least, and that makes me very tired.

I don't like our room a bit. I wanted one downstairs that opened on the piazza and had roses all over the window, and such pretty old-fashioned chintz hangings[14]! But John would not hear of it.

He said there was only one window and not room for two beds, and no near room for him if he took another.

He is very careful and loving, and hardly lets me stir without special direction.

I have a schedule prescription for each hour in the day; he takes all care from me, and so I feel basely ungrateful not to value it more.

He said we came here solely on my account, that I was to have perfect rest and all the air I could get. "Your exercise depends on your strength, my dear," said he, "and your food somewhat on your appetite; but air you can absorb all the time." So we took the nursery[15] at the top of the house.

Annotations

1. **ancestral** = relating to a person's family from the past
2. **felicity** = happiness, luck
3. **queer** = *here*: strange, suspicious
4. **untenanted** = not being inhabited or rented
5. **to scoff** = to speak about sth in a way that shows you think it's stupid
6. **tonic** = a liquid medicine that makes you feel better
7. **congenial** = pleasant, enjoyable
8. **sly** = dishonest, clever at deceiving people
9. **box** = *Buchs(baum)*
10. **grape** = *Weintraube*
11. **arbor** (AE) = *Laube*
12. **ghostliness** = the quality of being pale and transparent or seeming unreal
13. **draught** (BE) = a current of cold air
14. **chintz hangings** = large, slightly shiny pieces of cloth with flowery patterns that are put on a wall for decoration
15. **nursery** = a room in a family home where small children sleep or play

Short stories — The Yellow Wallpaper

It is a big, airy room, the whole floor nearly, with windows that look all ways, and air and sunshine galore[16].

It was nursery first and then playroom and gymnasium[17], I should judge; for the windows are barred for little children, and there are rings and things in the walls.

The paint and paper look as if a boys' school had used it. It is stripped off – the paper – in great patches all around the head of my bed, about as far as I can reach, and in a great place on the other side of the room low down. I never saw a worse paper in my life.

One of those sprawling[18] flamboyant[19] patterns committing every artistic sin.

It is dull enough to confuse the eye in following, pronounced enough to constantly irritate and provoke study, and when you follow the lame uncertain curves for a little distance they suddenly commit suicide – plunge[20] off at outrageous angles, destroy themselves in unheard of contradictions.

The color is repellant[21], almost revolting; a smouldering[22] unclean yellow, strangely faded by the slow-turning sunlight.

It is a dull yet lurid[23] orange in some places, a sickly sulphur[24] tint[25] in others.

No wonder the children hated it! I should hate it myself if I had to live in this room long.

There comes John, and I must put this away – he hates to have me write a word.

...

We have been here two weeks, and I haven't felt like writing before, since that first day.

I am sitting by the window now, up in this atrocious[26] nursery, and there is nothing to hinder my writing as much as I please, save lack of strength.

John is away all day, and even some nights when his cases are serious.

I am glad my case is not serious!

But these nervous troubles are dreadfully depressing.

John does not know how much I really suffer. He knows there is no *reason* to suffer, and that satisfies him.

Of course it is only nervousness. It does weigh on me so not to do my duty in any way!

I meant to be such a help to John, such a real rest and comfort, and here I am a comparative burden already! Nobody would believe what an effort it is to do what little I am able – to dress and entertain, and order things.

It is fortunate Mary is so good with the baby. Such a dear baby!

And yet I *cannot* be with him, it makes me so nervous.

I suppose John never was nervous in his life. He laughs at me so about this wallpaper!

At first he meant to repaper the room, but afterwards he said that I was letting it get the better of me, and that nothing was worse for a nervous patient than to give way to such fancies.

He said that after the wallpaper was changed it would be the heavy bedstead[27], and then the barred windows, and then that gate at the head of the stairs, and so on.

"You know the place is doing you good," he said, "and really, dear, I don't care to renovate the house just for a three months' rental."

"Then do let us go downstairs," I said, "there are such pretty rooms there."

Then he took me in his arms and called me a blessed little goose, and said he would go down cellar, if I wished, and have it whitewashed[28] into the bargain[29].

But he is right enough about the beds and windows and things.

It is as airy and comfortable a room as any one need wish, and, of course, I would not be so silly as to make him uncomfortable just for a whim[30].

I'm really getting quite fond of the big room, all but that horrid paper.

Out of one window I can see the garden, those mysterious deep-shaded arbors, the riotous[31] old-fashioned flowers, and bushes and gnarly[32] trees.

Out of another I get a lovely view of the bay and a little private wharf[33] belonging to the estate. There is a beautiful shaded lane that runs down there from the house. I always fancy I see people walking in these numerous paths and arbors, but John has cautioned me not to give way to fancy in the least. He says that with my imaginative power and habit of story-making, a nervous weakness like mine is sure to lead to all manner of excited fancies, and that I ought to use my will and good sense to check the tendency. So I try.

Annotations
[16] **galore** = in great numbers or quantity
[17] **gymnasium** = a large room equipped for sports and physical training
[18] **sprawling** = spreading out, reaching across a large area
[19] **flamboyant** = noticeable, brightly coloured
[20] to **plunge** = to fall or move suddenly
[21] **repellant** = causing disgust or strong dislike
[22] **smouldering** (BE) = burning slowly without flames
[23] **lurid** = too brightly coloured
[24] **sulphur** (BE) = *Schwefel*
[25] **tint** = a shade of a colour
[26] **atrocious** = very bad, horrible
[27] **bedstead** = the framework of a bed
[28] to **whitewash** = to paint walls white
[29] **into the bargain** = additionally
[30] **whim** = a sudden idea or wish
[31] **riotous** = wild or very colourful
[32] **gnarly** = rough and twisted, strangely shaped (usually because sth is old)
[33] **wharf** = a platform built beside a river or the sea where ships can be tied

I think sometimes that if I were only well enough to write a little it would relieve the press of ideas and rest me.

But I find I get pretty tired when I try.

It is so discouraging not to have any advice and companionship about my work. When I get really well, John says we will ask Cousin Henry and Julia down for a long visit; but he says he would as soon put fireworks in my pillow-case as to let me have those stimulating people about now.

I wish I could get well faster.

But I must not think about that. This paper looks to me as if it *knew* what a vicious[34] influence it had!

There is a recurrent spot where the pattern lolls[35] like a broken neck and two bulbous[36] eyes stare at you upside down.

I get positively angry with the impertinence of it and the everlastingness[37]. Up and down and sideways they crawl, and those absurd, unblinking eyes are everywhere. There is one place where two breadths[38] didn't match, and the eyes go all up and down the line, one a little higher than the other.

I never saw so much expression in an inanimate[39] thing before, and we all know how much expression they have! I used to lie awake as a child and get more entertainment and terror out of blank walls and plain furniture than most children could find in a toy-store.

I remember what a kindly wink the knobs[40] of our big, old bureau[41] used to have, and there was one chair that always seemed like a strong friend.

I used to feel that if any of the other things looked too fierce I could always hop into that chair and be safe.

The furniture in this room is no worse than inharmonious[42], however, for we had to bring it all from downstairs. I suppose when this was used as a playroom they had to take the nursery things out, and no wonder! I never saw such ravages[43] as the children have made here. The wallpaper, as I said before, is torn off in spots, and it sticketh closer than a brother[44] – they must have had perseverance as well as hatred.

Then the floor is scratched and gouged[45] and splintered, the plaster itself is dug out here and there, and this great heavy bed, which is all we found in the room, looks as if it had been through the wars.

But I don't mind it a bit – only the paper.

There comes John's sister. Such a dear girl as she is, and so careful of me! I must not let her find me writing.

She is a perfect and enthusiastic housekeeper, and hopes for no better profession. I verily[46] believe she thinks it is the writing which made me sick!

But I can write when she is out, and see her a long way off from these windows.

There is one that commands the road, a lovely shaded winding road, and one that just looks off over the country. A lovely country, too, full of great elms[47] and velvet meadows.

This wallpaper has a kind of sub-pattern in a different shade, a particularly irritating one, for you can only see it in certain lights, and not clearly then.

But in the places where it isn't faded and where the sun is just so – I can see a strange, provoking, formless sort of figure, that seems to skulk[48] about behind that silly and conspicuous front design.

There's sister on the stairs!

...

Well, the Fourth of July is over! The people are all gone and I am tired out. John thought it might do me good to see a little company, so we just had mother and Nellie and the children down for a week.

Of course I didn't do a thing. Jennie sees to everything now.

But it tired me all the same.

John says if I don't pick up faster he shall send me to Weir Mitchell in the fall.

But I don't want to go there at all. I had a friend who was in his hands once, and she says he is just like John and my brother, only more so!

Besides, it is such an undertaking to go so far.

I don't feel as if it was worth while to turn my hand over for anything, and I'm getting dreadfully fretful[49] and querulous[50].

I cry at nothing, and cry most of the time.

Of course I don't when John is here, or anybody else, but when I am alone.

And I am alone a good deal just now. John is kept in town very often by serious cases, and Jennie is good and lets me alone when I want her to.

---

[34] **vicious** = bad, evil, harmful
[35] to **loll** = to hang loosely
[36] **bulbous** = bulging, round and fat (in a rather ugly way)
[37] **everlastingness** = lasting forever, eternity
[38] **breadth** = the distance from side to side
[39] **inanimate** = lifeless
[40] **knob** = a round handle
[41] **bureau** = *(AE)* a chest of drawers; *(BE)* a writing desk with drawers and a lid
[42] **inharmonious** = not harmonious, unpleasant
[43] **ravage** = damage or destruction
[44] **sticketh closer than a brother** = reference to the Bible (Proverbs 18:24): implying a deep relationship or strong commitment
[45] to **gouge** = to make a hole or a long cut in sth, usually in a rough or violent way
[46] **verily** = truly
[47] **elm** = *Ulme (Laubbaum)*
[48] to **skulk** = to hide or move around quietly
[49] **fretful** = uncomfortable, irritable or upset
[50] **querulous** = complaining a lot

So I walk a little in the garden or down that lovely lane, sit on the porch under the roses, and lie down up here a good deal.

255 I'm getting really fond of the room in spite of the wallpaper. Perhaps *because* of the wallpaper.

It dwells in my mind so!

I lie here on this great immovable bed – it is nailed down, I believe – and follow that pattern about by the hour. It 260 is as good as gymnastics, I assure you. I start, we'll say, at the bottom, down in the corner over there where it has not been touched, and I determine for the thousandth time that I *will* follow that pointless pattern to some sort of a conclusion.

265 I know a little of the principle of design, and I know this thing was not arranged on any laws of radiation[51], or alternation, or repetition, or symmetry, or anything else that I ever heard of.

It is repeated, of course, by the breadths, but not 270 otherwise.

Looked at in one way each breadth stands alone, the bloated curves and flourishes – a kind of "debased[52] Romanesque[53]" with *delirium tremens*[54] – go waddling[55] up and down in isolated columns of fatuity[56].

275 But, on the other hand, they connect diagonally, and the sprawling outlines run off in great slanting waves of optic horror, like a lot of wallowing sea-weeds[57] in full chase.

The whole thing goes horizontally, too, at least it seems 280 so, and I exhaust myself in trying to distinguish the order of its going in that direction.

They have used a horizontal breadth for a frieze[58], and that adds wonderfully to the confusion.

There is one end of the room where it is almost intact, 285 and there, when the crosslights fade and the low sun shines directly upon it, I can almost fancy radiation after all – the interminable grotesques seem to form around a common centre and rush off in headlong plunges[59] of equal distraction.

290 It makes me tired to follow it. I will take a nap I guess.

. . .

I don't know why I should write this.

I don't want to.

I don't feel able.

And I know John would think it absurd. But I *must* say 295 what I feel and think in some way – it is such a relief!

But the effort is getting to be greater than the relief.

Half the time now I am awfully lazy, and lie down ever so much.

John says I mustn't lose my strength, and has me take 300 cod liver oil[60] and lots of tonics and things, to say nothing of ale and wine and rare meat.

Dear John! He loves me very dearly, and hates to have me sick. I tried to have a real earnest reasonable talk with him the other day, and tell him how I wish he would let 305 me go and make a visit to Cousin Henry and Julia.

But he said I wasn't able to go, nor able to stand it after I got there; and I did not make out a very good case for myself, for I was crying before I had finished.

It is getting to be a great effort for me to think straight. 310 Just this nervous weakness I suppose.

And dear John gathered me up in his arms, and just carried me upstairs and laid me on the bed, and sat by me and read to me till it tired my head.

He said I was his darling and his comfort and all he had, 315 and that I must take care of myself for his sake, and keep well.

He says no one but myself can help me out of it, that I must use my will and self-control and not let any silly fancies run away with me.

320 There's one comfort, the baby is well and happy, and does not have to occupy this nursery with the horrid wallpaper.

If we had not used it, that blessed child would have! What a fortunate escape! Why, I wouldn't have a child of 325 mine, an impressionable little thing, live in such a room for worlds.

I never thought of it before, but it is lucky that John kept me here after all, I can stand it so much easier than a baby, you see.

330 Of course I never mention it to them any more – I am too wise – but I keep watch of it all the same.

There are things in that paper that nobody knows but me, or ever will.

Behind that outside pattern the dim shapes get clearer 335 every day.

It is always the same shape, only very numerous.

And it is like a woman stooping down and creeping about behind that pattern. I don't like it a bit. I wonder – I begin to think – I wish John would take me away from here!

. . .

Annotations
[51] **radiation** = spreading from a central point
[52] **debased** = worse, less valuable
[53] **Romanesque** = an architectural style in western and southern Europe around the 11th century employing curves and rounded arches
[54] ***delirium tremens*** = a physical condition in which sb shakes and sees imaginary things (often resulting from alcoholism)
[55] to **waddle** = to walk with short steps
[56] **fatuity** = stupidity, foolishness
[57] **seaweed** = a plant that grows in or close to the sea
[58] **frieze** = a piece of decoration along a wall
[59] **plunge** = a sudden movement or fall

[60] **cod liver oil** = *Lebertran*

It is so hard to talk with John about my case, because he is so wise, and because he loves me so.

But I tried it last night.

It was moonlight. The moon shines in all around just as the sun does.

I hate to see it sometimes, it creeps so slowly, and always comes in by one window or another.

John was asleep and I hated to waken him, so I kept still and watched the moonlight on that undulating[61] wallpaper till I felt creepy.

The faint figure behind seemed to shake the pattern, just as if she wanted to get out.

I got up softly and went to feel and see if the paper *did* move, and when I came back John was awake.

"What is it, little girl?" he said. "Don't go walking about like that – you'll get cold."

I thought it was a good time to talk, so I told him that I really was not gaining here, and that I wished he would take me away.

"Why, darling!" said he, "our lease[62] will be up in three weeks, and I can't see how to leave before.

"The repairs are not done at home, and I cannot possibly leave town just now. Of course if you were in any danger, I could and would, but you really are better, dear, whether you can see it or not. I am a doctor, dear, and I know. You are gaining flesh and color, your appetite is better, I feel really much easier about you."

"I don't weigh a bit more," said I, "nor as much; and my appetite may be better in the evening when you are here, but it is worse in the morning when you are away!"

"Bless her little heart!" said he with a big hug, "she shall be as sick as she pleases! But now let's improve the shining hours by going to sleep, and talk about it in the morning!"

"And you won't go away?" I asked gloomily[63].

"Why, how can I, dear? It is only three weeks more and then we will take a nice little trip of a few days while Jennie is getting the house ready. Really, dear, you are better!"

"Better in body perhaps –" I began, and stopped short, for he sat up straight and looked at me with such a stern[64], reproachful[65] look that I could not say another word.

"My darling," said he, "I beg of you, for my sake and for our child's sake, as well as for your own, that you will never for one instant let that idea enter your mind! There is nothing so dangerous, so fascinating, to a temperament like yours. It is a false and foolish fancy. Can you not trust me as a physician when I tell you so?"

So of course I said no more on that score[66], and we went to sleep before long. He thought I was asleep first, but I wasn't, and lay there for hours trying to decide whether that front pattern and the back pattern really did move together or separately.

...

On a pattern like this, by daylight, there is a lack of sequence, a defiance[67] of law, that is a constant irritant to a normal mind.

The color is hideous[68] enough, and unreliable enough, and infuriating enough, but the pattern is torturing.

You think you have mastered it, but just as you get well underway in following, it turns a back-somersault[69] and there you are. It slaps you in the face, knocks you down, and tramples upon you. It is like a bad dream.

The outside pattern is a florid[70] arabesque[71], reminding one of a fungus[72]. If you can imagine a toadstool[73] in joints, an interminable[74] string of toadstools, budding and sprouting in endless convolutions[75] – why, that is something like it.

That is, sometimes!

There is one marked peculiarity about this paper, a thing nobody seems to notice but myself, and that is that it changes as the light changes.

When the sun shoots in through the east window – I always watch for that first long, straight ray – it changes so quickly that I never can quite believe it.

That is why I watch it always.

By moonlight – the moon shines in all night when there is a moon – I wouldn't know it was the same paper.

At night in any kind of light, in twilight, candlelight, lamplight, and worst of all by moonlight, it becomes bars! The outside pattern, I mean, and the woman behind it is as plain as can be.

I didn't realize for a long time what the thing was that showed behind, that dim sub-pattern, but now I am quite sure it is a woman.

By daylight she is subdued[76], quiet. I fancy it is the pattern that keeps her so still. It is so puzzling. It keeps me quiet by the hour.

---

[61] **undulating** = moving in waves or having the shape of waves
[62] **lease** = a contract by which facilities are rented for a specified period of time
[63] **gloomy** = unhappy and hopeless
[64] **stern** = severe, serious and strict
[65] **reproachful** = expressing criticism
[66] **on that score** = concerning this matter
[67] **defiance** = resistance or disregard
[68] **hideous** = extremely ugly or horrible
[69] **somersault** = an acrobatic movement in which you perform a roll in the air
[70] **florid** = excessively ornamented, flowery
[71] **arabesque** = a decorative pattern, a design of flowing lines
[72] **fungus** = *Pilz*
[73] **toadstool** = *Giftpilz*
[74] **interminable** = endless
[75] **convolution** = twist
[76] **subdued** = quiet and sad or worried

Short stories — The Yellow Wallpaper

I lie down ever so much now. John says it is good for me, and to sleep all I can.

Indeed he started the habit by making me lie down for an hour after each meal.

It is a very bad habit, I am convinced, for you see I don't sleep.

And that cultivates[77] deceit[78], for I don't tell them I'm awake – O no!

The fact is I am getting a little afraid of John.

He seems very queer[79] sometimes, and even Jennie has an inexplicable[80] look.

It strikes me occasionally, just as a scientific hypothesis, that perhaps it is the paper!

I have watched John when he did not know I was looking, and come into the room suddenly on the most innocent excuses, and I've caught him several times *looking at the paper!* And Jennie too. I caught Jennie with her hand on it once.

She didn't know I was in the room, and when I asked her in a quiet, a very quiet voice, with the most restrained[81] manner possible, what she was doing with the paper – she turned around as if she had been caught stealing, and looked quite angry – asked me why I should frighten her so!

Then she said that the paper stained everything it touched, that she had found yellow smooches[82] on all my clothes and John's, and she wished we would be more careful!

Did not that sound innocent? But I know she was studying that pattern, and I am determined that nobody shall find it out but myself!

...

Life is very much more exciting now than it used to be. You see I have something more to expect, to look forward to, to watch. I really do eat better, and am more quiet than I was.

John is so pleased to see me improve! He laughed a little the other day, and said I seemed to be flourishing in spite of my wallpaper.

I turned it off with a laugh. I had no intention of telling him it was *because* of the wallpaper – he would make fun of me. He might even want to take me away.

I don't want to leave now until I have found it out. There is a week more, and I think that will be enough.

...

I'm feeling ever so much better! I don't sleep much at night, for it is so interesting to watch developments; but I sleep a good deal in the daytime.

In the daytime it is tiresome and perplexing.

There are always new shoots on the fungus, and new shades of yellow all over it. I cannot keep count of them, though I have tried conscientiously[83].

It is the strangest yellow, that wallpaper! It makes me think of all the yellow things I ever saw – not beautiful ones like buttercups, but old foul, bad yellow things.

But there is something else about that paper – the smell! I noticed it the moment we came into the room, but with so much air and sun it was not bad. Now we have had a week of fog and rain, and whether the windows are open or not, the smell is here.

It creeps all over the house.

I find it hovering[84] in the dining-room, skulking[85] in the parlor, hiding in the hall, lying in wait for me on the stairs.

It gets into my hair.

Even when I go to ride, if I turn my head suddenly and surprise it – there is that smell!

Such a peculiar odor, too! I have spent hours in trying to analyze it, to find what it smelled like.

It is not bad – at first, and very gentle, but quite the subtlest[86], most enduring odor I ever met.

In this damp weather it is awful, I wake up in the night and find it hanging over me.

It used to disturb me at first. I thought seriously of burning the house – to reach the smell.

But now I am used to it. The only thing I can think of that it is like is the *color* of the paper! A yellow smell.

There is a very funny mark on this wall, low down, near the mopboard[87]. A streak[88] that runs round the room. It goes behind every piece of furniture, except the bed, a long, straight, even *smooch*[89], as if it had been rubbed over and over.

I wonder how it was done and who did it, and what they did it for. Round and round and round – round and round and round – it makes me dizzy!

...

I really have discovered something at last.

Through watching so much at night, when it changes so, I have finally found out.

Annotations

[77] to **cultivate** = to foster, to encourage
[78] **deceit** = deception, fraud
[79] **queer** = *here*: strange, suspicious
[80] **inexplicable** = unable to be explained or understood
[81] **restrained** = calm and controlled
[82] **smooch** = kiss; *here*: smudge
[83] **conscientious** = very careful, with a lot of effort
[84] to **hover** = to stay in one place in the air
[85] to **skulk** = to hide or move around quietly
[86] **subtle** = not immediately noticeable
[87] **mopboard** (AE) = *Sockelleiste*
[88] **streak** = a long stripe or mark
[89] **smooch** = kiss; *here*: smudge

The front pattern *does* move – and no wonder! The woman behind shakes it!

Sometimes I think there are a great many women behind, and sometimes only one, and she crawls around fast, and her crawling shakes it all over.

Then in the very bright spots she keeps still, and in the very shady spots she just takes hold of the bars and shakes them hard.

And she is all the time trying to climb through. But nobody could climb through that pattern – it strangles[90] so; I think that is why it has so many heads.

They get through, and then the pattern strangles them off and turns them upside down, and makes their eyes white!

If those heads were covered or taken off it would not be half so bad.

. . .

I think that woman gets out in the daytime!

And I'll tell you why – privately – I've seen her!

I can see her out of every one of my windows!

It is the same woman, I know, for she is always creeping, and most women do not creep by daylight.

I see her in that long shaded lane, creeping up and down. I see her in those dark grape arbors, creeping all around the garden.

I see her on that long road under the trees, creeping along, and when a carriage comes she hides under the blackberry vines.

I don't blame her a bit. It must be very humiliating to be caught creeping by daylight!

I always lock the door when I creep by daylight. I can't do it at night, for I know John would suspect something at once.

And John is so queer now, that I don't want to irritate him. I wish he would take another room! Besides, I don't want anybody to get that woman out at night but myself.

I often wonder if I could see her out of all the windows at once.

But, turn as fast as I can, I can only see out of one at one time.

And though I always see her, she *may* be able to creep faster than I can turn!

I have watched her sometimes away off in the open country, creeping as fast as a cloud shadow in a high wind.

. . .

If only that top pattern could be gotten off from the under one! I mean to try it, little by little.

I have found out another funny thing, but I shan't[91] tell it this time! It does not do to trust people too much.

There are only two more days to get this paper off, and I believe John is beginning to notice. I don't like the look in his eyes.

And I heard him ask Jennie a lot of professional questions about me. She had a very good report to give.

She said I slept a good deal in the daytime.

John knows I don't sleep very well at night, for all I'm so quiet!

He asked me all sorts of questions, too, and pretended to be very loving and kind.

As if I couldn't see through him!

Still, I don't wonder he acts so, sleeping under this paper for three months.

It only interests me, but I feel sure John and Jennie are secretly affected by it.

. . .

Hurrah! This is the last day, but it is enough. John had to stay in town over night, and won't be out until this evening.

Jennie wanted to sleep with me – the sly[92] thing! – but I told her I should undoubtedly rest better for a night all alone.

That was clever, for really I wasn't alone a bit! As soon as it was moonlight and that poor thing began to crawl and shake the pattern, I got up and ran to help her.

I pulled and she shook, I shook and she pulled, and before morning we had peeled off yards of that paper.

A strip about as high as my head and half around the room.

And then when the sun came and that awful pattern began to laugh at me, I declared I would finish it to-day!

We go away to-morrow, and they are moving all my furniture down again to leave things as they were before.

Jennie looked at the wall in amazement, but I told her merrily[93] that I did it out of pure spite[94] at the vicious thing.

She laughed and said she wouldn't mind doing it herself, but I must not get tired.

How she betrayed herself that time!

But I am here, and no person touches this paper but me – not *alive*!

---

[90] to **strangle** = to choke, to suffocate
[91] **shan't** = shall not
[92] **sly** = dishonest, clever at deceiving people
[93] **merry** = happy, cheerful
[94] **spite** = maliciousness

She tried to get me out of the room – it was too patent[95]! But I said it was so quiet and empty and clean now that I believed I would lie down again and sleep all I could; and not to wake me even for dinner – I would call when I woke.

So now she is gone, and the servants are gone, and the things are gone, and there is nothing left but that great bedstead nailed down, with the canvas mattress we found on it.

We shall sleep downstairs to-night, and take the boat home to-morrow.

I quite enjoy the room, now it is bare again.

How those children did tear about here!

This bedstead is fairly gnawed[96]!

But I must get to work.

I have locked the door and thrown the key down into the front path.

I don't want to go out, and I don't want to have anybody come in, till John comes.

I want to astonish him.

I've got a rope up here that even Jennie did not find. If that woman does get out, and tries to get away, I can tie her!

But I forgot I could not reach far without anything to stand on!

This bed will *not* move!

I tried to lift and push it until I was lame, and then I got so angry I bit off a little piece at one corner – but it hurt my teeth.

Then I peeled off all the paper I could reach standing on the floor. It sticks horribly and the pattern just enjoys it! All those strangled heads and bulbous eyes and waddling fungus growths just shriek with derision[97]!

I am getting angry enough to do something desperate. To jump out of the window would be admirable exercise, but the bars are too strong even to try.

Besides, I wouldn't do it. Of course not. I know well enough that a step like that is improper[98] and might be misconstrued[99].

I don't like to *look* out of the windows even – there are so many of those creeping women, and they creep so fast.

I wonder if they all come out of that wallpaper as I did?

But I am securely fastened now by my well-hidden rope – you don't get *me* out in the road there!

I suppose I shall have to get back behind the pattern when it comes night, and that is hard!

It is so pleasant to be out in this great room and creep around as I please!

I don't want to go outside. I won't, even if Jennie asks me to.

For outside you have to creep on the ground, and everything is green instead of yellow.

But here I can creep smoothly on the floor, and my shoulder just fits in that long smooch around the wall, so I cannot lose my way.

Why, there's John at the door!

It is no use, young man, you can't open it!

How he does call and pound!

Now he's crying for an axe.

It would be a shame to break down that beautiful door!

"John, dear!" said I in the gentlest voice, "the key is down by the front steps, under a plantain[100] leaf!"

That silenced him for a few moments.

Then he said – very quietly indeed, "Open the door, my darling!"

"I can't," said I. "The key is down by the front door under a plantain leaf!"

And then I said it again, several times, very gently and slowly, and said it so often that he had to go and see, and he got it of course, and came in. He stopped short by the door.

"What is the matter?" he cried. "For God's sake, what are you doing!"

I kept on creeping just the same, but I looked at him over my shoulder.

"I've got out at last," said I, "in spite of you and Jane! And I've pulled off most of the paper, so you can't put me back!"

Now why should that man have fainted? But he did, and right across my path by the wall, so that I had to creep over him every time!

Annotations

[95] **patent** = obvious
[96] **to gnaw** = to bite or chew repeatedly
[97] **derision** = mockery, scorn, ridicule
[98] **improper** = inappropriate, unsuitable
[99] **to misconstrue** = to misinterpret, to misunderstand
[100] **plantain** = *Wegerich (Gewächs)*

The Yellow Wallpaper — Short stories

WHILE READING

3 Read the short story. Decide whether the statements below are true or false. Give evidence from the text.

	Statement	True	False	Evidence
1	The narrator has moved to a rented summer country estate to cure her nerves.			
2	John is the narrator's primary doctor.			
3	The narrator spends most of the time in a nursery upstairs.			
4	The narrator has to stay in a bed bolted to the floor.			
5	The narrator's baby is staying with its grandparents.			
6	The narrator begins to think she has to free a woman behind the wallpaper and strips the paper off the wall.			
7	Because the woman behind the wallpaper scares her, the narrator is happy when her husband arrives home.			
8	The narrator believes to have become the woman behind the yellow wallpaper herself.			

4 While reading, pay close attention to the narrator's description and perception of her surroundings. Fill in the grid below with information from the short story.

How the narrator describes …	Evidence from the text
her room:	
the wallpaper in the room:	
her husband:	
her illness:	

Short stories: The Yellow Wallpaper

1

How the narrator describes …	Evidence from the text
herself:	

5

a) **Pair work** Choose some adjectives from the box that best describe your impression of the narrator. Explain your choice to a partner.

> lonely | arrogant | crazy | nervous | disappointed | stressed | angry | introverted | fussy | pessimistic | bossy | impatient | stubborn | unreliable | mad | self-centred | afraid

b) In the course of the plot, the narrator goes through different emotional states. Use the quotes below and explain these states. The order of the quotes is the same as in the story.

	Quote from the story	Explanation
1	Still I will proudly declare that there is something queer about it.	
2	Personally, I believe that congenial work, with excitement and change, would do me good.	
3	We have been here two weeks, and I haven't felt like writing before, since that first day. I am sitting by the window now, up in this atrocious nursery, and there is nothing to hinder my writing as much as I please, save lack of strength.	
4	Of course it is only nervousness. It does weigh on me so not to do my duty in any way!	
5	I think sometimes that if I were only well enough to write a little it would relieve the press of ideas and rest me. But I find I get pretty tired when I try.	
6	I'm getting really fond of the room in spite of the wallpaper. Perhaps *because* of the wallpaper. It dwells in my mind so!	
7	John was asleep and I hated to waken him, so I kept still and watched the moonlight on that undulating wallpaper till I felt creepy.	
8	Life is very much more exciting now than it used to be. You see I have something more to expect, to look forward to, to watch.	
9	But I am here, and no person touches this paper but me – not *alive!*	
10	"I've got out at last," said I, "in spite of you and Jane! And I've pulled off most of the paper, so you can't put me back!"	

6

Analyse whether or not the narrator is a reliable narrator. Give proof from the text.

> Info
>
> ### Reliable vs. unreliable narrator
>
> An **unreliable narrator** is usually a first-person narrator and character within the story whose narration and perception are not completely credible due to the character's affected mental condition or maturity. As a result, this narrator has a distorted view of events, gives illogical or contradicting information, speaks with a bias or even lies.
> Accordingly, a **reliable narrator** is considered a credible storyteller being fully aware of the circumstances around him/her. His/Her perception of the world is trustworthy and coherent.
> Reliable and unreliable narration has been widely debated within literary scholarship, since some literary critics argue that there is no such thing as a reliable first-person narrator at all. According to them, every literary character is affected by his or her past experiences and perception in the telling of a story. However, generally most first-person narrators attempt to give the most accurate and therefore reliable version of the events told in the story. One reason for creating an unreliable narrator is to make the reader reconsider their point of view and create dramatic suspense by making the truth unclear.

7

What makes John faint at the end of the story? Explain.

POST-READING

8

Analyse the narrative perspective of the short story. How does it influence the reader's perceptions of the story and its characters?

9

Speculate: What is the narrator doing when she is "creeping"?

10 Pair work

Why do you think the narrator thinks that her room in the rented home was once a nursery?
Consider other things that it could have been. Discuss with a partner.

11

Explain why John and Jennie are worried about the wallpaper.

12

What is the significance of the colour of the wallpaper in the short story? Discuss in class.

13 CHOOSE

Creative writing:
Find an alternative ending to the short story. Include information the narrator deliberately left out.
OR
Imagine John writes a letter to the narrator's primary doctor about his wife's mental condition.
What would he write? How would he assess his wife's health and the success of the treatment so far?
Write John's letter.

The Story of an Hour – A short story (1894)

PRE-READING

1

First read the information about the characters from the short story. Try to predict what their roles in the plot of the story might be.

- Louise Mallard: married to Brently Mallard, suffering from a heart disease

_____

_____

- Brently Mallard: husband to Louise Mallard, supposedly involved in a train accident

_____

_____

- Josephine: Louise's sister, worried about her

_____

_____

- Richards: Brently's friend, coming with some ominous information

_____

_____

The Story of an Hour

by Kate Chopin

Knowing that Mrs. Mallard was afflicted with a heart trouble, great care was taken to break to her as gently as possible the news of her husband's death.

It was her sister Josephine who told her, in broken sentences; veiled¹ hints that revealed in half concealing. Her husband's friend Richards was there, too, near her. It was he who had been in the newspaper office when intelligence² of the railroad disaster was received, with Brently Mallard's name leading the list of "killed." He had only taken the time to assure himself of its truth by a second telegram, and had hastened to forestall³ any less careful, less tender friend in bearing the sad message.

She did not hear the story as many women have heard the same, with a paralyzed inability to accept its significance. She wept at once, with sudden, wild abandonment, in her sister's arms. When the storm of grief had spent itself she went away to her room alone. She would have no one follow her.

There stood, facing the open window, a comfortable, roomy armchair. Into this she sank, pressed down by a physical exhaustion⁴ that haunted⁵ her body and seemed to reach into her soul.

She could see in the open square before her house the tops of trees that were all aquiver⁶ with the new spring life. The delicious breath of rain was in the air. In the

---

Annotations

¹ **veiled** = disguised, concealed
² **intelligence** = information, news
³ **to forestall** = to anticipate sth and prevent it from happening
⁴ **exhaustion** = the state of being extremely tired and having no energy left
⁵ **to haunt** = to appear repeatedly, to cause repeated anxiety or suffering
⁶ **aquiver** = shaking or trembling, often because of strong emotion

street below a peddler[7] was crying his wares[8]. The notes of a distant song which some one was singing reached her faintly, and countless sparrows[9] were twittering in the eaves.

There were patches of blue sky showing here and there through the clouds that had met and piled one above the other in the west facing her window.

She sat with her head thrown back upon the cushion of the chair, quite motionless, except when a sob came up into her throat and shook her, as a child who has cried itself to sleep continues to sob in its dreams.

She was young, with a fair, calm face, whose lines bespoke[10] repression and even a certain strength. But now there was a dull stare in her eyes, whose gaze was fixed away off yonder[11] on one of those patches of blue sky. It was not a glance of reflection, but rather indicated a suspension of intelligent thought.

There was something coming to her and she was waiting for it, fearfully. What was it? She did not know; it was too subtle and elusive[12] to name. But she felt it, creeping out of the sky, reaching toward her through the sounds, the scents[13], the color that filled the air.

Now her bosom[14] rose and fell tumultuously[15]. She was beginning to recognize this thing that was approaching to possess her, and she was striving to beat it back with her will – as powerless as her two white slender[16] hands would have been.

When she abandoned herself a little whispered word escaped her slightly parted lips. She said it over and over under her breath: "free, free, free!" The vacant[17] stare and the look of terror that had followed it went from her eyes. They stayed keen and bright. Her pulses beat fast, and the coursing blood warmed and relaxed every inch of her body.

She did not stop to ask if it were or were not a monstrous joy that held her. A clear and exalted[18] perception enabled her to dismiss the suggestion as trivial.

She knew that she would weep again when she saw the kind, tender hands folded in death; the face that had never looked save with love upon her, fixed and gray and dead. But she saw beyond that bitter moment a long procession of years to come that would belong to her absolutely. And she opened and spread her arms out to them in welcome.

There would be no one to live for her during those coming years; she would live for herself. There would be no powerful will bending hers in that blind persistence with which men and women believe they have a right to impose[19] a private will upon a fellow-creature. A kind intention or a cruel intention made the act seem no less a crime as she looked upon it in that brief moment of illumination[20].

And yet she had loved him – sometimes. Often she had not. What did it matter! What could love, the unsolved mystery, count for in face of this possession of self-assertion[21] which she suddenly recognized as the strongest impulse of her being!

"Free! Body and soul free!" she kept whispering.

Josephine was kneeling before the closed door with her lips to the keyhole, imploring[22] for admission. "Louise, open the door! I beg; open the door – you will make yourself ill. What are you doing, Louise? For heaven's sake open the door."

"Go away. I am not making myself ill." No; she was drinking in a very elixir[23] of life through that open window.

Her fancy was running riot along those days ahead of her. Spring days, and summer days, and all sorts of days that would be her own. She breathed a quick prayer that life might be long. It was only yesterday she had thought with a shudder that life might be long.

She arose at length and opened the door to her sister's importunities[24]. There was a feverish triumph in her eyes, and she carried herself unwittingly like a goddess of Victory. She clasped her sister's waist, and together they descended the stairs. Richards stood waiting for them at the bottom.

Some one was opening the front door with a latchkey[25]. It was Brently Mallard who entered, a little travel-stained[26], composedly carrying his grip-sack[27] and umbrella. He had been far from the scene of accident, and did not even know there had been one. He stood amazed at Josephine's piercing cry[28]; at Richards' quick motion to screen him from the view of his wife.

But Richards was too late.

When the doctors came they said she had died of heart disease – of joy that kills.

---

[7] **peddler** = a person who sells small goods, usually in the street or by going from door to door
[8] **ware** = goods
[9] **sparrow** = *Spatz*
[10] to **bespeak** = to show, to indicate
[11] **yonder** = over there
[12] **elusive** = difficult to describe, hard to grasp
[13] **scent** = a pleasant natural smell
[14] **bosom** = a person's chest
[15] **tumultuous** = highly agitated, confused or disturbed
[16] **slender** = thin and graceful
[17] **vacant** = empty, blank
[18] **exalted** = sublime, powerful

[19] to **impose** sth **on** sb = to force sth on sb
[20] **illumination** = spiritual enlightenment
[21] **self-assertion** = insistence on your own opinions, needs and wishes
[22] to **implore** = to beg
[23] **elixir** = a liquid with magical powers to preserve or improve sth
[24] **importunity** = persistence in demanding sth in a forceful and annoying way
[25] **latchkey** = a key for an outer door or gate
[26] **travel-stained** = dirty as a result of travelling
[27] **gripsack** (AE) = travel bag
[28] **piercing cry** = a loud, high-pitched and very sharp sound

1 Short stories — The Story of an Hour

WHILE READING

2
Read the short story. Match the sentence parts. Write the letters A–F in the boxes.

1 Richards …

2 After hearing about Brently's death, …

3 Louise …

4 Even though she loved him, …

5 Heading back downstairs, …

6 Being shocked at the sight of Brently, …

A has a heart disease.

B Louise dies from a heart attack.

C Louise witnesses Brently coming home.

D tells Louise that her husband has been killed in an accident.

E Brently's death means a new sense of freedom for Louise.

F Louise reacts with immediate grief.

3
Short stories often follow a certain scheme. Look at the main elements and features of typical short stories. Then fill in the grid for "The Story of an Hour".

A typical short story		"The Story of an Hour"
1	… has an exposition or quickly throws the reader into the story without a lot of explanations.	
2	… has a theme.	
3	… focuses on one or two protagonists.	
4	… may have further characters.	
5	… has a single or limited setting.	
6	… is less complex and has a limited plot.	
7	… mostly includes a conflict.	
8	… doesn't contain a lot of development.	
9	… has a climax.	
10	… has an open ending.	
11	… has a limited number of words.	
12	… isn't divided into chapters.	
13	… doesn't show a lot of development of the characters. However, the story depicts an important moment in the characters' lives.	
14	… needs to be read more than once so that the reader can delve deeper into it and read between the lines. (Give examples.)	

POST-READING

4 Group work

Discuss: What is the main idea of "The Story of an Hour"?

5

Analyse the setting of the story: Why is it essential to the story? Could the story have taken place somewhere else?

6 Group work

What does the final phrase "joy that kills" (l. 111) mean? Explain.

7

The 'heart' appears to be a central symbol in the short story. Analyse in which contexts it is used in the story and what it could stand for.

8

The short story was originally published under the title "The Dream of an Hour".
Speculate why it has been changed to "The Story of an Hour".

9 CHOOSE

Creative writing: Brently's reaction to his wife's death is not shown in Kate Chopin's short story.
Continue the story by adding information about Brently experiencing the incident.

OR

Create a comic strip: Retell the story in five cartoon sketches with captions or speech/thought bubbles.
Focus on the following scenes:
- Richards coming to tell Louise about her husband's death
- Louise's first reaction to the news
- going up to her room and her second reaction to the news
- Josephine getting Louise back downstairs
- Brently walking in and Louise having a heart attack

Weekend – A short story (1978)

PRE-READING

1

What are your first associations with the word 'weekend'?
Write an acrostic poem by using the letters as initials or placing them in the middle of a word or sentence.

W
E
E
K
E
N
D

Info

Acrostic

An acrostic is a poem in which particular letters, for example the first letters of each line, make a new word or phrase.

2

What do you expect a short story titled "Weekend" to deal with?
Note down your ideas.

_____

_____

_____

Weekend

by Fay Weldon

By seven-thirty they were ready to go. Martha had everything packed into the car and the three children appropriately dressed and in the back seat, complete with educational games and wholewheat¹ biscuits. When everything was ready in the car Martin would switch off the television, come downstairs, lock up the house, front and back, and take the wheel.

Weekend! Only two hours' drive down to the cottage on Friday evenings: three hours' drive back on Sunday nights. The pleasures of greenery² and guests in between. They reckoned themselves fortunate, how fortunate!

On Fridays Martha would get home on the bus at six-twelve and prepare tea and sandwiches for the family: then she would strip four beds and put the sheets and quilt covers in the washing machine for Monday: take the country bedding from the airing basket, plus the books and the games, plus the weekend food – acquired³ at intervals throughout the week, to lessen the load – plus her own folder of work from the office, plus Martin's drawing materials (she was a market researcher in an advertising agency, he a freelance⁴ designer) plus hairbrushes, jeans, spare T-shirts, Jolyon's antibiotics (he suffered from sore throats), Jenny's recorder, Jasper's cassette player and so on – ah, the so on! – and would pack them all, skilfully and quickly, into the boot. Very little could be left in the cottage during the week. ('An open invitation to burglars⁵': Martin) Then Martha would run round the house tidying and wiping, doing this and that, finding the cat at one neighbour's and delivering it to another, while the others ate their tea; and would usually, proudly, have everything finished by the time they had eaten their fill. Martin would just catch the BBC2 news, while Martha cleared away the tea table, and the children tossed⁶ up for the best positions in the car. 'Martha,' said Martin, tonight, 'you ought to get Mrs Hodder to do more. She takes advantage of you.'

Mrs Hodder came in twice a week to clean. She was over seventy. She charged two pounds an hour. Martha paid her out of her own wages: well, the running of the house was Martha's concern. If Martha chose to go out to work – as was her perfect right, Martin allowed, even though it wasn't the best thing for the children, but that must be Martha's moral responsibility – Martha must surely pay her domestic stand-in. An evident truth, heard loud and clear and frequent in Martin's mouth and Martha's heart. 'I expect you're right,' said Martha. She did not want to argue. Martin had had a long hard week, and now had to drive. Martha couldn't. Martha's licence had been suspended⁷ four months back for drunken driving. Everyone agreed that the suspension was unfair; Martha seldom drank to excess: she was for one thing usually too busy pouring drinks for other people or washing other people's glasses to get much inside herself. But Martin had taken her out to dinner on her birthday, as was his custom, and exhaustion⁸ and excitement mixed had made her imprudent⁹, and before she knew where she was, why there she was, in the dock¹⁰, with a distorted lamp-post to pay for and a new bonnet¹¹ for the car and six months' suspension.

So now Martin had to drive her car down to the cottage, and he was always tired on Fridays, and hot and sleepy on Sundays, and every rattle¹² and clank¹³ and bump in the engine she felt to be somehow her fault.

Martin had a little sports car for London and work: it could nip in and out of the traffic nicely: Martha's was an old estate car, with room for the children, picnic baskets, bedding, food, games, plants, drink, portable television and all the things required by the middle classes for weekends in the country. It lumbered¹⁴ rather than zipped and made Martin angry. He seldom spoke a harsh word, but Martha, after the fashion of wives, could detect his mood from what he did not say rather than what he did, and from the tilt¹⁵ of his head, and the way his crinkly¹⁶ merry eyes seemed crinklier and merrier still – and of course from the way he addressed Martha's car.

'Come along, you old banger¹⁷ you! Can't you do better than that? You're too old, that's your trouble. Stop complaining. Always complaining, it's only a hill. You're too wide about the hips. You'll never get through there.'

Annotations

¹ **wholewheat** = made from flour that contains all the natural features of the wheat grain
² **greenery** = green plants, vegetation
³ to **acquire** = to get, buy or obtain
⁴ **freelance** = self-employed, doing pieces of work for different organizations
⁵ **burglar** = a thief who enters a building to steal things
⁶ to **toss up** = to gamble or to throw a coin in the air in order to make a decision between two alternatives
⁷ **suspended** = stopped from being active; *here:* not allowed to drive as a form of punishment for drunken driving
⁸ **exhaustion** = a state of extreme tiredness
⁹ **imprudent** = thoughtless, not considering the consequences
¹⁰ **in the dock** = in court
¹¹ **bonnet** = the metal cover over a car engine
¹² **rattle** = a series of short, sharp knocking sounds
¹³ **clank** = a sharp, metallic sound
¹⁴ to **lumber** = to move slowly and clumsily
¹⁵ **tilt** = a sloping position
¹⁶ **crinkly** = full of small lines and folds
¹⁷ **banger** = *(infml.)* an old car in very bad condition

Martha worried about her age, her tendency to complain, and the width of her hips. She took the remarks personally. Was she right to do so? The children noticed nothing: it was just funny lively laughing Daddy being witty about Mummy's car. Mummy, done for drunken driving. Mummy, with the roots of melancholy somewhere deep beneath the bustling, busy, everyday self. Busy: ah so busy!

Martin would only laugh if she said anything about the way he spoke to her car and warn her against paranoia. 'Don't get like your mother, darling.' Martha's mother had, towards the end, thought that people were plotting against her. Martha's mother had led a secluded[18], suspicious life, and made Martha's childhood a chilly and a lonely time. Life now, by comparison, was wonderful for Martha. People, children, houses, conversations, food, drink, theatres – even, now, a career. Martin standing between her and the hostility[19] of the world – popular, easy, funny Martin, beckoning the rest of the world into earshot[20].

Ah, she was grateful: little earnest Martha, with her shy ways and her penchant[21] for passing boring exams – how her life had blossomed out! Three children too – Jasper, Jenny and Jolyon – all with Martin's broad brow and open looks, and the confidence born of her love and care, and the work she had put into them since the dawning[22] of their days.

Martin drives. Martha, for once, drowses[23].

The right food, the right words, the right play. Doctors for the tonsils[24]: dentists for the molars[25]. Confiscate guns: censor television: encourage creativity. Paints and paper to hand: books on the shelves: meetings with teachers. Music teachers. Dancing lessons. Parties. Friends to tea. School plays. Open days. Junior orchestra.

Martha is jolted awake[26]. Traffic lights. Martin doesn't like Martha to sleep while he drives.

Clothes. Oh, clothes! Can't wear this: must wear that. Dress shops. Piles of clothes in corners: duly[27] washed, but waiting to be ironed, waiting to be put away.

Get the piles off the floor, into the laundry baskets. Martin doesn't like a mess.

Creativity arises out of order, not chaos. Five years off work while the children were small: back to work with seniority[28] lost. What, did you think something was for nothing? If you have children, mother, that is your reward. It lies not in the world.

Have you taken enough food? Always hard to judge.

Food. Oh, food! Shop in the lunch-hour. Lug[29] it all home. Cook for the freezer on Wednesday evenings while Martin is at his car-maintenance[30] evening class, and isn't there to notice you being unrestful. Martin likes you to sit down in the evenings. Fruit, meat, vegetables, flour for home-made bread. Well, shop bread is full of pollutants[31]. Frozen food, even your own, loses flavour. Martin often remarks on it. Condiments[32]. Everyone loves mango chutney. But the expense!

London Airport to the left. Look, look, children! Concorde? No, idiot, of course it isn't Concorde.

Ah, to be all things to all people: children, husband, employer, friends! It can be done: yes, it can: super woman.

Drink. Home-made wine. Why not? Elderberries[33] grown thick and rich in London: and at least you know what's in it. Store it in high cupboards: lots of room: up and down the step-ladder. Careful! Don't slip. Don't break anything. No such thing as an accident. Accidents are Freudian slips[34]: they are wilful, bad-tempered things.

Martin can't bear bad temper. Martin likes slim ladies. Diet. Martin rather likes his secretary. Diet. Martin admires slim legs and big bosoms[35]. How to achieve them both? Impossible. But try, oh try, to be what you ought to be, not what you are. Inside and out.

Martin brings back flowers and chocolates: whisks[36] Martha off for holiday weekends. Wonderful! The best husband in the world: look into his crinkly, merry, gentle eyes; see it there. So the mouth slopes away into something of a pout[37]. Never mind. Gaze into the eyes. Love. It must be love. You married him. *You*. Surely *you* deserve true love?

Salisbury Plain[38]. Stonehenge[39]. Look, children, look! Mother, we've seen Stonehenge a hundred times. Go back to sleep.

Cook! Ah cook. People love to come to Martin and Martha's dinners. Work it out in your head in the lunch-

---

[18] **secluded** = quiet, private and quite isolated
[19] **hostility** = unfriendly or aggressive behaviour
[20] **earshot** = the distance within which a sound or voice can be heard
[21] **penchant** = a special liking for sth
[22] **dawning** = daybreak; beginning
[23] to **drowse** = to be almost asleep or to sleep lightly
[24] **tonsil** = one of two small organs situated on each side of the throat at the back of the mouth
[25] **molar** = a large tooth at the back of the mouth
[26] to **jolt** sb **awake** = to wake sb up suddenly and violently
[27] **duly** = properly, as expected

[28] **seniority** = a higher rank and privileged position earned at work
[29] to **lug** = (infml.) to carry or drag sth with effort (because it is heavy)
[30] **car maintenance** = the activity of checking a vehicle regularly and, when necessary, repairing it
[31] **pollutant** = a harmful substance
[32] **condiment** = any spice or sauce that is added to food to improve its taste
[33] **elderberry** = *Holunderbeere*
[34] **Freudian slip** = accidentally saying sth that reveals your hidden thoughts
[35] **bosom** = a woman's breasts
[36] to **whisk** = to take sb or sth somewhere else quickly
[37] **pout** = a position of the lips that shows displeasure or annoyance
[38] **Salisbury Plain** = a large area of flat land north of Salisbury in southern England
[39] **Stonehenge** = a circle of very large stones, a famous prehistoric monument in southern England

hour. If you get in at six-twelve, you can seal the meat while you beat the egg white while you feed the cat while you lay the table while you string the beans while you set out the cheese, goat's cheese, Martin loves goat's cheese, Martha tries to like goat's cheese – oh, bed, sleep, peace, quiet.

Sex! Ah sex. Orgasm, please. Martin requires it. Well, so do you. And you don't want his secretary providing a passion you neglected[40] to develop. Do you? Quick, quick, the cosmic bond. Love. Married love.

Secretary! Probably a vulgar suspicion: nothing more.

Probably a fit of paranoics, à la mother, now dead and gone.

At peace.

RIP.

Chilly, lonely mother, following her suspicions where they led.

Nearly there, children. Nearly in paradise, nearly at the cottage. Have another biscuit.

Real roses round the door.

Roses. Prune[41], weed[42], spray, feed, pick. Avoid thorns. One of Martin's few harsh words.

'Martha, you can't not want roses! What kind of person am I married to? An anti-rose personality?'

Green grass. Oh, God, grass. Grass must be mowed. Restful lawns, daisies bobbing[43], buttercups glowing. Roses and grass and books. Books.

Please, Martin, do we have to have the two hundred books, mostly twenties' first editions, bought at Christie's book sale on one of your afternoons off? Books need dusting.

Roars of laughter from Martin, Jasper, Jenny and Jolyon.

Mummy says we shouldn't have the books: books need dusting!

Roses, green grass, books and peace.

Martha woke up with a start when they got to the cottage, and gave a little shriek which made them all laugh. Mummy's waking shriek, they called it.

Then there was the car to unpack and the beds to make up, and the electricity to connect, and the supper to make, and the cobwebs[44] to remove, while Martin made the fire. Then supper – pork chops in sweet and sour sauce ('Pork is such a *dull* meat if you don't cook it properly': Martin), green salad from the garden, or such green salad as the rabbits had left ('Martha, did you really net them properly? Be honest now!': Martin) and sauté[45] potatoes.

Mash is so stodgy[46] and ordinary, and instant mash unthinkable. The children studied the night sky with the aid of their star map. Wonderful, rewarding children!

Then clear up the supper: set the dough to prove for the bread: Martin already in bed: exhausted by the drive and lighting the fire. ('Martha, we really ought to get the logs[47] stacked properly. Get the children to do it, will you?': Martin) Sweep and tidy: get the TV aerial[48] right. Turn up Jasper's jeans where he has trodden the hem[49] undone. ('He can't go around like *that*, Martha. Not even Jasper': Martin)

Midnight. Good night. Weekend guests arriving in the morning. Seven for lunch and dinner on Saturday. Seven for Sunday breakfast, nine for Sunday lunch. ('Don't fuss[50], darling. You always make such a fuss': Martin) Oh, God, forgotten the garlic squeezer. That means ten minutes with the back of a spoon and salt. Well, who wants *lumps* of garlic? No one. Not Martin's guests. Martin said so. Sleep.

Colin and Katie. Colin is Martin's oldest friend. Katie is his new young wife. Janet, Colin's other, earlier wife, was Martha's friend.

Janet was rather like Martha, quieter and duller than her husband. A nag[51] and a drag[52], Martin rather thought, and said, and of course she'd let herself go, everyone agreed. No one exactly excused Colin for walking out, but you could see the temptation.

Katie versus Janet.

Katie was languid[53], beautiful and elegant. She drawled when she spoke. Her hands were expressive: her feet were little and female. She had no children.

Janet plodded[54] round on very flat, rather large feet. There was something wrong with them. They turned out slightly when she walked. She had two children. She was, frankly, boring. But Martha liked her: when Janet came down to the cottage she would wash up. Not in the way that most guests washed up – washing dutifully and setting everything out on the draining board[55], but actually drying and putting away too. And Janet would wash the bath and get the children all sat down, with chairs for everyone, even the littlest, and keep them quiet and satisfied so the grown-ups – well, the men – could get on with their conversation and their jokes and their

---

Annotations

[40] to **neglect** = to fail to give enough care or attention to sb or sth
[41] to **prune** = to cut off parts from a plant to make it grow better
[42] to **weed** = to remove wild (unwanted) plants from a place in a garden or field
[43] to **bob** = to move up and down
[44] **cobweb** = a net made by a spider
[45] **sauté** = fried quickly in a little oil or fat
[46] **stodgy** = heavy and difficult to digest
[47] **log** = a piece of wood cut for burning on a fire
[48] **aerial** = a piece of metal wire that can receive or send out radio or television signals
[49] **hem** = the edge of a piece of cloth that is folded over and sewn
[50] to **fuss** = to give too much attention to unimportant matters
[51] **nag** = a person who is always complaining or criticizing
[52] **drag** = (infml.) a person who is unpleasant and boring
[53] **languid** = showing little energy or interest (often in an attractive way)
[54] to **plod** = to walk slowly and heavily
[55] **draining board** = the place next to a sink where the dishes are left to dry after they have been washed

love of country weekends, while Janet stared into space, as if grateful for the rest, quite happy.

Janet would garden, too. Weed the strawberries, while the men went for their walk; her great feet standing firm and square and sometime crushing a plant or so, but never mind, oh never mind. Lovely Janet; who understood.

Now Janet was gone and here was Katie.

Katie talked with the men and went for walks with the men, and moved her ashtray rather impatiently when Martha tried to clear the drinks round it.

Dishes were boring, Katie implied[56] by her manner, and domesticity[57] was boring, and anyone who bothered with that kind of thing was a fool. Like Martha. Ash should be allowed to stay where it was, even if it was in the butter, and conversations should never be interrupted.

Knock, knock. Katie and Colin arrived at one-fifteen on Saturday morning, just after Martha had got to bed. 'You don't mind? It was the moonlight. We couldn't resist it. You should have seen Stonehenge! We didn't disturb you? Such early birds!'

Martha rustled up a quick meal of omelettes. Saturday nights' eggs. ('Martha makes a lovely omelette': Martin) ('Honey, make one of your mushroom omelettes: cook the mushrooms separately, remember, with lemon. Otherwise the water from the mushrooms gets into the egg, and spoils everything.') Sunday supper mushrooms. But ungracious[58] to say anything.

Martin had revived wonderfully at the sight of Colin and Katie. He brought out the whisky bottle. Glasses. Ice. Jug[59] for water. Wait. Wash up another sinkful, when they're finished. 2 a.m.

'Don't do it tonight, darling.'

'It'll only take a sec.' Bright smile, not a hint of self-pity[60]. Self-pity can spoil everyone's weekend.

Martha knows that if breakfast for seven is to be manageable the sink must be cleared of dishes. A tricky meal, breakfast. Especially if bacon, eggs, and tomatoes must all be cooked in separate pans. ('Separate pans mean separate flavours!': Martin)

She is running around in her nightie[61]. Now if that had been Katie – but there's something so *practical* about Martha. Reassuring, mind; but the skimpy[62] nightie and the broad rump[63] and the thirty-eight years are all rather embarrassing. Martha can see it in Colin and Katie's eyes. Martin's too. Martha wishes she did not see so much in other people's eyes. Her mother did, too. Dear, dead mother. Did I misjudge[64] you?

This was the second weekend Katie had been down with Colin but without Janet. Colin was a photographer: Katie had been his accessorizer. First Colin and Janet: then Colin, Janet and Katie: now Colin and Katie!

Katie weeded with rubber gloves on and pulled out pansies[65] in mistake for weeds and laughed and laughed along with everyone when her mistake was pointed out to her, but the pansies died. Well, Colin had become with the years fairly rich and fairly famous, and what does a fairly rich and famous man want with a wife like Janet when Katie is at hand?

On the first of the Colin/Janet/Katie weekends Katie had appeared out of the bathroom. 'I say,' said Katie, holding out a damp[66] towel with evident distaste, 'I can only find this. No hope of a dry one?' And Martha had run to fetch a dry towel and amazingly found one, and handed it to Katie who flashed her a brilliant smile and said, 'I can't bear damp towels. Anything in the world but damp towels,' as if speaking to a servant in a time of shortage of staff, and took all the water so there was none left for Martha to wash up.

The trouble, of course, was drying anything at all in the cottage. There were no facilities for doing so, and Martin had a horror of clothes lines which might spoil the view. He toiled and moiled[67] all week in the city simply to get a country view at the weekend. Ridiculous to spoil it by draping it with wet towels! But now Martha had bought more towels, so perhaps everyone could be satisfied. She would take nine damp towels back on Sunday evenings in a plastic bag and see to them in London.

On this Saturday morning, straight after breakfast, Katie went out to the car – she and Colin had a new Lamborghini; hard to imagine Katie in anything duller – and came back waving a new Yves St Laurent towel. 'See! I brought my own, darlings.'

They'd brought nothing else. No fruit, no meat, no vegetables, not even bread, certainly not a box of chocolates. They'd gone off to bed with alacrity[68], the night before, and the spare room rocked and heaved: well, who'd want to do washing-up when you could do that, but what about the children? Would they get confused? First Colin and Janet, now Colin and Katie?

Martha murmured something of her thoughts to Martin, who looked quite shocked. 'Colin's my best friend. I don't expect him to bring anything,' and Martha felt mean.

---

[56] to **imply** = to express sth indirectly
[57] **domesticity** = life at home, family life
[58] **ungracious** = rude, impolite
[59] **jug** = a container for liquids
[60] **self-pity** = a feeling of unhappiness or sadness for yourself
[61] **nightie** *(infml.)* = nightdress
[62] **skimpy** = not large enough, made of too little material
[63] **rump** = a person's bottom

[64] to **misjudge** = to form an unfair opinion or a wrong idea about sb or sth
[65] **pansy** = *Stiefmütterchen (Pflanze)*
[66] **damp** = slightly wet
[67] to **toil and moil** = to work hard
[68] **with alacrity** = quickly and eagerly

Short stories — Weekend

'And good heavens, you can't protect the kids from sex for ever: don't be so prudish[69],' so that Martha felt stupid as well. Mean, complaining, and stupid.

Janet had rung Martha during the week. The house had been sold over her head, and she and the children had been moved into a small flat. Katie was trying to persuade Colin to cut down on her allowance[70], Janet said.

'It does one no good to be materialistic,' Katie confided. 'I have nothing. No home, no family, no ties, no possessions. Look at me! Only me and a suitcase of clothes.' But Katie seemed highly satisfied with the me, and the clothes were stupendous. Katie drank a great deal and became funny. Everyone laughed, including Martha. Katie had been married twice. Martha marvelled at how someone could arrive in their mid-thirties with nothing at all to their name, neither husband, nor children, nor property and not mind.

Mind you, Martha could see the power of such helplessness. If Colin was all Katie had in the world, how could Colin abandon her? And to what? Where would she go? How would she live? Oh, clever Katie.

'My teacup's dirty,' said Katie, and Martha ran to clean it, apologizing, and Martin raised his eyebrows, at Martha, not Katie.

'I wish *you'd* wear scent[71],' said Martin to Martha, reproachfully[72]. Katie wore lots. Martha never seemed to have time to put any on, though Martin bought her bottle after bottle. Martha leapt out of bed each morning to meet some emergency – miaowing cat, coughing child, faulty alarm clock, postman's knock – when was Martha to put on scent? It annoyed Martin all the same. She ought to do more to charm him.

Colin looked handsome and harrowed[73] and younger than Martin, though they were much the same age. 'Youth's catching,' said Martin in bed that night. 'It's since he found Katie.' Found, like some treasure. Discovered; something exciting and wonderful, in the dreary[74] world of established spouses[75].

On Saturday morning Jasper trod on a piece of wood ('Martha, why isn't he wearing shoes? It's too bad': Martin) and Martha took him into the hospital to have a nasty splinter removed. She left the cottage at ten and arrived back at one, and they were still sitting in the sun, drinking, empty bottles glinting in the long grass. The grass hadn't been cut. Don't forget the bottles. Broken glass means more mornings at the hospital. Oh, don't fuss. Enjoy yourself. Like other people. Try.

But no potatoes peeled, no breakfast cleared, nothing. Cigarette ends still amongst old toast, bacon rind[76] and marmalade. 'You could have done the potatoes,' Martha burst out. Oh, bad temper! Prime sin. They looked at her in amazement and dislike. Martin too.

'Goodness,' said Katie. 'Are we doing the whole Sunday lunch bit on Saturday? Potatoes? Ages since I've eaten potatoes. Wonderful!'

'The children expect it,' said Martha.

So they did. Saturday and Sunday lunch shone like reassuring beacons[77] in their lives. Saturday lunch: family lunch: fish and chips. ('So much better cooked at home than bought': Martin) Sunday. Usually roast beef, potatoes, peas, apple pie. Oh, of course. Yorkshire pudding. Always a problem with oven temperatures. When the beef's going slowly, the Yorkshire should be going fast. How to achieve that? Like big bosom and little hips.

'Just relax,' said Martin. 'I'll cook dinner, all in good time. Splinters always work their own way out: no need to have taken him to hospital. Let life drift over you, my love. Flow with the waves, that's the way.'

And Martin flashed Martha a distant, spiritual smile. His hand lay on Katie's slim brown arm, with its many gold bands.

'Anyway, you do too much for the children,' said Martin. 'It isn't good for them. Have a drink.'

So Martha perched[78] uneasily on the step and had a glass of cider, and wondered how, if lunch was going to be late, she would get cleared up and the meat out of the marinade for the rather formal dinner that would be expected that evening. The marinaded lamb ought to cook for at least four hours in a low oven; and the cottage oven was very small, and you couldn't use that and the grill at the same time and Martin liked his fish grilled, not fried. Less cholesterol[79].

She didn't say as much. Domestic details like this were very boring, and any mild complaint was registered by Martin as a scene. And to make a scene was so ungrateful. This was the life. Well, wasn't it? Smart friends in large cars and country living and drinks before lunch and roses and bird song – 'Don't drink *too* much,' said Martin, and told them about Martha's suspended driving licence.

The children were hungry so Martha opened them a can of beans and sausages and heated that up. ('Martha, do they have to eat that crap? Can't they wait?': Martin)

Annotations
[69] **prudish** = easily shocked by rude things or anything relating to sex
[70] **allowance** = money that is given to sb on a regular basis, financial support
[71] **scent** = perfume
[72] **reproachful** = expressing criticism
[73] **harrowed** = looking as if you have suffered
[74] **dreary** = boring, dull and depressing
[75] **spouse** = husband or wife
[76] **bacon rind** = the outer edge of a slice of bacon
[77] **beacon** = a light or fire that acts as a signal
[78] to **perch** = to sit down on the edge of sth
[79] **cholesterol** = *Cholesterin*

Katie was hungry: she said so, to keep the children in face. She was lovely with children – most children. She did not particularly like Colin and Janet's children. She said so, and he accepted it. He only saw them once a month now, not once a week.

'Let me make lunch,' Katie said to Martha. 'You do so much, poor thing!'

And she pulled out of the fridge all the things Martha had put away for the next day's picnic lunch party – Camembert cheese and salad and salami and made a wonderful tomato salad in two minutes and opened the white wine – 'not very cold, darling. Shouldn't it be chilling?' – and had it all on the table in five amazing competent minutes. 'That's all we need, darling,' said Martin. 'You are funny with your fish-and-chip Saturdays! What could be nicer than this? Or simpler?'

Nothing, except there was Sunday's buffet lunch for nine gone, in place of Saturday's fish for six, and would the fish stretch? No. Katie had had quite a lot to drink. She pecked[80] Martha on the forehead. 'Funny little Martha,' she said. 'She reminds me of Janet. I really do like Janet.' Colin did not want to be reminded of Janet, and said so. 'Darling, Janet's a fact of life,' said Katie. 'If you'd only think about her more, you might manage to pay her less.' And she yawned and stretched her lean[81], childless body and smiled at Colin with her inviting, naughty little girl eyes, and Martin watched her in admiration.

Martha got up and left them and took a paint pot and put a coat of white gloss on the bathroom wall. The white surface pleased her. She was good at painting. She produced a smooth, even surface. Her legs throbbed[82]. She feared she might be getting varicose veins[83].

Outside in the garden the children played badminton. They were bad-tempered, but relieved to be able to look up and see their mother working, as usual: making their lives for ever better and nicer: organizing, planning, thinking ahead, side-stepping disaster, making preparations, like a mother hen, fussing and irritating: part of the natural boring scenery of the world.

On Saturday night Katie went to bed early: she rose from her chair and stretched and yawned and poked her head into the kitchen where Martha was washing saucepans. Colin had cleared the table and Katie had folded the napkins into pretty creases[84], while Martin blew at the fire, to make it bright. 'Good night,' said Katie.

Katie appeared three minutes later, reproachfully holding out her Yves St Laurent towel, sopping wet. 'Oh dear,' cried Martha. 'Jenny must have washed her hair!' And Martha was obliged to rout[85] Jenny out of bed to rebuke[86] her, publicly, if only to demonstrate that she knew what was right and proper. That meant Jenny would sulk[87] all weekend, and that meant a treat or an outing mid-week, or else by the following week she'd be having an asthma attack. 'You fuss the children too much,' said Martin. 'That's why Jenny has asthma.' Jenny was pleasant enough to look at, but not stunning. Perhaps she was a disappointment to her father? Martin would never say so, but Martha feared he thought so.

An egg and an orange each child, each day. Then nothing too bad would go wrong. And it hadn't. The asthma was very mild. A calm, tranquil environment, the doctor said. Ah, smile, Martha smile. Domestic happiness depends on you. 21 x 52 oranges a year. Each one to be purchased, carried, peeled and washed up after. And what about potatoes. 12 x 52 pounds a year? Martin liked his potatoes carefully peeled. He couldn't bear to find little cores of black in the mouthful. ('Well, it isn't very nice, is it?': Martin).

Martha dreamt she was eating coal, by handfuls, and liking it.

Saturday night. Martin made love to Martha three times. Three times? How virile[88] he was, and clearly turned on by the sounds from the spare room. Martin said he loved her. Martin always did. He was a courteous[89] lover; he knew the importance of foreplay. So did Martha. Three times.

Ah, sleep. Jolyon had a nightmare. Jenny was woken by a moth[90]. Martin slept through everything. Martha pottered[91] about the house in the night. There was a moon. She sat at the window and stared out into the summer night for five minutes, and was at peace, and then went back to bed because she ought to be fresh for the morning.

But she wasn't. She slept late. The others went out for a walk. They'd left a note, a considerate note: 'Didn't wake you. You looked tired. Had a cold breakfast so as not to make too much mess. Leave everything 'til we get back.' But it was ten o'clock, and guests were coming at noon, so she cleared away the bread, the butter, the crumbs, the smears[92], the jam, the spoons, the spilt sugar, the cereal, the milk (sour by now) and the dirty plates, and swept

---

[80] to **peck** = *here:* to give sb a quick, light kiss
[81] **lean** = thin and in good physical condition
[82] to **throb** = to pulsate
[83] **varicose veins** = a condition in which the veins, especially in the legs, are swollen and can be seen on the skin
[84] **crease** = a line on cloth or paper where it has been folded
[85] to **rout** sb **out** = to force or drive out
[86] to **rebuke** = to speak severely or angrily to sb because they have said or done sth that you think is wrong
[87] to **sulk** = to be silent and bad-tempered because you are angry about sth
[88] **virile** = masculine, full of strength and sexual energy
[89] **courteous** = polite and respectful
[90] **moth** = an insect which usually flies at night and is attracted to light
[91] to **potter about/around** (BE) = to move around or do unimportant things without hurrying, in a pleasant way
[92] **smear** = a dirty mark

the floors, and tidied up quickly, and grabbed a cup of coffee, and prepared to make a rice and fish dish, and a chocolate mousse and sat down in the middle to eat a lot of bread and jam herself. Broad hips. She remembered the office work in her file and knew she wouldn't be able to do it. Martin anyway thought it was ridiculous for her to bring work back at the weekends. 'It's your holiday,' he'd say. 'Why should they impose[93]?' Martha loved her work. She didn't have to smile at it. She just did it.

Katie came back upset and crying. She sat in the kitchen while Martha worked and drank glass after glass of gin and bitter lemon. Katie liked ice and lemon in gin. Martha paid for all the drink out of her wages. It was part of the deal between her and Martin – the contract by which she went out to work. All things to cheer the spirit, otherwise depressed by a working wife and mother, were to be paid for by Martha. Drink, holidays, petrol, outings, puddings, electricity, heating: it was quite a joke between them. It didn't really make any difference: it was their joint[94] money, after all. Amazing how Martha's wages were creeping up, almost to the level of Martin's. One day they would overtake. Then what?

Work, honestly, was a piece of cake[95].

Anyway, poor Katie was crying. Colin, she'd discovered, kept a photograph of Janet and the children in his wallet. 'He's not free of her. He pretends he is, but he isn't. She has him by a stranglehold[96]. It's the kids. His bloody kids. Moaning Mary and that little creep Joanna. It's all he thinks about. I'm nobody.'

But Katie didn't believe it. She knew she was somebody all right. Colin came in, in a fury. He took out the photograph and set fire to it, bitterly, with a match. Up in smoke they went. Mary and Joanna and Janet. The ashes fell on the floor. (Martha swept them up when Colin and Katie had gone. It hardly seemed polite to do so when they were still there.) 'Go back to her,' Katie said. 'Go back to her. I don't care. Honestly, I'd rather be on my own. You're a nice old fashioned thing. Run along then. Do your thing, I'll do mine. Who cares?'

'Christ, Katie, the fuss! She only just happens to be in the photograph. She's not there on purpose to annoy. And I do feel bad about her. She's been having a hard time.'

'And haven't you, Colin? She twists a pretty knife, I can tell you. Don't you have rights too? Not to mention me. Is a little loyalty too much to expect?'

They were reconciled[97] before lunch, up in the spare room. Harry and Beryl Elder arrived at twelve-thirty. Harry didn't like to hurry on Sundays; Beryl was flustered with apologies for their lateness. They'd brought artichokes from their garden. 'Wonderful,' cried Martin. 'Fruits of the earth? Let's have a wonderful soup! Don't fret[98], Martha. I'll do it.'

'Don't fret.' Martha clearly hadn't been smiling enough. She was in danger, Martin implied, of ruining everyone's weekend. There was an emergency in the garden very shortly – an elm[99] tree which had probably got Dutch elm disease – and Martha finished the artichokes. The lid flew off the blender and there was artichoke purée everywhere. 'Let's have lunch outside,' said Colin. 'Less work for Martha.'

Martin frowned at Martha: he thought the appearance of martyrdom[100] in the face of guests to be an unforgivable offence.

Everyone happily joined in taking the furniture out, but it was Martha's experience that nobody ever helped to bring it in again.

Jolyon was stung by a wasp. Jasper sneezed and sneezed from hay fever[101] and couldn't find the tissues and he wouldn't use loo[102] paper. ('Surely you remembered the tissues, darling?': Martin)

Beryl Elder was nice. 'Wonderful to eat out,' she said, fetching the cream for her pudding, while Martha fished a fly from the liquefying[103] Brie[104] ('You shouldn't have bought it so ripe, Martha': Martin) – 'except it's just some other woman has to do it. But at least it isn't *me*.' Beryl worked too, as a secretary, to send the boys to boarding school, where she'd rather they weren't. But her husband was from a rather grand family, and she'd been only a typist when he married her, so her life was a mass of amends[105], one way or another. Harry had lately opted out of the stockbroking[106] rat race and become an artist, choosing integrity rather than money, but that choice was his alone and couldn't of course be inflicted on the boys. Katie found the fish and rice dish rather strange, toyed[107] at it with her fork, and talked about Italian restaurants she knew. Martin lay back soaking in the sun: crying, 'Oh, this is the life.' He made coffee, nobly, and the lid

---

Annotations

[93] to **impose** = to expect sb to do sth that is inconvenient
[94] **joint** = belonging to two or more people
[95] **a piece of cake** = *here:* sth that is easily accomplished
[96] **stranglehold** = a position of complete control over sb or sth
[97] to **be reconciled with** sb = to become friendly again after a quarrel or disagreement
[98] to **fret** = to be worried or unhappy about sth
[99] **elm** = *Ulme (Laubbaum)*
[100] **martyrdom** = great suffering
[101] **hay fever** = an allergic reaction to pollen
[102] **loo** *(infml.)* = toilet
[103] **liquefying** = becoming liquid
[104] **Brie** = a soft and creamy French cheese with a white skin
[105] **amends** = recompense or compensation for some mistake such as an injury or insult
[106] **stockbroking** = the job of buying and selling stocks and shares for clients
[107] to **toy** = to play, to fiddle

flew off the grinder[108] and there were coffee beans all over the kitchen especially in amongst the row of cookery books which Martin gave Martha Christmas by Christmas. At least they didn't have to be brought back every weekend. ('The burglars won't have the sense to steal those': Martin)

Beryl fell asleep and Katie watched her, quizzically[109]. Beryl's mouth was open and she had a lot of fillings, and her ankles were thick and her waist was going, and she didn't look after herself. 'I love women,' sighed Katie. 'They look so wonderful asleep. I wish I could be an earth mother.' Beryl woke with a start and nagged her husband into going home, which he clearly didn't want to do, so didn't. Beryl thought she had to get back because his mother was coming round later. Nonsense! Then Beryl tried to stop Harry drinking more home-made wine and was laughed at by everyone. He was driving, Beryl couldn't, and he did have a nasty scar on his temple from a previous road accident. Never mind.

'She does come on strong, poor soul,' laughed Katie when they'd finally gone. 'I'm never going to get married,' – and Colin looked at her yearningly[110] because he wanted to marry her more than anything in the world, and Martha cleared the coffee cups.

'Oh don't *do* that,' said Katie, 'do just sit *down*, Martha, you make us all feel bad,' and Martin glared at Martha who sat down and Jenny called out for her and Martha went upstairs and Jenny had started her first period and Martha cried and cried and knew she must stop because this must be a joyous occasion for Jenny or her whole future would be blighted[111], but for once, Martha couldn't. Her daughter Jenny: wife, mother, friend.

[108] **grinder** = a kitchen device for crushing food into small pieces or a powder
[109] **quizzically** = in a way that seems to ask a question
[110] **yearningly** = in a way that expresses a strong desire for sth
[111] **blighted** = spoiled, ruined

WHILE READING

3

Read the short story and answer the following questions.

a) Where are Martha, Martin and their children heading for the weekend?

_____

_____

b) What do they carry with them to their destination?

_____

_____

c) Who turns up unexpectedly for the weekend?

_____

_____

d) What is Martha's reaction to the surprise visit? What is Martin's?

_____

_____

e) Who is Janet?

_____

_____

Short stories — Weekend

f) What happens on Saturday?

_____

_____

g) More visitors turn up for Sunday lunch. Who are they?

_____

_____

4
Choose the best adjectives to describe Martha's relationship with Martin. Explain your choice in class.

> affectionate | dependent | intimate | strong | disdaining | special | selfish | traditional | fussy | difficult | close | supportive | submissive | inferior | committed | devoted

5
Reread the short story. Pay special attention to Martin's comments which are inserted in brackets. Speculate what they might suggest.

6
Explain why Martha cries at the end of the story.

POST-READING

7 Group work (3)
Read the short story again. Work in a group of three. Each of you chooses one of the following characters: Martha, Martin or Katie.

a) Use the grid below to note down what you have learned about them and provide evidence from the text.

b) Present your results to the other members of your group and add the missing information.

	Martha	Martin	Katie
Outer appearance (e.g. physical features, clothes, body language)			
Behaviour (how the character acts)			

	Martha	Martin	Katie
Mood (the emotional state of the character)			
Relationship to other people (how the character interacts with others and is perceived by them)			
Evidence from the text			

c) Write a coherent characterization of one of the characters using appropriate quotations from the short story.
→ **Workshop:** Analysing characters → **S12:** Checklist: Analysis – prose → **S23:** How to quote

Language support

Writing a characterization

The protagonist is described/depicted as … | He/She seems to be … | He/She appears to be … | He/She likes to be … | He/She is portrayed as … | His/Her behaviour clearly indicates that … | The fact that he/she … reveals/proves that … | It is quite apparent that …

8
Compare Martha and Katie.

9 CHOOSE

Pair work Imagine a conversation in the car as Martha and Martin drive back to London. What will Martin say about the weekend? What is Martha's response? Write and act out their conversation.
OR
The story is told from Martha's point of view. Describe what happened at the weekend from Martin's point of view.

1 Short stories — The First Feminists

10 Pair work

Create a freeze-frame portraying Martha's and Martin's relationship.

11

Do you think there are typical jobs around the house that should be done by women/men? Why (not)? Form a double circle and discuss.

The First Feminists – A short story (2020)

PRE-READING

1

Look at the picture and think of a caption.

Info

Feminism

Feminism is a social, political and economic movement based on the belief that women all over the world should have equal social, economic and political rights and freedoms. It stresses and advocates the equality of the sexes. No person should be denied certain rights – such as the right to vote – because of their sex and gender. Yet, feminism goes beyond basic rights and seeks deeper cultural shifts like rethinking gender norms, sexism and self-expression. Since the late 18th century, there have been public campaigns for women's rights fighting for educational, professional and interpersonal improvement for women. Among feminism's successes are important personal rights such as owning property and receiving education. However, these rights are not guaranteed in every country of the world. This is also true for legal access to contraception and legal abortion, or protection from domestic violence. Feminism is manifested worldwide and keeps on fighting against societal obstacles preventing women from equal rights and treatment.

2

After having looked at the picture and having read the information in the box, outline your expectations of the short story "The First Feminists".

_____

_____

_____

_____

The First Feminists

by Bernardine Evaristo

we were there when you were just becoming human, unaware that we were carrying the futures of countless billions of souls in our yet to be discovered DNA, unaware we would go on reproducing ever-evolving[1] versions of ourselves, that as the reason for the foetus in every mother's womb[2], we were the Founding Mothers[3] of the Human Gene Pool

of that we are so proud, we say, when we get together for our annual Founding Mother's Reunion, it dominates the conversation – the human race is here because of us, we boast, only to ourselves, sadly, because nobody can see us, which is a shame, what with the obsession with ancestry DNA these days, we'd love to present ourselves to the world, in the flesh – sashaying[4] down the runway of time in our glad rags[5], as weird and wonderful role models from pre-history

we were there when you were just becoming human, although we didn't know it back then, we didn't know that humans were beginning to evolve into existence, after the planet's land mass had floated apart and reformed into continents, after the world had gone into a deep freeze during the ice ages, and ice sheets covered the earth and sea, after mountainous[6] icebergs rose up into the cold, blue landscape, sucking the water of the seas into their peaks and freezing them, draining the waterways, which became hollow basins, exposing the continental shelves[7] hidden several miles below in the underground world of oceans, after the ice melted, and the world re-emerged, and the glacial plains[8] of the Sahara thawed[9] out and burst forth with the green and glorious colours of tropical vegetation and impenetrable[10] rainforest, and became ripe with all the fruits and teeming[11] with all the wildlife

we were the first tribes, the first clans, we were the original trailblazers[12], after enough of us had developed a maternal instinct towards our offspring[13], after we stopped walking away from the curious thing that had ejected itself from our bodies, after enough of us learned that the children born out of siblings copulating[14] with each other, and also with their parents, would, in two or three generations, be born with a terrible weakness passed on for generations to come, after we learned to trek[15] and hunt in search of food, and discovered there was more land to be found out there in The Great Unknown, after we became intelligent enough to create fire, a powerful, artificial heat, and to work with bone and stone, after our brains expanded, our arms shortened, our legs lengthened until finally we became fully upright and slowly made progress with The Great Migration of Humankind, and eventually arrived at a location near you – Asia, America, Australasia[16], the Arctic, Europe, and all over Africa, our homeland, where we all began

it was tough in the early years, we like to remind each other at our decennial[17] Founding Mother's Reunion, we love indulging[18] in 21st Century social customs like pretending to drink tea and eating biscuits, playacting[19] at being contemporary humans, when we've actually been around for mega-annums[20], in one form or another, and how we laughed at the millennium celebrations just the other day, marking the transition from the 20th to the 21st Century, as if it was such a big deal, our descendants really haven't lived at all, unlike us

we who risked extinction[21] over and over again from lack of food or water, from too much heat or too much cold, we who risked extinction from the relentless[22] battles, especially when our food sources dried up, or when others came onto the territory we'd claimed as ours, and when our tribal squabbles[23] led to internecine

---

Annotations

[1] **ever-evolving** = developing continuously
[2] **womb** = the organ inside the body of a woman (or female mammal) in which a baby grows before it is born
[3] **founding mother/father** = a person who establishes an important institution, movement or idea
[4] **to sashay** = to walk gracefully and confidently, in a way that attracts attention
[5] **glad rags** *(infml.)* = best clothes or clothes for special occasions
[6] **mountainous** = having or relating to mountains; very large, huge
[7] **continental shelf** = the edge of a continent that lies under the ocean
[8] **glacial plains** = a flat mass of sand, mud and other material deposited by a moving or melting glacier
[9] **to thaw out** = to get warm gradually after being very cold
[10] **impenetrable** = impossible to enter or get through
[11] **to teem with** = to be full of
[12] **trailblazer** = pioneer, the first person to do sth
[13] **offspring** = a person's children or the young of an animal
[14] **to copulate** = to have sexual intercourse
[15] **to trek** = to walk a long way over land
[16] **Australasia** = the region of Australia, New Zealand and neighbouring islands in the Pacific Ocean
[17] **decennial** = occurring every ten years
[18] **to indulge in** = to allow oneself to enjoy the pleasure of sth
[19] **to playact** = to make believe
[20] **mega-annum** = a period of 1 million years
[21] **extinction** = the death of all living members of a species
[22] **relentless** = harsh and persistent
[23] **squabble** = a noisy quarrel over an unimportant matter

warfare[24] about who was boss, once we discovered the power of power, once we realised that having it meant a better chance of survival, and being in control could be intoxicating

we women were all alpha females back in the day, we had to be to survive, we were so formidable, we'd have it out with anyone who gave us grief, whether male or female, and believe us when we say, you didn't mess with the Founding Mothers, the First Ladies of Humanity, because we gave as good as we got, we fought back like the beasts we all were, we women didn't run screaming when we were confronted with human foes and expect men to defend us, we often attacked first, it was in us, we had the primal energy to do combat[25], we owned our physical strength

the concepts of femininity and masculinity did not exist back in the day, the idea of women behaving in a "'ladylike'" fashion took ages to become normalised, we first humans of Planet Earth shat where we were, farted and burped with impunity, modesty was a future concept, we sexed whenever we felt like it, wore no clothes, not even animal skins or tree barks, not at first, and when we menstruated, we left a trail of blood

we women were equal to men, it was only mothering that tethered[26] our ambitions, when it became our sole responsibility because men liked power so much they wanted to keep it all for themselves, but before then, childrearing[27] was shared equally between all of us, shared between our clan, until the males among us began to pack more muscle density and grow taller, and began to assume the upper hand, demanding we stay with the children rather than go hunting for dinner, for our family, for our clan

we women fought back, we never stopped fighting back, sometimes we won and men were forced to live in a matriarchal[28] society, other times men won and we lived in a patriarchy, sometimes neither dominated and we were egalitarian[29], which was ideal, we were the first communists, but it never lasted long because the human desire to dominate each other prevailed[30], among us were the first control freaks, dictators, emotional manipulators, domestic abusers – and we women survived it all, we women survived everything pre-civilisation had to throw at us, we were the ultimate survival experts, we survived on nuts and berries, in the early days of human life, could go days without water, we slept rough, lived dangerously, fought wild animals, protected our young

luckily for the human race, dinosaurs died out 64 million years before we emerged, we could not have co-existed on the same planet, our small communities roaming[31] the plains on two legs would have ended up as their hors d'oeuvres[32], eaten live, eaten raw

we were the world's first female leaders, the first feminists, the badass bitches of evolution, whose names will never be remembered because we had no names, we were anonymous, we will never be recognised as individuals for our incredible global achievements in ensuring the continuation of the human race, although we lived long before egos became part of being human, we do want to be remembered for what we achieved, and we are saddened that we have been reduced to a few fossils and the imaginations of archaeologists who haven't really got a clue about our lives, how we lived, the different ways in which we died – death by disease, before herbs, incantations[33], health and safety regulations, and medicine, and death by murder, death by tribal warfare, and death by religious sacrifice, once we started to worship deities[34] – animate and inanimate, seen and unseen, once we became intelligent enough to want to make sense of the world we lived in and imagined supreme, all knowing beings who could help us in times of crisis

for the longest time we mated without love, we did not know the meaning of it, although in time we evolved to have feelings for each other, the modern-day concept of love still amuses us, all the songs sung about it when companionship and compatibility[35] are more important, we all agree on that, love is a feeling but if the human race is to survive then we all have to get along

Annotations

[24] **internecine warfare** = destructive fighting which takes place between opposing groups in a country or organization
[25] **combat** = a fight or a battle
[26] **to tether** = to tie sth (especially an animal) with a rope or chain to restrict its movement
[27] **childrearing** = the process of bringing up children
[28] **matriarchal** = controlled by women
[29] **egalitarian** = believing that all people are equal and should have the same rights and opportunities
[30] **to prevail** = to predominate
[31] **to roam** = to move around without a particular purpose
[32] **hors d'oeuvre** = a small dish that is usually served as an appetizer before the main part of a meal
[33] **incantation** = a series of words said or sung as a magic spell
[34] **deity** = a god or goddess
[35] **compatibility** = the ability to exist or work together successfully with sth or sb else

it might seem odd telling you all this now when it was eons[36] ago, but our lives were important to us and we have been so overlooked, so misunderstood, and we are the only ones who know it, sometimes at our Founding Mothers Reunion, after we've had a few gin and tonics and feel relaxed and comforted by our company, we all fall silent and return to our pre-language selves, to a time when we humans were hyper-sensitive to each other, when we sensed more than we thought, when that was enough, when our first sounds were inarticulate grunts, it took an age for words to come into being and many hundreds of thousands of years for us to create language, to join the words up into sentences, and many more for writing to be invented

imagine a world where there are no words to describe your fellow human beings, no words for animals, to describe the trees, the forest, the sea, a child, imagine a world where there was no word for the concept of family, now we know all the words in all the languages, thousands of them, we have so much knowledge stored in our infinite memory banks, we are knowledge and because we take the long view, we worry about what the future holds, we look up into the exploding stars from a society we never imagined and wonder aloud – what will the human race become? how will we evolve?

we discuss our fears that the human race will annihilate[37] itself before too long, dehydrate the planet so that it once more dies of thirst, all plant and animal life withered[38] in the heat, we worry that cannibalism will return, which is what happens when starving people have to resort to desperate measures, we worry about the appearance of new diseases that science cannot control, we worry that humans will detonate[39] themselves into inexistence with the last great wars of this civilisation, perhaps there'll be a global Armageddon[40] of megalomaniacal[41] warlords[42] who are capable of human eradication[43], of planetary destruction, we worry that hackers encoded encryptions[44] will one day collapse the cybers-structures without which this society cannot function – the internet virus that finally closed the world down – the civilisation you are looking for is no longer available

we worry that everything we fought for might one day no longer be here, except for us, hovering in the air, a ghostly presence neither seen, heard or felt by modern human beings who have lost their extra sensory perception, and we will feel so sad that our endeavours over millions of years might one day come to an end, and then we decide to cheer ourselves up by wallowing in nostalgia, because we are happiest in the past, when we were younger, more truly alive and everything was new

we remember a time before the internet, before computers, before laws
before cars, aeroplanes, bicycles, penny farthings[45] and horse-drawn carriages
before factories, before politics, before royalty, before money, before houses
before agriculture, before the idea of work, before marriage, before enslavement
before the formation of countries, governments, before leisure and social lives
before cooked food, before sophisticated cognitive reasoning, before science
before pollution, before manufacture, education, dancing, poetry
before we could plan ahead, could think outside of ourselves
before we were able to tell our own stories
before our songs were sung
we were there
we were there
we were there

---

[36] **eon** = an indefinitely long period of time
[37] to **annihilate** = to destroy completely
[38] **withered** = dry and decaying, losing vitality
[39] to **detonate** = to explode or to cause sth to explode
[40] **Armageddon** = a catastrophic and extremely destructive conflict; the end of the world
[41] **megalomaniacal** = having a very strong desire for power
[42] **warlord** = a military leader who controls an area
[43] **eradication** = complete destruction
[44] **encryption** = the process of converting information into a secret code
[45] **penny farthing** = a type of bicycle with a very large front wheel and a small back wheel which was used in the past

Short stories — Post-reading

WHILE READING

3

Read the short story.
a) Divide the story into meaningful parts.
b) Give every part a heading.
c) Summarize the story.

4

Explain the following quote:
"we worry that everything we fought for might one day no longer be here, except for us [...]" (ll. 189–190)

5

Describe the role of women as depicted in the short story. Do men play any role?

POST-READING

6

a) **Think:** Make a list of three themes you consider central to your understanding of the short story.
b) **Pair:** Explain your choices to a partner and agree on three major themes.
c) **Share:** Discuss your results in a small group and agree on three themes, giving reasons for your choice by presenting examples from the short story.

7

Bernardine Evaristo hardly uses any punctuation in her short story.
a) Rewrite the short story using punctuation.
b) How do you decide where to put a comma, question mark or full stop?
c) How does it change the understanding and meaning of the text if more punctuation is used?
d) Discuss in class why Bernardine Evaristo might have decided to leave out most of the punctuation.

Post-reading: The short stories

1

Compare the short stories you have read. What similarities are there and what differences can you identify?

Similarities	Differences

Post-reading — Short stories

2

Look at the quotes taken from the short stories. Choose the one you like best or consider most relevant. Explain the context of the quote and analyse its relevance for the short story.

> And yet she had loved him – sometimes. Often she had not. What did it matter! What could love, the unsolved mystery, count for in face of this possession of self-assertion which she suddenly recognized as the strongest impulse of her being!
> *("The Story of an Hour")*

> She didn't say as much. Domestic details like this were very boring, and any mild complaint was registered by Martin as a scene. And to make a scene was so ungrateful.
> *("Weekend")*

> […] before then, childrearing was shared equally between all of us, shared between our clan, until the males among us began to pack more muscle density and grow taller, and began to assume the upper hand, […]
> *("The First Feminists")*

> Personally, I disagree with their ideas.
> Personally, I believe that congenial work, with excitement and change, would do me good.
> But what is one to do?
> *("The Yellow Wallpaper")*

> It is so hard to talk with John about my case, because he is so wise, and because he loves me so.
> *("The Yellow Wallpaper")*

> There would be no powerful will bending hers in that blind persistence with which men and women believe they have a right to impose a private will upon a fellow-creature.
> *("The Story of an Hour")*

> we women fought back, we never stopped fighting back, sometimes we won and men were forced to live in a matriarchal society, other times men won and we lived in a patriarchy, sometimes neither dominated and we were egalitarian, […]
> *("The First Feminists")*

> If Martha chose to go out to work – as was her perfect right, Martin allowed, even though it wasn't the best thing for the children, but that must be Martha's moral responsibility – Martha must surely pay her domestic stand-in.
> *("Weekend")*

3

Discuss in class what the quotes tell us about female roles and gender equality.

Topic: The individual and society

The individual and society

QUESTIONS OF IDENTITY – AMBITIONS AND OBSTACLES

1 Pair work

Look at the diagram and the photos below. What do they tell you in terms of people's ambitions and obstacles in society? Discuss with a partner.

Half or more say being poor, Muslim, black or Hispanic puts people at a disadvantage in our society

% saying being each of the following helps/hurts people's ability to get ahead in our country these days

Being …	Hurts a lot	Hurts a little	Helps a little	Helps a lot	Neither helps nor hurts
White	4	7	21	38	28
Asian	3	18	26	8	44
Native American	16	22	16	7	37
Hispanic	17	35	11	6	30
Black	25	30	10	7	26
Evangelical Christian	5	10	19	11	54
Jewish	4	16	15	8	55
Muslim	31	32	5	3	27
A man	3	7	28	38	24
A woman	10	41	15	8	25
Wealthy	2	2	11	78	7
Poor	66	20	3	2	8

Note: Share of respondents who didn't offer an answer not shown.
Source: Survey of U.S. adults conducted Jan. 22-Feb. 5, 2019.
"Race in America 2019"
PEW RESEARCH CENTER

> **Language support**
>
> The survey shows … / Photo number … shows …
> There are a lot of obstacles concerning …
> It hurts a little/a lot to be …
> In contrast to …
> If you compare people's ambitions and obstacles in society, one can say …

1

2

3

4

The individual and society — Topic 1

2 Pair work

Describe and analyse the infographic below.

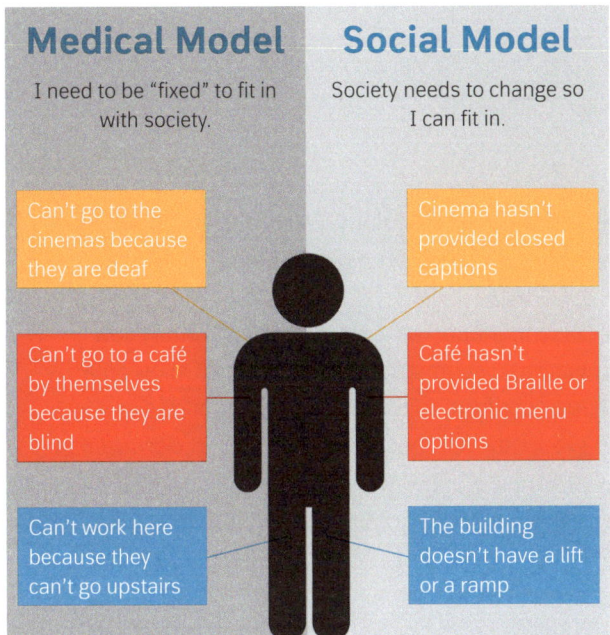

3 Pair work

a) List obstacles that people with disabilities face in their work life.
b) Find solutions to the obstacles listed in a).

4

Milling around: Talk to at least five classmates about your ambitions and goals in life.
Find out whether your classmates give the same or similar answers to your own.

5

a) Do some research on the term "from rags to riches".
b) Write a short entry on "from rags to riches" for an online dictionary.
c) **Group work** Discuss: Do you think that a "from rags to riches" story is still possible? If so, find famous persons as examples.

QUESTIONS OF IDENTITY – CONFORMITY VS. INDIVIDUALISM

6 → **Workshop:** Analysing a cartoon   → **S17:** How to work with cartoons

a) Look at the cartoon and describe it.
b) Analyse its message.
c) Comment on the message of the cartoon.

"What's wrong with you?"

Topic: The individual and society

7

Read the following extract from an online article.

The Dangers of Conformity

By Paul Sloane   24/07/2023

Conformity can be defined as the act of following social norms, rules, or expectations in order to fit in or be accepted by a group.
While conformity can be beneficial in some situ-
5 ations, such as following traffic rules to ensure safety, there are also dangers associated with conformity, including:
- Loss of individuality: Conformity can lead to a loss of individuality as people may suppress
10 their own opinions and ideas in order to fit in with a group. This can result in a lack of creativity and innovation, as well as a failure to address important issues.
- Groupthink: Conformity can lead to groupthink,
15 which is a situation where a group of people makes decisions based on maintaining group harmony rather than objective analysis of the situation. This can lead to poor decision-making
20 and can be particularly dangerous in situations where the stakes are high, such as in politics or business.
- Discrimination and prejudice: Conformity can lead to discrimination and prejudice as people may conform to the beliefs and attitudes of a
25 group, even if those beliefs and attitudes are discriminatory or prejudiced.
- Inhibition of personal growth: Conformity can inhibit personal growth as people may avoid taking risks or pursuing their own goals in
30 order to conform to societal norms or group expectations.
- Failure to question authority: Conformity can result in a failure to question authority, which can lead to acceptance of unjust or unethical
35 practices.
[...]

a) **Pair work** Write down four questions about the text to test your partner's knowledge.
b) Answer each other's questions.
c) Find at least one example for each danger of conformity described in the article.
d) Discuss in class: What are the dangers of individualism? Can you think of any?

CHANCES AND CHALLENGES FOR SOCIETY – GENDER ISSUES

8

Look at the word cloud. What challenges for today's society can you spot?

9

a) What other challenges for society can you think of?
b) **Group work** Compare your results in your group.
c) Share your results in class and discuss which of the challenges can also be seen as chances for our future.

10

a) Describe the picture.

b) Look up unknown gender and orientation icons and create a legend for all of them.

11

What's the difference between 'gender' and 'sex'? Look up both terms and write a definition for each of them.

12

Comment on the following quote.

> "A gender-equal society would be one where the word 'gender' does not exist, where everyone can be themselves."
> – *Gloria Steinem*

| Topic | The individual and society |

13
You are going to listen to an extract from a *BBC* interview in which presenter Kim Chakanetsa talks to two women fighting for equality with men in their chosen sport. **Webcode** DSW-73698-01

First read the questions below. Then listen to the interview (up to 04:57) and answer the questions.

a) What is the big deal about equality for women's sports besides payment?

___

b) What did Kathryn Bertine successfully lobby for?

___

c) What makes Hajra Khan so special in her profession?

___

d) What is money in terms of equality in women's sport according to Hajra Khan?

___

e) What goes hand in hand according to Kathryn Bertine?

___

f) Where did Hajra Khan use to train?

___

g) How was the enormous pay gap between male and female football players justified?

___

h) Until when were women in cycling denied a bigger salary?

___

14 Group work
Have a formal debate on the following statement: "Female athletes deserve equal pay to men."
- Get into six groups and prepare the debate. Three groups collect arguments in favour of the statement, the other three groups collect arguments against it.
- Choose a chairperson to act as a 'referee'. He/She opens the debate and keeps track of the time (e.g. a one-minute time limit for each speaker).
- Each group chooses their first speaker (the others can join the discussion later). Start the debate through the chairperson.
- Take turns in arguing for or against the statement. The chairperson always introduces the next speaker.
- Open the debate for questions from the floor.
- In the end, the chairperson closes the debate.

The individual and society — Topic 1

Language support

Useful phrases for the chairperson:
- Ladies and gentlemen, today's motion is equal pay in sports. Team A is going to argue in favour of the motion, team B is going to argue against it. May the best team win! We'll start with a first person in favour of the motion. ...
- The debate is now open to the floor. ...
- There are some questions from the audience. ...
- Now I would like to ask the audience to vote on the motion: Would those in favour of it please raise their hands? ... Would those against the motion please raise their hands? ... The motion is accepted/lost.

15 Pair work
What do you know about gender inequality? Talk to a partner.

16
Read five statements from *Human Rights Careers* on causes of gender inequality. What do you think? Match the given percentages and numbers to the statements below.

> 6 | 24.3% | 25% | 75% | 200

1. Around the world, women still have less access to education than men.

   _____ of young women between 15–24 will not finish primary school.

2. Only _____ countries in the world give women the same legal work rights as men.

3. In fact, most economies give women only _____ of the rights of men.

4. According to the World Health Organization, over _____ million women who don't want to get pregnant are not using contraception.

5. Of all national parliaments at the beginning of 2019, only _____ of seats were filled by women.

17 → **Workshop:** Mediation → **S19:** How to improve your mediation skills → **S7:** Checklist: Writing a blog post

Imagine you are an exchange student at a school in Britain. Your class is doing a project on gender roles around the world. You are asked to contribute a German perspective on the matter and found an opinion piece from *Deutschlandfunk Kultur*. Read the text below and use the information to write a blog post for the school website.

Gemeinsame Doppelnamen reichen nicht!

Ein Kommentar von Tanja Dückers • 03.04.2023

Soll es künftig beim Heiraten auch die Möglichkeit geben, die Nachnamen beider Partner zu verschmelzen? Dieser Vorschlag kam nicht in den aktuellen Entwurf des Justizministeriums. *Autorin und Journalistin Tanja Dückers findet das falsch.*

Topic: The individual and society

Bundesjustizminister Marco Buschmann (FDP) will das Namensrecht reformieren und es Eheleuten ermöglichen, künftig gemeinsame Doppelnamen zu führen. Auch die Grünen hatten eine Reform ins Gespräch gebracht: die Verschmelzung von Nachnamen.

Wie bei so manchen Vorschlägen der Grünen wurden sogleich in routiniert-reflexhafter Weise hämische Stimmen laut. Doch bei näherer Betrachtung erscheint die Idee nicht so abwegig: Sie erlaubt Ehepartnern einen egalitären Kompromiss ohne endlose Doppelnamen oder den Verzicht auf einen der beiden Nachnamen. Und doch wird eine Gemeinsamkeit betont, anders als bei dem Modell: Jeder behält den eigenen Namen, als wäre man nie miteinander in den Ehestand getreten.

Traditionelle Rollenbilder

In Ländern wie den USA oder Großbritannien ist dieses Meshing längst Praxis. Der ehemalige Bürgermeister von Los Angeles, Antonio Villaraigosa, hat seinen Nachnamen Villar mit dem seiner Frau Corina Raigosa verschmolzen. In vielen spanischsprachigen Ländern haben die Bürger in der Regel zwei Nachnamen: einen vom Vater, einen von der Mutter.

Auch wenn der Vorschlag in Deutschland sicher nicht mit Breitenwirkung umgesetzt werden wird, wirft er doch ein Licht auf ein wenig beachtetes Feld: Parität der Geschlechter herrscht in Deutschland bei der Annahme der Nachnamen nicht einmal entfernt.

Im Gegenteil: Allen bekannten Doppelnamen zum Trotz kann man größtenteils immer noch die tradierte Rollenaufteilung beobachten. Bis 1991 war es geltendes Recht, dass der Ehemann den Ehenamen bestimmen darf. Inzwischen ist es über 30 Jahre her, seit dieses Gesetz gekippt wurde und das Verfassungsgericht beschlossen hat, es sei unvereinbar mit dem Grundgesetz. Die angemahnte Reform trat drei Jahre später in Kraft: Seit 1994 können sich Ehepartnerinnen und -partner entscheiden, ihren Nachnamen zu behalten.

Nur sechs Prozent wählen den Namen der Frau

Aber wie sieht die Realität aus? Nur jedes achte Ehepaar nutzt die Möglichkeit, den jeweils eigenen Nachnamen weiterhin zu behalten. Laut einer Studie der Gesellschaft für deutsche Sprache von 2018 entscheidet sich ein Ehepaar in nur sechs Prozent der Fälle für den Nachnamen der Frau. Viel dürfte sich daran bisher nicht geändert haben. Dass sich nur so wenige Paare für den Namen der Ehefrau entscheiden, liegt sicher nicht daran, dass Frauen die hässlicheren Nachnamen mit in die Ehe bringen. Männer argumentieren laut der genannten Studie häufig mit der Tradition. Sie empfänden es als Zeichen von Schwäche oder Unmännlichkeit, den Namen der Frau anzunehmen. Frauen könnten jedoch ebenso argumentieren, etwa weil ein Name sonst in der Familienlinie aussterben würde oder weil er als wichtiger Teil der eigenen Identität begriffen wird.

Ein weiteres Argument für das Beibehalten des eigenen Namens laut Gesellschaft für deutsche Sprache: Wer schon Karriere gemacht hat, möchte seinen Namen nicht aufgeben. Bei Eheschließung sind Männer in Deutschland im Schnitt knapp drei Jahre älter als Frauen. Somit wiegt ihr „Karriereargument" schwerer als das ihrer Partnerinnen.

Mauer, Hattmann und Schauck

Die Kritik selbst ernannter Sprachästheten kann man bei der Frage nach der Nachnamensregelung getrost zurückweisen, wenn man sich einige der Doppelnamen-Wortungetüme von Personen des öffentlichen Lebens in Erinnerung ruft. Außerdem lässt sich über Geschmack bekanntlich nicht streiten. Es gibt Menschen, die ihre Kinder Rapunzel, Waterloo oder Bierstübl nennen dürfen – diese Vornamen wurden in Deutschland tatsächlich erlaubt.

Dagegen klingen Mauer (Angela Merkel und Joachim Sauer), Hattmann (Marco Buschmann und Janina Hatt) und Schauck (Joachim Gauck und Daniela Schadt, falls sie heiraten würden), doch vergleichsweise harmlos. Und Frau Leutheusser-Schnarrenberger könnte einfach Leutberger heißen – falls sie denn diesen Namen bevorzugen würde.

18 Group work

In our society, steps are being taken to improve gender equality and the equality of opportunities. Prepare a card survey: Think about supportive measures that could be used to improve gender equality. Note down your ideas on cards. Then present your ideas to the class and cluster the cards on the board.

19

Do some research on one of the following topics:
- violence against women
- empowerment of women
- balanced participation in decision-making
- gender mainstreaming
- gender stereotypes and sexism
- sex roles in contemporary western societies
- toys and games for boys and girls

Prepare a short presentation. You can also choose to record it as a podcast or to create a short video.

QUESTIONS OF IDENTITY AND GENDER ISSUES IN THE SHORT STORIES

Go back to the short stories you have read.

20

Name the different ambitions and obstacles the protagonists of the short stories have to deal with.

21

Provide as many examples of gender stereotypes and sexism from the short stories as you can.

22

Analyse the role of the institution of marriage in the short stories.

23 Pair work

Discuss which of the short stories present the most conformative character and the most individualized character. Give reasons for your choice.

24

Explain why all of the short stories can be considered feminist literature. Discuss your results in class.

25

Do you think it is important to read feminist literature at school? Why (not)?
Have a fishbowl discussion.

Info

Fishbowl discussion

A fishbowl discussion is an efficient way to practice group discussions.

Four to six students sit in a circle, the "fishbowl". Each of them first presents their arguments and then starts actively discussing the topic. The other students sit outside the "fishbowl" and listen carefully to their classmates' discussion.

There are two ways to organize a fishbowl discussion: a closed and an open "fishbowl".

In a closed "fishbowl", all chairs inside the "fishbowl" are occupied by students. The audience outside the circle listens and takes notes on who had the best arguments.

In an open "fishbowl", however, one or two chairs in the "fishbowl" remain empty and any member of the audience can, at any time, occupy an empty chair and join the discussion.

Students usually take turns in a fishbowl discussion to practice both discussing a topic and giving feedback to the contributors.

2 Novel — Behold the Dreamers

Pre-reading

1

You are going to read the novel *Behold the Dreamers* (2016) by Imbolo Mbue.

a) Examine the title and the book cover below.
   You can look at more book covers online:
   Webcode DSW-73698-02
   Try to paraphrase the title of the novel and assess the choice of words.

> **Info**
>
> According to *Oxford Languages*, the verb **behold** means "*(archaic, literary)* see or observe (someone or something, especially of remarkable or impressive nature)".
> Example: "behold your lord and prince!"

Publisher: Random House
(Penguin Random House LLC), 2016

b) Based on your observations, speculate what the novel could be about.
   Make a mind map and note down your first ideas about the plot.

(Behold the Dreamers)

Behold the Dreamers | **Novel**

While reading

Info

A **reading map** will help you follow and keep track of the novel throughout the reading process, so you can review the plot easily and quickly, and access passages about characters, themes and motifs when working on specific topic tasks. Highlighting thoroughly saves you time and effort when analysing the novel.

2

While you read the novel, create your own reading guide through the narrative in the form of a reading map.

Use …
- **sticky notes** to summarize each chapter in as many sentences or bullet points as you need.
- **smaller strips** to mark passages in the book where important topics and motifs are mentioned.
- **different colours** to highlight crucial information about the characters, key words, sentences or passages.
- **symbols and abbreviations** to mark aspects such as topics and motifs which are weaved into the novel.

Examples:

☁	dream motif (a significant or recurrent theme)
☺ / ☹	themes of happiness/sadness
↔	dichotomies (for example, rich – poor, black – white, …)
$	information on somebody's job situation or financial background information
"…"	important quotes
!	crucial events
?!	indignation concerning an event or situation, surprise, or point for discussion
R / Cl–J	relationships (for example, between Clark and Jende)
pol / gov	issues that concern politics or the government
US	descriptions and perceptions of the United States

47

Novel — Behold the Dreamers

CHAPTER ONE

3

a) Describe the behaviour and feelings of Jende and Clark during their first encounter. Provide textual evidence and write the words and quotes around the characters below.

Language support

Adjectives to describe behaviour

condescending | respectful | submissive | nervous | insecure | rude | relieved | tense | busy | desperate | arrogant | demanding | undignified | disrespectful | benevolent | gracious | polite | welcoming | interested | ...

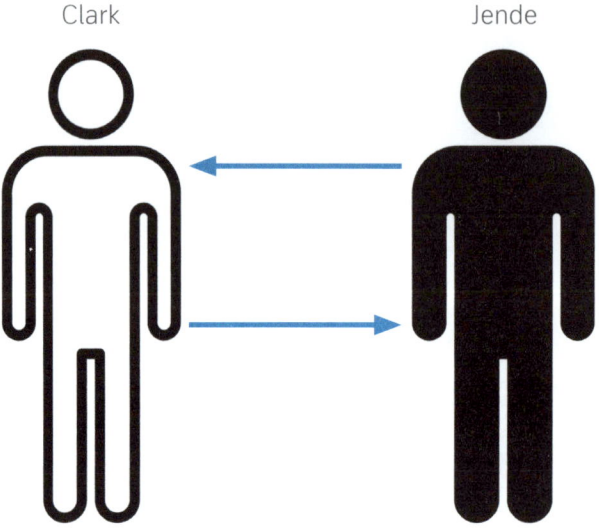

Clark   Jende

b) Assess Jende's and Clark's behaviour.

CHAPTERS TWO – THREE

4

Describe Neni's and Jende's dreams. Include quotes.

Neni   Jende

48

Behold the Dreamers | Novel

CHAPTERS FOUR – SIX

5
Create a (digital) web diagram about the family dynamics in the Edwards family.

6
Contrast Jende's descriptions of Limbe (Cameroon, Central Africa) and America.

Limbe:
_____
_____
_____
_____
_____
_____
_____
_____
_____
_____
_____
_____

America:
_____
_____
_____
_____
_____
_____
_____
_____

Novel — Behold the Dreamers

CHAPTERS SEVEN – THIRTEEN

7 Summarize Leah's concerns about the Wall Street firm, Lehman Brothers.

8 Describe Neni's work ethic and the effect life in America has on her.

9 Explain the consequences of Jende's application for asylum not being approved.

10 Pair work
In order to recapitulate important issues and information in chapters 11 and 12, use the words in the boxes below and exchange information with your partner. You may also give opinions, add extra information, do some quick research, or raise questions. Be prepared to share your results in class.

Partner A: | truth and love | work permit | Obama | Hillary | police |

Partner B: | Professor | homosexuality | transgender | dishonesty | domestic violence |

11
a) Note down what you find out about Cindy's character in chapter 13.
b) Add what you find out from Cindy's phone conversation about Clark to your family dynamics web diagram from task 5.

CHAPTER FOURTEEN

12 Describe the situation in the bar and Neni's observations about 'belonging'.

13 → **S21:** How to succeed in oral exams
While waiting for Neni to come to the US, Jende "[…] often wondered if leaving home in search of something as fleeting as fortune was ever worthwhile." (p. 70)
Comment on his statement, using the think – pair – share method.

> **Info**
> **Method: Think – pair – share**
> **Think:** What do you think? Make a list of pros and cons.
> **Pair:** Based on your results, present your opinion and listen to your partner's.
> **Share:** Discuss in a group of four.

✓ It is worth it because …	✗ It is not worth it because …

Behold the Dreamers | Novel

CHAPTERS FIFTEEN – SIXTEEN

14

a) Describe the difficulties that Lehman Brothers is facing.

b) Contrast Tom's stance with Clark's on how to deal with the issues at Lehman Brothers.

15 → **S9:** How to structure a text → **S23:** How to quote

a) Analyse Vince's description of America.

b) Compare it to Jende's description in chapter 6.

CHAPTERS SEVENTEEN – TWENTY-FIVE

16 → **S12:** Checklist: Analysis – prose

a) Characterize Cindy Edwards. → **Workshop:** Analysing characters

b) Analyse which concepts of 'home' are presented in these chapters.

CHAPTERS TWENTY-SIX – THIRTY-FOUR

17

a) Read the information about Lehman Brothers from the online encyclopedia *Britannica*.

b) Describe Jende's dream and the significant economic event.

c) List the consequences of the collapse.

d) Explain Jende's predicament concerning the Edwards family.

> **Info**
>
> **Bankruptcy of Lehman Brothers,** collapse of the investment bank Lehman Brothers that occurred on September 15, 2008. It was the largest bankruptcy in U.S. history at that time, and it was among the most significant events of the financial crisis of 2007–08. […]

CHAPTERS THIRTY-FIVE – FORTY-THREE

18

Answer the following questions.

a) What important document does Jende receive?

_____

_____

b) What does Neni do to deal with the situation?

_____

_____

c) How does Jende perceive himself and his behaviour?

_____

_____

d) What does Clark need to see Jende about?

_____

_____

Novel — Behold the Dreamers

e) What are the effects of the new situation on Jende and Neni individually?

f) What are the effects on their relationship?

g) What does Neni do at the Edwards' home?

CHAPTERS FORTY-FOUR – FIFTY-FOUR

19 → **S12:** Checklist: Analysis – prose → **Workshop:** Analysing characters → **S8:** How to improve your text

a) Characterize Neni.
b) What is Neni considering doing in order to ensure that she and her family can stay in America? (Refer to chapters 44, 51 and 53.)

c) **Group work (3)** Work in groups of three. One of you is Neni, one of you tries to assert that her idea is beneficial, and one of you tries to convince her that it would be a fatal mistake. Write the dialogue and perform the role play.

d) Assess Neni's behaviour.
e) Neni says, "Maybe I'm becoming another person." (p. 229) Comment on her statement.

20

Decide whether the statements below are true or false. Provide evidence from the text for each statement.

	Statement	True	False	Evidence
1	Cindy Edwards dies due to the consumption of drugs in combination with alcohol.			
2	Neni feels guilty about Cindy's death because of her blackmail.			
3	The dean is very helpful and supports Neni's ambitions.			
4	Neni is grateful for the dean's realistic advice.			
5	Watching videos of the funeral after Pa Jonga's death makes up for the fact that Jende wasn't able to be there.			
6	Neni and Jende agree that they should leave the US.			
7	Before Neni arrived in the US, America was synonymous with happiness to her.			
8	Jende is remorseful after hitting Neni.			
9	Neni doesn't understand why Jende has turned into an abuser and can never forgive him.			
10	Jende applies for voluntary departure.			

21

a) Describe Jende's changed attitude towards America.
b) "I'm ready to go back home," (p. 212) Jende states. Explain what led to his decision.
c) Explain why Neni wants to stay in the US.

CHAPTERS FIFTY-FIVE – SIXTY-TWO

22

Describe the impact that Cindy's death has on Clark, Vince and Mighty.

23

Explain what Vince criticizes about American society.

24

Describe Jende's and Neni's thoughts concerning their future life in Cameroon and their present life in America after the request for voluntary departure has been granted.

25

Comment on this statement about Neni:
"[…] she was not one of them – she was now a woman of class […]." (p. 261)

Novel — Behold the Dreamers

26

Analyse the meaning of the final question in the novel:

> "What did you say, Papa?" a drowsy and awakening Liomi asked.
> Jende turned from the front seat and looked at his son. "Guess where we are," he whispered.
> "Where?" Liomi asked, struggling to open his eyes.
> "Guess," Jende whispered again.
> The boy opened his eyes and said, "Home?" (p. 261)

Post-reading

27

Analyse how the relationship between Jende and Neni changes throughout the novel.

28

a) Examine what 'home' means to Jende and Clark.
b) Comment on the fact that the Jongas return to Limbe.
   → **Workshop:** Writing a comment   → **S6:** How to write a discussion/comment

29   → **S12:** Checklist: Analysis – prose   → **Workshop:** Analysing characters   → **S8:** How to improve your text

Choose one of the following characters and write a characterization:
- Vince Edwards
- Jende Jonga
- Clark Edwards

30

a) Describe the relationship between Vince and his parents.
b) Examine the importance of family for Clark and Cindy Edwards.

31

A lot of things distinguish the Edwards family from the Jongas. Define the differences and then focus on what they have in common.

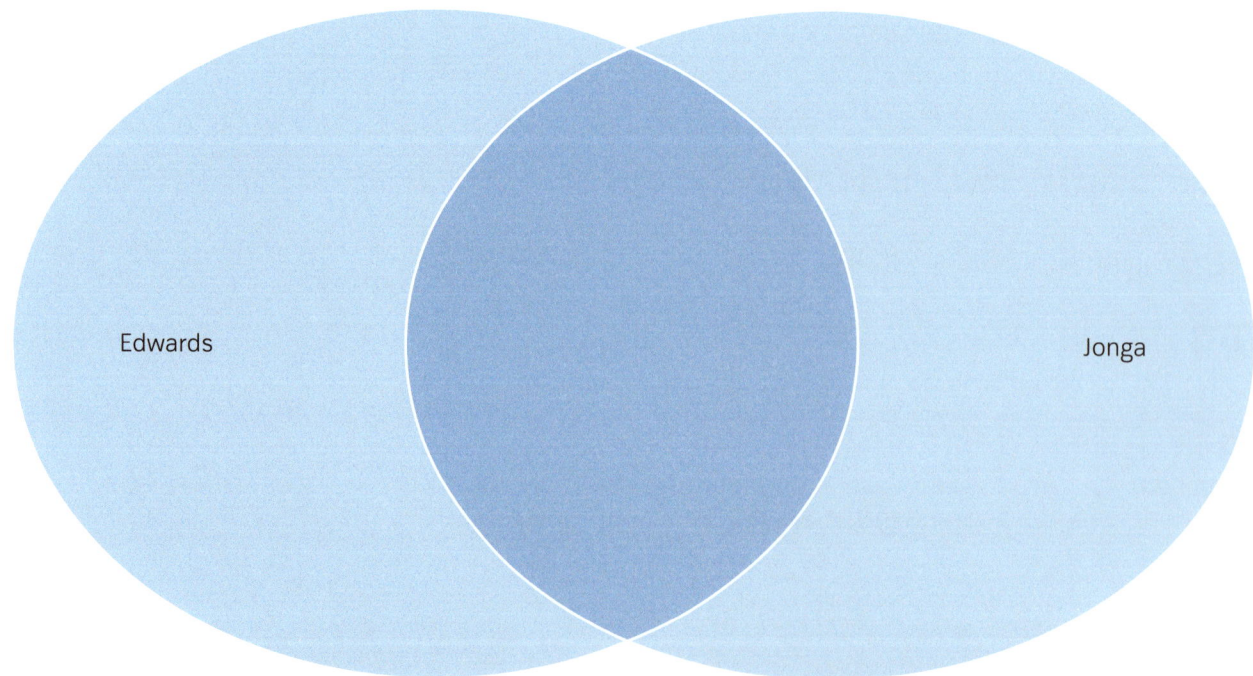

32

Compare Jende's to Neni's relationship with the Edwards family.

33

Describe the role of the church community for Neni and her family.

34

Examine the role of women in the novel.

35 → **S15:** How to describe pictures

a) Look at the two photos below. Describe the pictures and relate them to the novel.

1

2

b) Discuss whether the depiction of Clark and Jende in the novel reinforces stereotypes.

36

a) Discuss the thematic focus of the novel. Is the novel about …?

immigration | finances | dreams | social class | equality | racism | the pursuit of happiness

b) Compare your findings to your expectations from task 1 on p. 46. Decide which book cover you think is most suitable to convey what the novel is about. Give reasons for your choice.

c) Create your own book cover based on your assessment.

37

a) Read the following text by Aaron Bady and outline his critique.

Has Imbolo Mbue Written the Great American Novel?
How an Unknown Cameroonian Novelist Followed in the Footsteps of Jonathan Franzen

By Aaron Bady October 26, 2016

[…] At the start of the novel, Africa is given as a place to flee, an abjection to be abjured. When his employer idly asks him what his home village is like, he [Jende Jonga] is damningly unequivocal:

Everyone wants to come to America, sir. Everyone. To be in this country, sir. To live in this country. Ah! It is the greatest thing in the world … my country is no good. It is nothing like America. I stay in my country, I would have become nothing. I would have remained nothing. My son will grow up and remain poor like me, just like I was poor like my father. But in America, sir? I can become something. I can

Novel — Behold the Dreamers

even become a respectable man. My son can be a respectable man.

His dream of America, then, is this very particular story of Obama: the dream that the son of an African might cease to be African. Instead of becoming nothing – instead of being reduced to being a function of his own lies – he might become *something*.

The extent to which Jende Jonga buys into this version of the American dream – America as Not-Africa – makes the novel, frankly, a bit racist. To put it bluntly, it confirms and displays an uncomfortably large number of stereotypes about Africa and Africans. If you make a list of words to describe Jende Jonga, you get an image of the African as: simple, good, hopeless, ignorant, confused, earnest, happy, selfless, patriarchal, incurious, faithful, dependable, and dependent. If he is sympathetic, the depth of his pathos is matched and facilitated by his shallowness of intellect; his American dream is always, also, his totalizing self-negation as African. He is many things, but one of them is a figure of Fanonian[1] abjection; if his is the story of the American dream, it is also the story of African self-hate.

To be clear: Jende Jonga and his wife, Neni, are rendered with sympathy and warmth, and it is their lives which concern us as readers. But they are also caricatures of the good-hearted, ignorant immigrant. Their misconceptions about America are played throughout for light comedy – as when Neni describes lingerie as the American version of love potions – and the many small confusions and humiliations which form Jende's life as a rich man's chauffeur never result in anything approaching resentment or hostility. His love for his employer – and the depth of his gratitude and satisfaction – is unsettling.

But maybe it's meant to be. I don't know. A caricature can be warm-hearted, coming from a place of sympathy and love. It can also be minstrelsy[2]. And this is the question, the problem with the novel: is it "problematic," or does it expose the problem with the American dream, and its exceptionalist presumptions? Without Obama's claim that "in no other country on earth is my story even possible" – a line in his 2004 convention speech which panders to soft racism and xenophobia – would his presidency have been thinkable?

To believe in that American story – as Jende Jonga wholeheartedly does, at the beginning of the novel – one must accept its racist premise: to become a person with an American future, Jende Jonga must scrub away his African past. He must insist that America *is* the promised land, for which he would give anything; Africa is the bondage in Egypt from which his family must flee. And so he does.

But this is not where the novel ends. What saves it, for me, is the distance *Behold the Dreamers* eventually creates between its subjects and their dreams, between the dream they think they are living and the lives they ultimately wake up to. It does this through a simple act of narrative framing: we never leave the minds of the novel's African protagonists. For all its apparent fascination with a rich, white, American-born family – as our protagonists eavesdrop and peer into the lives they aspire to live – the book never leaves the perspective of their servants, never sees the one percent except from the perspective of their employees; for all the hyper-American signifiers that get thrown around – immigration, the American dream, even New York City itself – the novel only ever sees America through their eyes. We never see the dreamers through America's.

This is important. Who is laughing clarifies who this comedy of manners and errors is laughing *with*. There is gentle mockery, here, of their pretensions and misconceptions – as when Neni aspires, someday, to purchase a fine suit from "a fine white people store" like Target – but the naiveté of their aspirations to nouveau riches is also their innocent belief in America itself. And the novel ultimately mocks both beliefs as naïve. Imbolo Mbue became an American success story when she wrote this novel, but her novel never tells this story. Jende Jonga's son will not grow up to be Obama.

Instead, the novel uses the destruction of a family to represent the failure of the American dream.

Annotations
[1] **Fanonian** = relating to Frantz Fanon (1925–1961), French-Martiniquais psychologist and philosopher
[2] **minstrelsy** = A minstrel was a travelling musician and singer in medieval times. The term can also refer to minstrel shows, in which white performers wore dark make-up to imitate black people through stereotypes and caricatures. (For more information cf. the box on p. 81.)

Behold the Dreamers — Novel

100 But the family that splinters is not Jende Jonga's: while the lives of the one percent fall apart, Jende Jonga's story continues even *after* its American chapter comes to a conclusion. [...] life is about irresolution, about questions, about change. And 105 [...] this novel ends with a question mark (literally) and with the question of what is to come next.

Behold the Dreamers is about the consequences of dreaming too long, too recklessly, and too credulously, but even more, it's about waking up from 110 that dream, and living, [...]. In the warm comedy of an immigrant family, we find a different story, a story that in its very irresolution, continues to have a future.

b) Comment on Aaron Bady's review. → **Workshop:** Writing a comment → **S6:** How to write a discussion/comment

38

a) You are a German student spending a year abroad in America. You have read the novel *Behold the Dreamers* in your high school literature class. Your teacher has asked the class to submit articles which show how the novel was received internationally. You have chosen an article from the German newspaper *FAZ*. Read the text below and use the information to write an English article in which you outline the strengths and weaknesses of the novel. → **Workshop:** Mediation → **S19:** How to improve your mediation skills

---

Imbolo Mbues neuer Roman
So hat Amerika die Einwanderer immer gebraucht
In „Das geträumte Land" bricht die Autorin Imbolo Mbue mit dem Klischee des amerikanischen Traums. Nun erscheint ihr in Amerika gefeierter Debütroman auf Deutsch. Eine Begegnung.

Von Annabelle Hirsch – 11.02.2017 – Aktualisiert am 15.02.2017, 13:17 Uhr

In der Nacht der amerikanischen Wahl saß Imbolo Mbue vor ihrem Fernseher in New York und schrie: „No! Florida! What's wrong with you?", „Iowa! OMG! What are you doing?", „Michigan, please don't!" Sie 5 zitterte und wütete, beschimpfte das Gerät, ging zu Bett und beschloss, erst einmal gar nicht mehr zu reden. Vielleicht weil man der Realität ihre Wirkungskraft ganz gut verweigert, solange man sie nicht benennt, vielleicht aber auch einfach weil, 10 na ja, worüber auch? Mit welchen Worten erfasst man eine Wirklichkeit, der man bis vor kurzem keine Chance eingeräumt hat?
Es sei ja gar nicht so, dass man es sich nicht hätte denken können, sagt sie, als wir uns zehn Tage 15 nach der Wahl an einem regnerischen Vormittag im „Whole Foods" des Times Warner Center in Manhattan treffen. Natürlich habe sie es irgendwie auch geahnt, so wie retrospektiv die meisten, aber man habe eben gehofft: „Wir hätten unseren Mäd-20 chen sagen können: Schau, eine Frau im Weißen Haus!" Die Tatsache, dass das Land, in das sie all ihre Hoffnung und Liebe gesteckt hat, dieses Land, in das sie vor über zehn Jahren aus ihrem kamerunischen Heimatort Limbé gekommen ist, um ein 25 besseres Leben zu finden, nun einen Mann wählt, der Menschen wie sie, also Frauen, Schwarze, Einwanderer, beschimpft und verachtet, sei ziemlich bitter. Die Tatsache, dass dieses Land, an das sie glaubt, offensichtlich an einen Mann wie 30 Donald Trump glaubt und ihn zum 45. Präsident der Vereinigten Staaten von Amerika macht, wiederum sehr ernüchternd.
Noch ein paar Wochen zuvor hatte Mbue in der „New York Times" darüber geschrieben, wie 35 glücklich und stolz sie sei, nach all den Jahren auf amerikanischem Boden endlich dazuzugehören, endlich Amerikanerin zu sein, endlich wählen zu können, überhaupt zum ersten Mal in ihrem Leben (in Kamerun zu wählen sei ziemlich witzlos). Und 40 darüber, wie komplex es dann aber auch sei, es zu tun, die konkurrierenden Gefühle der „von woanders Gekommenen" und der „Dazugehörenden", den Wunsch nach Offenheit mit dem nach Schutz in Einklang zu bringen: „Während die Bürgerin in 45 mir versteht, dass Amerika nicht jedem Einwanderer die Möglichkeiten geben kann, die er sich wünscht, und auch, dass Amerika sich erst einmal um Amerikaner kümmern muss, hofft die Ein-

wanderin in mir auf Gesetze, die Amerika als den ‚Traum, den Träumer träumten' erhält."

Über diesen Traum oder, besser gesagt, über die, wie sie meint, bis heute ungebrochene Anziehungskraft der Marke „American Dream" hat Imbolo Mbue ein Buch, ihr erstes, geschrieben: „Behold the Dreamers", das jetzt in Deutschland unter dem etwas uninspiriert trockenen Titel „Das geträumte Land" erscheint. Es wurde in den Vereinigten Staaten im vergangenen Herbst als Überraschungserfolg gefeiert, „the one book Donald Trump should read right now". Zum einen, weil Mbue für diesen Erstlingsroman einen Vorschuss von einer Million Euro bekommen hatte, was Berichterstatter fast immer begeistert, auch wenn es über den Roman nicht viel mehr sagt, als dass er einen guten Agenten hatte (in dem Fall eine gute Agentin, nämlich die von Jonathan Franzen). Zum anderen, weil sie einen Nerv der Zeit getroffen hatte – und das auf sehr kluge, differenzierte Art und Weise.

Für kurze Zeit vereint

Mbue erzählt in ihrem Roman die Geschichte der Jongas, die von Jende, seiner Frau Neni und ihrem Sohn Liomi, einer Einwandererfamilie aus Limbé, Kamerun, die in New York im Jahr 2008 ihr Glück und eine dauerhafte Aufenthaltsgenehmigung suchen. Jende arbeitet als Chauffeur für den Lehmann-Brothers-Top-Manager, Clark Edwards, Neni studiert in der Hoffnung, irgendwann Apothekerin zu werden, arbeitet nebenbei als Putzfrau und einen idyllischen Sommer lang als Haushälterin im Wochenend-Hamptons-Haus der Edwards. Sie sind arm, sie haben es nicht leicht, aber sie sind gewillt, hart zu arbeiten und alles zu tun für ihren Traum: Einem Leben in Amerika, dem „greatest country on earth", wie Jende Jonga, im Einklang mit Barack Obamas letztem Video, seinem Chef auf langen Autofahrten durch Manhattan immer wieder mit glänzenden Augen erklärt. Fast zwei Jahre lang scheint es, als würde alles gut ausgehen. Die Jongas und die Edwards brauchen sich, so wie Amerika seine Einwanderer immer brauchte. Das jeweilige Glück der Familien hängt, wenn auch in sehr unterschiedlicher existentieller Gewichtung, voneinander ab. In dieser Zeit wird auch noch Obama zum ersten schwarzen Präsidenten der Vereinigten Staaten gewählt, nichts kann mehr schiefgehen, denken die Jongas und träumen natürlich noch mehr, hören gar nicht mehr hin, wenn der Cousin erklärt, in Amerika sei die Polizei nur für weiße Mitbürger da, nicht für die schwarzen, wenn einer ganz visionär erzählt, irgendwann würde es eine Mauer geben und die Mexikaner stünden dann nur noch dumpf dreinschauend davor. Jende und Neni ignorieren diese Warnungen und denken bei aller Vorsicht schon fast, sie gehörten wirklich dazu. Zumindest kurz. Denn dann kommt der Wall-Street-Crash, und die Verzahnung der Leben dieser beiden so gegensätzlichen Familien zerbricht.

Märchen versus Realität

So zusammengefasst erzählt, mag das Ganze wie eine unerträgliche Anhäufung von Klischees klingen. Wie das Märchen vom guten Wilden und dem herzlosen Kapitalisten. Man könnte versucht sein, Imbolo Mbues Roman für eine Anklageschrift gegen die Amerikaner zu halten, die den Fremden akzeptieren, solange er ihnen nützt, und ihn wegschmeißen, sobald er lästig wird. Nur umgeht die Autorin diese Falle mühelos. Denn auch wenn sie kaum verbergen kann (oder will), dass ihr Herz für die Jongas schlägt, die aus ihrer Heimatstadt kommen, wie sie sprechen, wie sie essen und erleben, was sie erlebt hat, sind die Figuren, die sie sehr liebevoll, niemals grob, niemals urteilend zeichnet, allesamt weder gut noch böse, sondern beides zugleich. Alle versuchen das Richtige zu tun, aber verzweifeln an diesem amerikanischen Traum, der „größer als das Leben" ist, der alles verspricht und es nur für wenige hält.

Manche Leser hätten ihr das vorgeworfen, sagt Mbue, sie wollten lieber das Klischee. Sie hätten zum Beispiel nicht akzeptiert, dass Jende, dem man zuerst als gutherzigem Vater und Ehemann begegnet, irgendwann gewalttätig wird, weil er sich schämt, seiner Familie nicht mehr bieten zu können, weil die Ungerechtigkeit der Realität ihn bricht. Sie sage dann nur: „Männer aus meiner Stadt sind eben leider so." Nur geht es am Ende vielleicht weniger darum, wie Männer aus ihrem Dorf sind oder nicht sind, als darum, was bestimmte soziale und geschichtliche Situationen mit Menschen machen. Mit allen. Das wirklich Gute an Mbues Roman, der sich ein bisschen wie ein Traum artikuliert, in dem sich anfangs alles weich und beschützt anfühlt und die Geräusche der Außenwelt immer mehr stören, bis man schließlich aufwacht, liegt im Realismus, mit dem sie dieser Frage begegnet.

Ihre Figuren, die man übrigens alle sehr mag, zeigen sich anfangs kämpferisch und guten Willens, hoffnungsvoll und gerecht, können sich vor den Ängsten, die sie heimsuchen, aber nicht schützen. Da ist zum Beispiel Cindy Edwards, die hinter ihrer perfekten Fifth-Avenue-Society-Lady-Fassade noch immer darunter leidet, aus einem armen, gewalttätigen Elternhaus zu kommen, und die den Absturz so sehr fürchtet, dass sie ihre Gutherzigkeit dabei vergisst. Oder Fatou, Nenis Freundin, die zwar in New York bleiben darf, sich aber irgendwann fragt, ob ihre Kinder, die Amerikaner sind, sich vielleicht insgeheim schämen, weil sie Afrikanerin ist, und sich deshalb stärker an ihre Herkunftskultur klammert.

Statt sich ausufernd darauf zu konzentrieren, was den Einwanderer und den vermeintlichen „Native" unterscheidet, findet Imbolo Mbue ihre Gemeinsamkeiten, nämlich ihre Träume. Und entschuldigt damit auch vieles. Überhaupt scheint sie, die nach dem Börsencrash ihren Job verlor und damals, als sie schon fast daran dachte, nach Kamerun zurückzukehren, begann, an ihrem Roman zu schreiben, weniger kämpferisch als verständnisvoll. Sie findet es zum Beispiel nicht mehr schlimm, wenn irgendwelche Damen kreischen: „Wie toll! Die Tochter einer Freundin war letztens in Südafrika!", wenn sie sagt, sie komme aus Kamerun. Ja, das sei, als würde man einem Franzosen sagen: „Wie schön! Ich war mal in Polen!" Aber was soll's.

Vertrauen in Amerika

Sie findet es auch nicht schlimm, zu wissen, dass sie immer, auch wenn sie mittlerweile einen amerikanischen Pass besitzt, Schriftstellerin ist, ein gutes, integriertes Leben führt, in erster Linie eine Einwanderin bleiben wird: „Es ist ganz egal, wie lange ich hier bleibe, ob ich meinen Akzent verliere, ich werde immer von woanders gekommen sein. Und wenn ich es mal vergesse, weiß ich es spätestens wieder, wenn man mich nach meiner Herkunft fragt." Viel wichtiger sei doch, dass sie Vertrauen in Amerika und seine „greatness" hat. Auch jetzt noch, auch wenn sie damit etwas ganz anderes meint als Donald Trump.

Natürlich sei sie besorgt, nur hätten sich Sorgen und Ängste in der Geschichte noch nie als besonders gute Ratgeber erwiesen. Es sei an der Zeit, sich zu fragen, was sich die Menschen erhoffen, und zu verstehen, wie weit entfernt die Realisierung ihrer Wünsche scheinen muss, um so einen Wahlausgang möglich zu machen: „Wir mögen zwar nicht mit ihnen einverstanden sein, aber wir sollten ihre Träume ernst nehmen."

b) Write your own review of the novel. → **S8:** How to improve your text

Topic: Behold the Dreamers

The American Dream: Freedom, equality and the pursuit of happiness

1

a) What do you associate with the American Dream? Make a mind map.

The American Dream

b) Analyse the following quotes.

1
"[…] the American dream that has lured tens of millions of all nations to our shores in the past century has not been a dream of material plenty, though that has doubtless counted heavily. It has been much more than that. It has been a dream of being able to grow to fullest development as man and woman, unhampered by the barriers which had slowly been erected in older civilizations, unrepressed by social orders which had developed for the benefit of classes rather than for the simple human of any and every class."
– James Truslow Adams (1878–1949), American writer and historian who coined the term "American Dream" in his book *The Epic of America* (1931).

2
"We hold these truths to be self-evident, that all men are created equal, that they are endowed by their Creator with certain unalienable Rights, that among these are Life, Liberty and the pursuit of Happiness."
– United States Declaration of Independence, In Congress, July 4, 1776

3
"We don't see any American dream. We've experienced only the American nightmare."
– Malcolm X (1925–1965), American activist and supporter of Black empowerment, was a prominent figure during the civil rights era; he gave his speech "The Ballot or the Bullet" in Detroit on April 12, 1964.

4
"The reason they call it the American Dream is because you have to be asleep to believe in it."
– George Carlin (1937–2008), American comedian, actor and social critic

5
"Barack knows the American Dream because he's lived it … and he wants everyone in this country to have that same opportunity, no matter who we are, or where we're from, or what we look like, or who we love."
– Michelle Obama, First Lady of the United States from 2009 to 2017, giving a speech at the Democratic National Convention in Charlotte, N.C. on September 4, 2012. Barack Obama, 44th President of the United States, was the first African-American president in history.

6 "So even though we face the difficulties of today and tomorrow, I still have a dream. It is a dream deeply rooted in the American dream. I have a dream that one day this nation will rise up and live out the true meaning of its creed: We hold these truths to be self-evident, that all men are created equal. [...]
I have a dream that my four little children will one day live in a nation where they will not be judged by the color of their skin but by the content of their character. I have a dream today."
– Martin Luther King Jr. (1929–1968), "I Have a Dream", speech delivered during the March on Washington for Jobs and Freedom on August 28, 1963; Martin Luther King Jr. fought against racial segregation and discrimination and was one of the most prominent leaders in the American civil rights movement.

c) Add new aspects to your mind map above.

2

a) The promise of equality is an integral element of the concept of the American Dream. Read the definition from the online encyclopedia *Britannica*. Then state what areas of life and parts of society 'equality' affects.

Info

Equality

Generally, an ideal of uniformity in treatment or status by those in a position to affect either. Acknowledgment of the right to equality often must be coerced from the advantaged by the disadvantaged. Equality of opportunity was the founding creed of U.S. society, but equality among all peoples and between the sexes has proved easier to legislate than to achieve in practice. [...]

b) Imagine that you have spent a year in the US and you are surprised at your perception of the reality of the American Dream. You have found an article in the German newspaper *Süddeutsche Zeitung* that seems to be in line with what you experienced, and you want to share the main points about social inequality in the US in an English blog post. Read the article below and use the information to write the blog post.
→ **Workshop:** Mediation   → **S19:** How to improve your mediation skills   → **S7:** Checklist: Writing a blog post

---

Soziale Gerechtigkeit
Die Illusion vom amerikanischen Traum
- In zwei Studien wurde untersucht, wie sich der Lebensstandard von Familien in den USA entwickelt hat.
- Sie zeigen: Das Versprechen vom sozialen Aufstieg gilt längst nicht mehr für jeden, und auch die Umverteilung durch den Staat bleibt weitgehend wirkungslos.

Von Catherine Hoffmann   27. Januar 2017, 20:00 Uhr

Der Glaube an den amerikanischen Traum ist angeschlagen. Die Wahl von Donald Trump zum US-Präsidenten wird von vielen Wissenschaftlern als die Rache der Abgehängten interpretiert, die
5 verbittert darüber sind, dass die Einkommensungleichheit seit Ausbruch der Finanzkrise im Jahr 2008 zugenommen hat. Trotz guter Wirtschaftszahlen haben die meisten amerikanischen Arbeiter und große Teile der Mittelschicht das Gefühl, dass
10 ihr Lebensstandard stagniert, während sich die Lage der Besserverdiener schnell erholt hat.

Zwei beachtliche Studien über die Entwicklung von Einkommen und Vermögen in den USA zeigen nun, dass dieses Gefühl nicht von ungefähr
15 kommt. Die Autoren zeichnen ein umfassendes Bild der sozialen Ungleichheit, die sich nicht erst mit der jüngsten Wirtschaftskrise verschärfte, sondern seit Generationen wächst. „The Fading American Dream" haben sechs Wissenschaftler
20 aus Stanford und Harvard über ihr Papier geschrieben, der verblassende amerikanische Traum.

Topic: Behold the Dreamers

Gemeint ist der Traum von einem Land, in dem das Leben für alle „besser und reicher und voller" sein sollte, wie es der amerikanische Publizist James Truslow Adams in seinem 1931 veröffentlichten Buch „The Epic of America" formulierte. Dieser Glaube, dass es jeder – wenn er nur hart genug dafür arbeitet – nach oben schaffen kann, hat die Vereinigten Staaten von Anfang an zusammengehalten. In den Jahrzehnten nach der Großen Depression wurde dieser Traum Wirklichkeit. Ein ungewöhnlich starkes Wirtschaftswachstum verbesserte den Lebensstandard aller Amerikaner, egal ob sie reich oder arm waren oder der Mittelschicht angehörten. 92 Prozent aller Kinder, die im Jahr 1940 in einem durchschnittlichen Haushalt geboren wurden, verdienten mit 30 Jahren mehr als ihre Eltern mit 30 verdient hatten. Auch den Kindern, denen dies nicht gelang, ging es oftmals gut: Sie waren nicht selten in einem reichen Haushalt aufgewachsen, der Vater Vorstand in einem Unternehmen, und arbeiteten selbst als Ärzte, Anwälte oder Professoren.

40 Jahre später gilt das Versprechen vom Aufstieg nicht mehr für alle: Nur die Hälfte der Kinder, die im Jahr 1980 geboren wurden, verdiente später mehr als ihre Eltern. „Im Grunde entscheidet ein Münzwurf, ob es einem besser geht als den Eltern", sagt Raj Chetty, Wirtschaftsprofessor und einer der Studienautoren. Aus dem Jahrgang 1950 gelang es immerhin noch fast 80 Prozent, den Wohlstand der Eltern zu übertreffen. Die Generationen der 1960 und 1970 Geborenen verwirklichten noch zu rund 60 Prozent die Hoffnungen auf ein besseres Leben. Der amerikanische Traum verblasst tatsächlich. Die Chance auf Teilhabe und Glück ist längst nicht mehr für alle Amerikaner gleich. Angesichts dieser Zahlen muss es niemanden überraschen, dass sich schleichend über viele Jahre und Jahrzehnte Frust aufgebaut hat. […]

Es kommt also weniger auf das Wachstum als vielmehr auf die Verteilung des erreichten Wohlstands an, will man das Versprechen vom Aufstieg der Fleißigen und Tüchtigen auch in der Gegenwart einlösen. Wie stark die Ungleichheit in den USA zugenommen hat, belegt auch eine Studie von Thomas Piketty, Emmanuel Saez und Gabriel Zucman. Die Wissenschaftler haben dafür nicht nur die Einkommen in den Blick genommen, sondern auch die Auswirkungen von Besteuerung, Sozialausgaben sowie die Einkünfte aus Kapitalanlagen. Ergebnis: Der Anteil der schlechter verdienenden Hälfte der amerikanischen Bevölkerung am Nationaleinkommen verharrt seit 1980 bei etwa 16 000 Dollar (vor Steuern). Das Einkommen der unteren Schichten stagniert also seit zwei Jahrzehnten.

In derselben Zeit steigerte der Durchschnitt der Amerikaner seinen Anteil um 60 Prozent auf 64 500 Dollar, während das eine Prozent der Spitzenverdiener sein Kuchenstück von 420 000 auf 1,3 Millionen Dollar vergrößern konnte. Das führt dazu, dass das Nationaleinkommen 2014 ungleicher verteilt ist als 1980: Der Anteil der schlechter verdienenden Bevölkerungshälfte schrumpfte von 20 auf zwölf Prozent, gleichzeitig schnellte der Anteil des einen Prozent der Spitzenverdiener am Nationaleinkommen von zwölf auf 20 Prozent.

Auch wenn man Steuern und Sozialleistungen berücksichtigt, ändert sich überraschend wenig an diesem Bild. Staatliche Umverteilung bleibt also weitgehend wirkungslos. Als wichtigsten Grund für die zunehmende Ungleichheit in jüngster Zeit machen die Ökonomen den rasanten Anstieg der Kapitaleinkünfte seit Ende der Neunzigerjahre aus, der vor allem den Spitzenverdienern zugutekam, die große Aktien- und Rentendepots besitzen.

Die neuen Studien erschüttern einmal mehr den Mythos von der sozialen Durchlässigkeit der amerikanischen Gesellschaft. Arbeit ist in den USA längst kein Garant mehr für Wohlstand und Gerechtigkeit, wie Adams noch gedacht hatte.

3

Read the interview with author Imbolo Mbue (on pp. 266–269, after the end of the novel) and summarize her story.

Behold the Dreamers | Topic **2**

4
Is the American Dream dead?
a) Use the grid below to collect arguments that support the idea that the American Dream is dead and arguments that support the idea that the American Dream is alive.
b) **Group work** Use your arguments to discuss the question.

Is the American Dream dead?	
For (✓)	Against (✗)

FREEDOM, EQUALITY AND THE PURSUIT OF HAPPINESS IN *BEHOLD THE DREAMERS*

5
a) **Pair work** The Declaration of Independence acknowledges the right to "the pursuit of happiness", which is an essential part of the concept of the American Dream. Define what happiness means to you.
b) Explain what happiness means for the characters in *Behold the Dreamers*.

6
Examine the relationship between Jende and Clark with respect to the concept of equality.

7
Describe the perceptions and experiences of the American Dream by the following characters:
- Vince Edwards
- Clark Edwards
- Jende Jonga
- Cindy Edwards
- Neni Jonga

8 → S23: How to quote   → S8: How to improve your text
Compare the points made in Catherine Hoffmann's article "Die Illusion vom amerikanischen Traum" (p. 61f.) to the perceptions of the American Dream in the novel.

9
Compare Jende and Neni's immigration story to Imbolo Mbue's.

10 → S23: How to quote   → S8: How to improve your text
Explain how the novel can be described as "a dissection of the American dream" (as Carmela Ciuraru phrased it in her 2016 article in *The New York Times*).

Topic: Behold the Dreamers

Questions of identity

1 Group work

a) Try to define 'identity'.

> **Info**
>
> ### Method: Placemat
>
> Get into groups of four and divide a big sheet of paper (in A3 format) as shown on the right.
> **Step 1:** Try to solve the task by yourself first and write down your results in your section.
> **Step 2:** Rotate the sheet and read each other's outcomes.
> **Step 3:** Decide on a definition together and write it down in the middle.

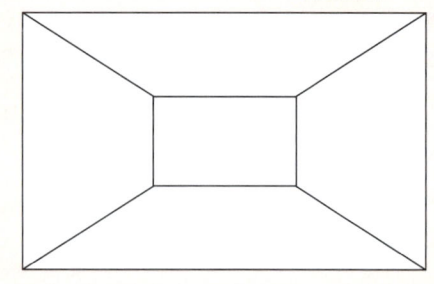

b) Visualize your results and present them in class.
c) Which aspects do you find most important? Rank them and explain your choices.

IDENTITY IN *BEHOLD THE DREAMERS*

2

Analyse what parts of Neni's and Jende's identities are stressed in the novel.

3

Comment on the quotes below.

> She'd waited too long to become something, and now, at thirty-three, she finally had, or was close enough to having, everything she'd ever wanted in life.
> *(narrator about Neni, p. 15)*

> "It is nothing like America. I stay in my country, I would have become nothing. I would have remained nothing. My son will grow up and be poor like me, just like I was poor like my father. But in America, sir? I can become something. [...]"
> *(Jende to Clark, p. 32)*

> "[...] And my son will grow up to be somebody, whatever he wants to be. [...]"
> *(Jende to Clark, p. 37)*

> "[...] Without school, you will be nothing. You will never be anybody. Me and Papa, we wake up every day and do everything we can so you can have a good life and become somebody one day, [...]"
> *(Neni to Liomi, p. 50)*

> Jende was going to be somebody in Limbe when they returned.
> *(narrator about Jende, p. 242)*

The financial crisis

1

Watch a video about the Great Recession and answer the questions below. **Webcode** DSW-73698-03

a) What are subprime mortgages and what is their significance to the financial crisis?

_____

_____

_____

b) What was the development in the housing market before 2007?

_____

_____

_____

c) What happened to the housing market after 2007?

_____

_____

_____

d) How did the bursting of the housing bubble affect the banks, the economy and people in America?

_____

_____

_____

_____

2

Read the article from *The New York Times* and outline the present and possible future consequences of the financial crisis.

From Trump to Trade, the Financial Crisis Still Resonates 10 Years Later

By Andrew Ross Sorkin   September 10, 2018

This week is the 10th anniversary of the inflection point of the financial crisis: the collapse of Lehman Brothers, the biggest bankruptcy in history. To some, it feels like a long time ago.

Yet, its effects still echo in the way we live today – in the attitudes that pervade our economy, our culture and our politics. It is hardly a stretch to suggest that President Trump's election was a direct result of the financial crisis.

The crisis was a moment that cleaved our country. It broke a social contract between the plutocrats[1] and everyone else. But it also broke a sense of trust, not just in financial institutions and the government that oversaw them, but in the very idea of experts and expertise. The past 10 years have seen an open revolt against the intelligentsia.

Mistrust led to new political movements: the Tea Party for those who didn't trust the government and Occupy Wall Street for those who didn't trust big business. These moved Democrats and Republicans away from each other in fundamental ways, and populist attitudes on both ends of the spectrum found champions in the 2016 presidential race in Senator Bernie Sanders and Donald J. Trump.

The depth of financial despair during the Great Recession and the invariably slow recovery have

Annotations   [1] **plutocrat** = sb who is powerful because they are rich

unleashed a sense of bitterness that dominates the political landscape, culminating in Mr. Trump's electoral victory.

"We are almost at each other's throats when times are good," said Ray Dalio, the founder of Bridgewater Associates, the largest hedge fund in the world with some $150 billion in assets, and the author of a new book, "A Template for Understanding Big Debt Crises," an exhaustive study of financial panics and the policies that both created and rescued them.

The deepest crises, he said, always lead to populism. And it should be no surprise that a crisis leads to conflict and, in some extreme cases, war. "I would be worried about the emergence of populism," he said, "because populists tend to want to fight with the other side rather than try to find ways of getting through it." Populists on every side of the political spectrum "have in common that they're confrontational," he said.

When I wrote "Too Big to Fail" nearly a decade ago, I knew that the crisis would redefine Wall Street and the economy, but I didn't appreciate how fundamentally it would redefine the political environment.

Amir Sufi, a professor of economics and public policy at University of Chicago's Booth School of Business and the co-author of "House of Debt," pointed to the financial crisis as the source of reduced civility a few months after Mr. Trump's victory. He conducted an analysis of 60 countries with his "House of Debt" co-author, Atif Mian of Princeton University, and Francesco Trebbi of the University of British Columbia. They found that such a response was "common and predictable," he wrote.

"Our conclusion: Financial crises tend to radicalize electorates," Mr. Sufi wrote. "After a banking, currency, or debt crisis, our data indicate, the share of centrists or moderates in a country went down, while the share of left- or right-wing radicals went up in most cases."

In the United States, the crisis exposed an economy that had been a charade – one that most Americans didn't understand or appreciate. The use of debt had masked the real problems underneath the surface: a significant decrease in worker participation, automation that would take jobs and stagnant wage growth.

These issues long predated the crisis. But as Warren Buffett famously said, "You only find out who is swimming naked when the tide goes out."

In truth, our economy today is in much better shape than you might expect, with unemployment at 3.9 percent – lower than it was before the crisis.

Yet debates persist about the way the government, first under President George W. Bush and then under President Barack Obama, chose to respond to the crisis. Should it have done more directly for homeowners? Should it have demanded more onerous terms for the hundreds of billions of dollars in loans to the banks and bankers, like restricting compensation and firing executives to demonstrate more accountability? Should some bankers have gone to jail?

For some, it is tempting to think that the government should have taken a more populist approach itself. If it had offered more help directly to the public rather than what was perceived as bailing out the banks, there is a suspicion that divisions could have been lessened, yielding a more united United States.

But would it?

In Britain, the government did all those politically popular things: It restricted banker pay, it fired executives, it lent money to banks on onerous terms, it restricted spending.

It didn't work. The British economy grew significantly slower than ours. And the resulting resentment and bitterness were much worse than our own, leading to a manifestation of populism even more drastic: the unimaginable vote to leave the European Union.

It's not popular to say, but it's clear that the financial crisis was so deep and so painful that whatever populist positions policymakers took, the positive feelings would have been short-lived.

Timothy F. Geithner, the Treasury secretary under Mr. Obama, recounted in his book "Stress Test" a conversation that he had with President Bill Clinton as he was considering a more populist approach. Mr. Clinton told him, "You could take Lloyd Blankfein into a dark alley, and slit his throat, and it would satisfy them for about two days. Then the blood lust would rise again."

It doesn't help that the economic medicine used by policymakers after a crisis exacerbates those feelings of anger. The most efficient fix – lowering interest rates – helps the wealthy because they end up with cheaper mortgages and enjoy the benefits that low rates have on corporate growth. Those lower on the economic ladder, on the other hand, get little in interest on their savings. The gap between the haves and the have-nots widens.

But that approach actually works, pulling everyone along with it, even if it is uneven and there are greater beneficiaries than others.

There is one question I get more than any other: "Will we have another crisis?" The answer, of course, is yes. But it's not a Wall Street crisis similar to 2008 that concerns me. I'm worried about something far bigger. When I wrote "Too Big to Fail," that phrase was only used in the context of financial institutions. Today, it is used to refer to cities, municipalities, states and countries. If you look at the buildup of debt, that's the place to keep an eye on.

Unmanageable debt is the match that lights the fire of every crisis. You can have as many bad actors on stage as you want – greedy bankers, inept regulators, conflicted credit rating agencies – but unless there is significant leverage in the system, there's little danger of a crisis. Our national debt is more than $21 trillion, and it increased a trillion dollars in just six months under Mr. Trump, who rode populist and anti-establishment sentiment to the White House but whose policy choices have largely favored the wealthy.

That's not the only cause for concern, either. If history tells us the political divisions we have seen since the financial crisis were predictable, then what does history have to say about what comes next?

Mr. Dalio pointed to the chilling of international relationships that happened after the Great Depression as a worrying example of the divisions that can widen when populism fosters protectionism. "We started to have economic tariffs and we started to have back-and-forths of those things," he said.

He paused for a moment, signaling he didn't want to contemplate what that later manifested. But he continued, "Which then, 10 years later, led to Pearl Harbor."

There are, of course, many steps between populism and war. But Mr. Dalio said he saw similarities between the global environment that preceded World War II and the one we see today.

That's reason enough to never forget this crisis and its lessons.

THE FINANCIAL CRISIS IN *BEHOLD THE DREAMERS*

3
Describe how the collapse of Lehman Brothers unfolds in the novel.

4
Relate Jende's dream about "money doublers" (pp. 119–120) in Limbe to the collapse of Lehman Brothers.

5
Examine the consequences of the financial crisis for the individual characters in the novel.

6
Imagine that Jende tries to explain to a friend in Limbe how the financial crisis began.
Create a dialogue between the two of them.

Political, cultural and social developments

1 Group work
Choose one of the topics below and research the most important facts on the Internet to illustrate their general ideals.
- Democrats
- Republicans
- Barack Obama
- Donald Trump
- Joe Biden

Info

Method: Jigsaw

Five students research the same topic respectively, for example A. They form an expert group (e.g. A, A, A, A, A), exchange results and prepare them for a presentation. Then the students get together in mixed groups (A, B, C, D, E) and inform each other on their topics.

Topic: Behold the Dreamers

2 → **Workshop:** Analysing a speech → **S14:** How to analyse a speech

Analyse the extract from Barack Obama's speech "The American Promise" (2008).

Address Accepting the Presidential Nomination at the Democratic National Convention in Denver: "The American Promise"

August 28, 2008

[...] Four years ago, I stood before you and told you my story – of the brief union between a young man from Kenya and a young woman from Kansas who weren't well-off or well-known, but shared a belief that in America, their son could achieve whatever he put his mind to.

It is that promise that has always set this country apart – that through hard work and sacrifice, each of us can pursue our individual dreams but still come together as one American family, to ensure that the next generation can pursue their dreams as well.

That's why I stand here tonight. Because for two hundred and thirty-two years, at each moment when that promise was in jeopardy, ordinary men and women – students and soldiers, farmers and teachers, nurses and janitors – found the courage to keep it alive.

We meet at one of those defining moments – a moment when our nation is at war, our economy is in turmoil, and the American promise has been threatened once more.

Tonight, more Americans are out of work and more are working harder for less. More of you have lost your homes and even more are watching your home values plummet. More of you have cars you can't afford to drive, credit card bills you can't afford to pay, and tuition that's beyond your reach.

[...] These are my heroes. Theirs are the stories that shaped me. And it is on their behalf that I intend to win this election and keep our promise alive as President of the United States.

What is that promise?

It's a promise that says each of us has the freedom to make of our own lives what we will, but that we also have the obligation to treat each other with dignity and respect.

It's a promise that says the market should reward drive and innovation and generate growth, but that businesses should live up to their responsibilities to create American jobs, look out for American workers, and play by the rules of the road.

Ours is a promise that says government cannot solve all our problems, but what it should do is that which we cannot do for ourselves – protect us from harm and provide every child a decent education; keep our water clean and our toys safe; invest in new schools and new roads and new science and technology.

Our government should work for us, not against us. It should help us, not hurt us. It should ensure opportunity not just for those with the most money and influence, but for every American who's willing to work.

That's the promise of America – the idea that we are responsible for ourselves, but that we also rise or fall as one nation; the fundamental belief that I am my brother's keeper[1]; I am my sister's keeper.

That's the promise we need to keep. That's the change we need right now.

[...] Passions fly on immigration, but I don't know anyone who benefits when a mother is separated from her infant child or an employer undercuts American wages by hiring illegal workers. This too is part of America's promise – the promise of a democracy where we can find the strength and grace to bridge divides and unite in common effort.

I know there are those who dismiss such beliefs as happy talk. They claim that our insistence on something larger, something firmer and more honest in our public life is just a Trojan Horse for higher taxes and the abandonment of traditional values. And that's to be expected. Because if you don't have any fresh ideas, then you use stale tactics to scare the voters. If you don't have a record to run on, then you paint your opponent as someone people should run from. You make a big election about small things.

And you know what – it's worked before. Because it feeds into the cynicism we all have about government. When Washington doesn't work, all its promises seem empty. If your hopes have been dashed again and again, then it's best to stop hoping, and settle for what you already know.

I get it. I realize that I am not the likeliest candidate for this office. I don't fit the typical pedigree, and I haven't spent my career in the halls of Washington. But I stand before you tonight because all across America something is stirring. What the nay-sayers don't understand is that this election has never been about me. It's been about you.

For eighteen long months, you have stood up, one by one, and said enough to the politics of the past.

Annotations
[1] This is a reference to the biblical story of Cain and Abel.

You understand that in this election, the greatest risk we can take is to try the same old politics with the same old players and expect a different result. You have shown what history teaches us – that at defining moments like this one, the change we need doesn't come from Washington. Change comes to Washington. Change happens because the American people demand it – because they rise up and insist on new ideas and new leadership, a new politics for a new time.

America, this is one of those moments. [...]

This country of ours has more wealth than any nation, but that's not what makes us rich. We have the most powerful military on Earth, but that's not what makes us strong. Our universities and our culture are the envy of the world, but that's not what keeps the world coming to our shores.

Instead, it is that American spirit – that American promise – that pushes us forward even when the path is uncertain; that binds us together in spite of our differences; that makes us fix our eye not on what is seen, but what is unseen, that better place around the bend.

That promise is our greatest inheritance. It's a promise I make to my daughters when I tuck them in at night, and a promise that you make to yours – a promise that has led immigrants to cross oceans and pioneers to travel west; a promise that led workers to picket lines, and women to reach for the ballot.

And it is that promise that forty-five years ago today, brought Americans from every corner of this land to stand together on a Mall in Washington, before Lincoln's Memorial, and hear a young preacher from Georgia speak of his dream.[2]

The men and women who gathered there could've heard many things. They could've heard words of anger and discord. They could've been told to succumb to the fear and frustration of so many dreams deferred. But what the people heard instead – people of every creed and color, from every walk of life – is that in America, our destiny is inextricably linked. That together, our dreams can be one.

"We cannot walk alone," the preacher cried. "And as we walk, we must make the pledge that we shall always march ahead. We cannot turn back."

America, we cannot turn back. Not with so much work to be done. Not with so many children to educate, and so many veterans to care for. Not with an economy to fix and cities to rebuild and farms to save. Not with so many families to protect and so many lives to mend. America, we cannot turn back. We cannot walk alone. At this moment, in this election, we must pledge once more to march into the future. Let us keep that promise – that American promise – and in the words of Scripture hold firmly, without wavering, to the hope that we confess.

Thank you, God bless you, and God bless the United States of America.

Annotations

[2] This is a reference to Martin Luther King Jr. and his speech "I Have a Dream", which he gave during the March on Washington for Jobs and Freedom on August 28, 1963.

3

a) Describe the photos → **S15:** How to describe pictures

1

2

3

4

Topic: Behold the Dreamers

Info

January 6 U.S. Capitol attack, storming of the United States Capitol on January 6, 2021, by a mob of supporters of Republican Pres. Donald J. Trump. The attack disrupted a joint session of Congress convened to certify the results of the presidential election of 2020, which Trump had lost to his Democratic opponent, Joe Biden. Because its object was to prevent a legitimate president-elect from assuming office, the attack was widely regarded as an insurrection or attempted coup d'état. The Federal Bureau of Investigation (FBI) and other law-enforcement agencies also considered it an act of domestic terrorism. For having given a speech before the attack in which he encouraged a large crowd of his supporters near the White House to march to the Capitol and violently resist Congress's certification of Biden's victory – which many in the crowd then did – Trump was impeached by the Democratic-led House of Representatives for "incitement of insurrection" (he was subsequently acquitted by the Senate). […] (From the online encyclopedia *Britannica*)

b) Analyse the cartoons. → **Workshop:** Analysing a cartoon → **S17:** How to work with cartoons

4

a) Go back to Annabelle Hirsch's article on p. 57ff. Summarize Imbolo Mbue's reaction to the presidential election of 2016, after which Donald Trump became the 45th President of the United States.
b) Identify the concept of identity that is revealed in her reaction.
c) Explain what Imbolo Mbue means by saying that the US needs to take care of Americans first.
d) Comment on the question of whether her hopes of America remaining 'the land of dreams' have come true.

5

Do some additional research on Donald Trump. Then comment on the title of Lucia Grave's 2016 article in *The Guardian*: "America's Trump nightmare has arrived".

6

Reread the information about equality in the box on p. 61. What kind of equality does the Black Lives Matter (BLM) movement envision?

7

Watch the video "Black Lives Matter – The history of a movement" from *Channel 4 News*.
Webcode DSW-73698-04
Answer the following questions about the BLM movement.

Behold the Dreamers — Topic 2

a) Which incident started the Black Lives Matter movement?

b) How did the slogan evolve?

c) What is the agenda of the BLM movement?

d) Where does the rallying cry "I can't breathe" originate from?

e) What happened in Ferguson?

f) What measures were taken by the Obama administration?

g) What reasons are given for the police officers "getting away with murder"?

h) What consequences for the BLM movement were there under the Trump administration?

Topic: Behold the Dreamers

8 → **Workshop:** Analysing a cartoon → **S17:** How to work with cartoons

Analyse the cartoons.

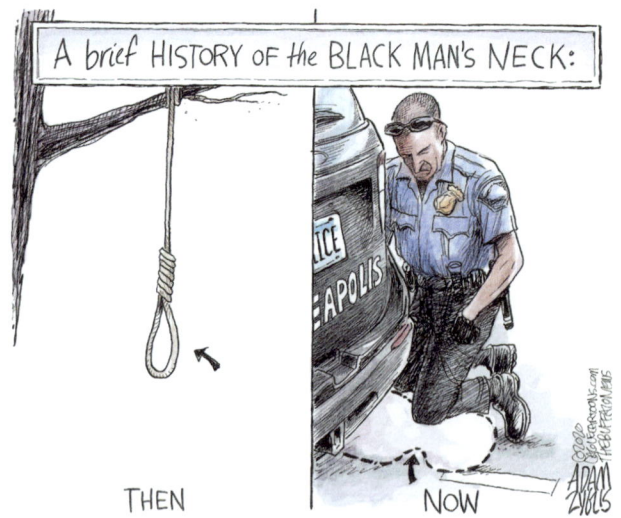

9

Watch two short extracts
(34:50–40:20 and 48:00–52:27)
from President Biden's address to Congress in 2021.

Webcode DSW-73698-05

Decide whether the statements below are true or false.

President Biden …		true	false
1	wants millionaires to pay their fair share of taxes.		
2	intends to reward work and not just wealth.		
3	plans to impose higher taxes on the middle class.		
4	is determined to grow the economy by supporting the middle class.		
5	remarks that the current pay gap between CEOs and their workers is extremely large.		
6	plans to fight white supremacy's terrorism.		
7	recounts that George Floyd's daughter said that her father had died in vain.		
8	believes that the trust in law enforcement needs to be re-established.		
9	vows to fight systemic racism, work towards real equity, and enable people to build generational wealth.		
10	supports the Equality Act to protect LGBTQ+ Americans.		

10

Compare the stances of Barack Obama, Donald Trump and Joe Biden on the major issues of immigration, integration and support of the middle class.

Stances on …	Barack Obama	Donald Trump	Joe Biden
immigration			
integration			
the middle class			

POLITICAL, CULTURAL AND SOCIAL ISSUES IN *BEHOLD THE DREAMERS*

11

Summarize the differing attitudes of Americans and American institutions towards immigrants in the novel.

12

Reread the short extract from Martin Luther King's speech on p. 61. Comment on whether you think that Martin Luther King's dream has been realized in the fictional reality of the novel.

13

Examine the depiction of Barack Obama in the novel.

14

Compare Obama's "American promise" (cf. p. 68f.) and his vision of America with Neni's and Jende's initial perceptions of America.

15 CHOOSE

Imagine that Neni and Jende have observed the political developments in America and they have a conversation about Donald Trump's presidency. Write their dialogue.

OR

Imagine that Neni writes an email to Mighty and Vince commenting on the presidential election of 2020, after which Joe Biden became the 46th President of the United States. Write her email.

3 Play — seven methods of killing kylie jenner

Pre-reading

1
Read the title of the play and The Premeditation. Speculate on what the play will be about.

2
a) Read the article from *The Standard* about the dramatist Jasmine Lee-Jones.
b) Find out more about her:
- age
- family background
- motivation for writing the play
- ideals
- personal experiences with theatre
- …

Jasmine Lee-Jones interview: I want people to come to the theatre like they watch Netflix

by Jessie Thompson

[…] Jasmine Lee-Jones's debut play, exploring female friendship, cultural appropriation and the internet, became one of the most talked-about plays of the year after a triumphant run at the Royal Court, picking up a trail of awards and an ecstatic stream of social media appreciation. […]

It's immediately obvious when talking to Lee-Jones IRL, […] that she is a deep and impressive thinker, often pausing for several seconds before she answers a question. […]

Born in North London, Lee-Jones became interested in theatre because of a strong connection she felt with words and language. "I always wanted to read things out loud," she says. "When I found theatre, I started to realise: oh, you can do a job where you're actually paid to speak words aloud, to really interrogate language." […]

The play's text is written in gifs, online acronyms, merging the IRL-world with the social media-sphere. It's the most original and successful way any writer has ever managed to capture the internet on stage, but Lee-Jones didn't do it on purpose – she just wanted it to feel real. "I think theatre can sometimes feel quite isolating like, oh, this is for someone else. We have a prestige about theatre and what should be on stage, like it's just for Shakespeare. And then you put something in from the internet that feels very casual and personal to people, and people are willing to give you more license," she says. […]

The online reaction to seven methods made it clear that the play was reaching new, more diverse audiences, something that matters greatly to Lee-Jones. "I want people to come to the theatre like they watch Netflix," she says. "I like watching reality TV and all of that as much as the next person. But one thing I find super interesting about TV is everyone will watch good, really thoroughly written, well-plotted TV. […] But when there's something really good in theatre on, people still feel like it's not for them. There's a universality to TV and film that theatre just hasn't created yet. It's still like, oh, it's meant for those people." […]

Having been nurtured as a writer by the Royal Court from the age of 17, Lee-Jones has always felt more comfortable there than at other theatres. But she had an experience a few years ago that shook that. She was watching a play with a friend, also a black woman, and they were waiting at the bar to get a drink. "This group of white people, I think maybe husband and wife, just went in front of us. I looked at my friend and was like, did you see that? And she just nodded, but eventually I realised they just didn't see us. They didn't think we were there to do something important or watch a show. They thought we were kind of just loitering," she tells me. "I think that was the first experience I had in this theatre where I realised – not because of the theatre, necessarily – but there's an audience that thinks this space belongs to them more than other people."

In the post-pandemic era, Lee-Jones thinks the theatre world will only bring in new audiences if it's really committed to doing so. "They have to keep programming the plays until people feel safe enough to come to the work. And what happened to me in the bar downstairs doesn't keep happening, because people realise: oh, this space is for everyone, it's not just for us." As she's telling me this, just behind her is the Royal Court's building; on the front of it, her name is written in neon lights. How thrilling that, right now, that one belongs to her. […]

seven methods of killing kylie jenner — Play — 3

3 Pair work

a) State what you know about Kylie Jenner, an American media celebrity.

b) Find out more about her on the Internet and decide whether the statements below are true or false. Correct the false statements.

statement	true	false	correction
1. Kylie Jenner is the daughter of Caitlyn and Kris Jenner.			
2. Kylie Jenner belongs to the Generation Alpha.			
3. She was part of the reality TV series *Keeping Up with the Kardashians* because she was adopted by Robert Kardashian.			
4. Jenner launched her own cosmetics line called *Kylie's BW lip kit*.			
5. In 2017, she was placed on the *Forbes* Celebrity 100 list, which made her the youngest person to be featured on the list.			
6. Kylie Jenner beat Mark Zuckerberg by two years when being announced the youngest self-made billionaire in 2019.			
7. Kylie Jenner is black.			

Language

4

a) **Pair work / Group work** Social media users don't normally use formal language. What abbreviations do you use?

`CHOOSE`

Write down the abbreviations that you use.

OR

Use a digital tool to do this task.

b) Rewrite the following comment in Standard English.

> **INCOGNEGRO** @INCOGNEGRO · Mar 5
> Errybody and they aunty need to quit fronting like Kylie killing it! She ain't killing shit! And tbh if I had it my way the only thing getting kilt would be that bitch! #kyliejennerfidead (p. 5)

5

Reading social media content in another language can be confusing. All the slang, idioms and abbreviations people use can make even simple sentences tricky to understand.

a) Get acquainted with the abbreviations the protagonists use in the play. Match the meanings from the box to the correct abbreviations and write them into the table.

3 Play — seven methods of killing kylie jenner

actually | big man ting (= seriously) | Don't piss me off! | Go on! | I don't care! | Kiss my teeth! | Never mind! | not gonna lie | Oh my days! | Say no more! | similar to LOL ✓ | Swear to God! | to be honest | What are you doing? | What the hell!

abbreviation	meaning
LEWL	similar to LOL
DPMO	
OMDS	
BMT	
IDC	
SNM	
S2G	
nvm	
wyd	
KMT	
ngl	
acc	
WTH	
tbh	
gwarn	

b) Now compare your results with the list of the most important abbreviations used in the play. You can find the list online. **Webcode** DSW-73698-06

c) While reading the play, add more abbreviations that are used by the protagonists to your list.

d) Rewrite the following email as a tweet by using as many abbreviations as possible.

> Hello, my best friend in the Twitter world!
> How are you today? I can't believe we're finally meeting each other. Have I told you that my mom believes you don't exist? That's extremely funny!!!!! However, I can't wait to meet you in real life. I'll see you in Berlin next week!
> Bye for now,
> your dearest friend

e) **CHALLENGE** You may add content to make the tweet sound more realistic.

f) **OPTIONAL** Rewrite the following hypothetical tweet into Standard English.

> Look @ her DP. What a QT! tbh, AFAIK – that's so fake! Never IRL! I'm BWL☺ Check X 4 more lies! And btw, DM next time!

seven methods of killing kylie jenner — Play 3

While reading

Info

The media in a fast-changing world

In 2022, billionaire Elon Musk (founder of SpaceX and other companies, product architect of Tesla) bought the social networking service Twitter and became its CEO. The platform has subsequently been criticized for an increase in content containing disinformation and hate speech. In the summer of 2023, Elon Musk announced that the name of **Twitter**, which had been in use since 2006, would be changed to **X**. He also introduced a new logo and wanted to get rid of associated words such as "tweet".

Jasmine Lee-Jones made changes to her play and published a new version in 2021, only two years after the first publication in 2019. At the time of her second publication, Twitter with its original name was still in practice.

---

6 CHOOSE

> Tip: Keeping a reading journal with the focus on summarizing the plot as well as adding information about the setting and relevant page numbers can be one option for remembering the content of a play.
> Taking notes with a specific focus (e.g. on one of the characters, topics, language, etc.) is another option to structure the content of a play.

Focus on one character's perspective: What aspects of Kylie's life are making Cleo furious? Take notes while reading.

OR

Focus on language: The playwright uses words from the black community, like "kiking" (p. 14), "bredrin" (p. 8), etc. Find more examples and explain their meanings.

OR

Focus on language: The play deals with serious topics but in a comical tone. Find examples from the text and evaluate the author's decision to make use of comic elements. Start a table like the one below and fill in your results.

quotation	topic	effect
1.		

THE PREMEDITATION (PP. 1–3)

7

a) Fill in the table.

1. **Who** are the characters?	
2. **When** do the scenes take place?	
3. **Where** does the action take place?	
4. **What** action is described?	
5. **What** references are made to the world outside the stage?	

77

3 Play — seven methods of killing kylie jenner

b) In the second version of her play from 2021, Jasmine Lee-Jones made considerable changes to The Premeditation from the original version from 2019 (see below). If you were Jasmine Lee-Jones and were asked by journalists why you made those changes to the play, apart from "A work of art is never finished" what would you answer?

> *The present.*
> *In the most present sense of the present tense.*
> *5th March 2019.*
> *Early morning. Outside. A park. Dark.*
>
> *KARA and CLEO drag something resembling a body onto the platform. They open the traps and throw it in. Cover it with earth. Suddenly they stop, standing over the body.*
>
> *Blackout.*

PART 1 (PP. 4–9): THE START

8

a) Cleo retweets a tweet by Forbes. Describe the Forbes tweet in your own words.

_____

b) Explain why Cleo is angry about the tweet.

_____

c) Cleo creates the hashtag #kyliejennerfidead as a response to the Forbes tweet and tweets hypothetical death threats against Kylie Jenner. Describe Cleo's methods in your own words.

Method #1: _____

Method #2: _____

d) Complete the sentence: With tweeting the first two methods of killing, Cleo wants to point out / criticize / make aware of the facts / aim at …

_____

e) Fill in the summary with the appropriate adjectives from the box.

> angry | crazy | happy | hypothetical | ingenious | real | surprise | worried

The first part of the plot describes developments in the Twitter world as well as in real life. When the action takes place in _____ life, Cleo gets a _____ visit from Kara. Kara has seen Cleo's tweets and wants to know why she is _____. Cleo plays down the seriousness of her _____ death threats and therefore wants to calm her _____ friend.

seven methods of killing kylie jenner — Play

PART 2 (PP. 10–27): TWITTERLUDE 1–2 AND IRL

9

Social media users are responding to Cleo's tweets (pp. 10–13).

a) **Pair work** List the words they are using.

_____

_____

b) Describe the tone of the tweets.

> **Language support**
>
> **Talking about tone**
> accusatory | admiring | aggressive | ambivalent | amused | appreciative | colloquial | concerned | critical | defensive | (dis)respectful | (dis)approving | judgmental | ...

> **Info**
>
> **Tone**
> Tone refers to an author's use of words and writing style to convey his or her attitude towards a topic. Tone is transported through the choice of words, viewpoint, syntax (grammar, how you put words together) and level of formality.

_____

_____

c) Explain the following quote in the play's context:

> "Inside that tweet is hundreds of years of anti-blackness, positive affirmations of capitalism, cultural appropriation ..." (p. 15)

d) Name and describe Method #3 in your own words.

_____

e) Describe the tone of the responses to Method #3.

_____

f) **Pair work** CHOOSE

Kara and Cleo have different opinions on various matters. They are having an argument about the importance of the tweet (p. 15). List their arguments.

Topic of discussion: "It's (just) a tweet."	
Kara	Cleo

79

3 Play — seven methods of killing kylie jenner

OR

Kara and Cleo are having an argument about the application of violence as an answer to oppression (p. 21). List their arguments.

Topic of discussion: "Violence is the answer to oppression."	
Kara	Cleo

g) Cleo has broken up with her boyfriend. Explain why his new girlfriend upsets Cleo.

h) **OPTIONAL**

Pair work Act out the scene in which the two girls talk about Cleo's boyfriend, the breakup and the new girlfriend.

OR

Group work (4) Create a freeze-frame in which the relationships between the following characters become apparent: Cleo, Cleo's boyfriend, the new girlfriend and Kara. You may also add up to three sentences that each character is saying.

The protagonists

10 Group work **CHOOSE**

What do you get to know about Cleo when reading the play? Write down her profile.
Note down the pages where you found the information.

Age: _____

Education: _____

Family and friends: _____

Topics of interest: _____

Political views: _____

Sexual orientation: _____

Black identity (appearance, language, etc.): _____

Character traits: _____

OR

What do you get to know about Kara when reading the play? Write down her profile.
Note down the pages where you found the information.

Age: _____

Education: _____

seven methods of killing kylie jenner | Play | 3

Family and friends: _____

Topics of interest: _____

Political views: _____

Sexual orientation: _____

Black identity (appearance, language, etc.): _____

Character traits: _____

PART 3 (PP. 28–53): TWITTERLUDE 3–5 AND IRL

11

a) Name and describe Method #4 in your own words.

_____

_____

b) Describe the tone of the responses to Method #4.

_____

_____

> **Info**
>
> ### Blackface
>
> The term "blackface" is used to refer to the practice of non-black performers wearing theatrical make-up to represent a caricature of black people on stage. This performance tradition was a popular form of entertainment in the US and Britain from around 1830 until the mid-20th century – especially in minstrel shows (for more information cf. the article on pp. 95–96). Today, it is regarded as highly offensive and racist.

c) By wanting Kylie to walk around in "whiteface" (p. 28), Cleo is referring to the term "blackface". Discuss whether the two terms can be compared.

12

In a video by the Darlinghurst Theatre Company, Dr Kathomi Gatwiri, a senior academic, researcher and psychotherapist, is talking about the term "gaslighting". **Webcode** DSW-73698-07

a) Watch the first part of Episode 1: "Racial Gaslighting" (00:00–03:23). Decide whether the following sentences are right or wrong. Correct the wrong statements.

statement	right	wrong	correction
1. Gaslighting is a form of physical abuse.			
2. People who are being gaslighted know that they are being manipulated and are therefore confident about their knowledge.			
3. The term refers to a movie in which a husband makes his wife think that she is just imagining the dimming of lights.			
4. Racial gaslighting is when people of colour are told that their experiences are acknowledged.			

81

3 Play — seven methods of killing kylie jenner

statement	right	wrong	correction
5. Racial gaslighting is deliberately used to maintain white supremacy.			
6. The more people of colour resist to this racial hierarchy the more acceptance they are experiencing in society.			

b) Explain Cleo's accusation: "My own bredrin gaslighting me!" (p. 32)

13
Which sentences about Kara's and Cleo's past are correct? Give proof from the text. → **S23:** How to quote

- The primary school teachers admired Cleo's curly hair.
- Cleo was always in Kara's shadow.
- Cleo had many boyfriends when she was young.
- Kara is satisfied with her appearance.
- Cleo accuses Kara of not having helped her at a party.

14
a) Name and describe Method #5.

b) Describe the tweets responding to Cleo's Method #5. What historical references are made? (Twitterludes 4 and 5)

PART 4 (PP. 54–78): TWITTERLUDE 6–11 AND IRL

15
a) Cleo's tweets get out of hand when one of her older tweets is retweeted by someone else.
- What gets retweeted and why?

- How does Cleo respond?

b) **Pair work** Both Cleo and Kara share stories from the past to explain when they felt misunderstood by each other.
- **Partner A:** Outline Cleo's story of #wiggate (pp. 45–48).
- **Partner B:** Outline Kara's story of "T'Sharn's 13th birthday party" (p. 66).
- Give feedback on how well the summary was performed by your partner.

c) **CHALLENGE** Comment on the following statement: "If they had acted differently in the past, their relationship now would be a different one." Justify your answer.

d) Name and describe Method #6.

e) Put these events into the right order:

☐ Cleo's identity in real life is revealed on Twitter.
☐ Cleo's IRL and Twitter identities merge into one.
☐ Cleo and Kara have a fight about Cleo's behaviour at T'Sharn's birthday party.
☐ Cleo is blocked from following Kara on Twitter.
☐ Someone retweets a comment by Cleo accusing her of being homophobic.
☐ Cleo apologizes for the two homophobic tweets from 2014.

f) In Method #7, Cleo wants Kylie Jenner to experience the same mistreatments that Saartjie must have gone through. Which mistreatments does Cleo mean? Describe the historical context Cleo is referring to.

THE END (PP. 79–83): THE POST-MORTEM

16

a) With the sentence "I just don't wanna feel heavy no more" (p. 79) Cleo describes a burden she is carrying. From what burden does Cleo need to be freed?

b) Saartjie's spirit is appearing. What are Kara and Cleo praising her for?

c) The image from The Premeditation of Cleo and Kara standing over a body reappears in The Post-Mortem.

Why do you think Jasmine Lee-Jones chose The Post-Mortem as the title for the last scene?

> **Info**
>
> **Post-mortem** (= "after death") refers to the time after a person has died. The term can also be applied to the post-mortem examination of a corpse in order to determine the cause of death.

Post-reading

Relationships

17

a) Describe the friendship between Kara and Cleo. Start a table like the one below.

> **Help** Look at the following pages: 7–9, 21–25, 32–40, 48–49, 59–60, 66, 69–73, 79ff.

section	content	description of their friendship / relationship

b) In the following quote Cleo makes a reference to slavery on a plantation:

> "Back in the old days I'd be the field nigger out shucking corn and you'd be in the house beating the master." (p. 39)

3 Play — seven methods of killing kylie jenner

- Explain the parallels she is drawing.
- What does the quote reveal about the friendship between Cleo and Kara?

c) Kara blocks Cleo from following @KARA and viewing her tweets. Describe Cleo's reaction. How would you feel if your best friend did that to you?

d) **Pair work** At the end of the play, Cleo and Kara share a spiritual encounter with Saartjie.
- Does this experience strengthen their friendship?
- Discuss: Will they stay friends?

18 Group work CHOOSE

Create five freeze-frames in which you show the development of Kara and Cleo's relationship. You may act between the freeze-frames.

OR

Choose a part of Cleo and Kara's conversation on pp. 32–35. Act out the scene.

19 Pair work

Talk for five minutes about the question in the bubble and come to a conclusion.

- same interests
- lives near you
- accepts you as you are
- is supportive
- ?

What are the three most important qualities of a good friend?

Characterization

20 CHOOSE

Write a characterization of Cleo (including her online and offline identity)

OR

Kara.

Consider the question of whether Cleo's and/or Kara's character develop throughout the play. Illustrate and prove your answers with the text. → **Workshop:** Analysing characters → **S23:** How to quote

> **Tip** You can find language support for writing a characterization in your textbook *Camden Town Oberstufe* on page 353.

Illustrations and graphic layout of the play's script

21

a) On social media, words are often flanked by photos, emojis, cartoons, etc. Look at the following pages: 4, 10, 12, 13, 17, 44. Explain the combined use of language and pictures in the Twittersphere. Start a table like the one below and fill in your findings.
- Define the type of picture. Is it a photo, a film still, an emoji, a gif, a meme, a cartoon, …?
- What are the pictures showing?
- How are pictures used to transport meaning?

Page	Type of picture	What does it show?	Why is it used? What is the meaning?
p. 4			

b) Find more examples and add them to your table.

c) CHALLENGE Describe the layout and the way some words are written. What could be the reason why people use such a layout?

_____

_____

d) **CHALLENGE** There are parts in the play where the Twittersphere seems to intersect with real life, e.g. pictures are shown IRL (pp. 22, 34, 45, 71–73). What could be the playwright's intention?

Putting the play on stage

22

A theatre director decides how elements of a play script can be transferred to the stage.

a) **Group work** Come up with an option for how the Twittersphere could be staged. Consider how light, sound, actors, props, stage and audience can play a role.
b) Watch the video of a theatre production. **Webcode** DSW-73698-08
Note down how the scene is staged. Explain the effect on the audience.
c) Take a look at the production photos from the version staged at the Royal Court Theatre in London. **Webcode** DSW-73698-09 Considering the elements on stage (ropes, purple-blue cloud, dark background) and the actors' gestures, what part of the play could be shown?

VIPs

23

Cleo and Kara make references to various famous people and characters.

| Joanne the Scammer | Cardi B | Angela Davis | Maxine Waters | MLK | Saartjie (Sarah Baartman) |

a) **Group work** Placemat: Work in groups using the placemat method:
- Each group member finds out about one person.
- Write your findings into your section of the placemat.
- Turn the placemat clockwise so that you can read your teammates' findings.
- Discuss and agree on a result, which you write into the group section in the middle.
- Present your results in front of the class.
b) Discuss: To what extent are these people important for the context of the play?

Body images

24

a) **CHOOSE** Choose a country (Iran, Japan, New Zealand, Brazil, France, Kenya, South Korea, Mauritania, Oman or United States) and prepare a two-minute talk on the beauty standard of this country as it is described in the video "How beauty standards differ around the world". **Webcode** DSW-73698-10
b) Who defines what beauty is? Read the extract from an online article from *Medical News Today*. Then explain the quote below in the context of body image as it is described in the article.

What is body image?

By Yvette Brazier   *Updated on May 25, 2023*
– Medically reviewed by Marney A. White, PhD, MS, Psychology

Body image refers to how an individual sees their body and their feelings with this perception. Positive body image relates to body satisfaction, while negative body image relates to dissatisfaction.

5 Many people have concerns about their body image. These concerns often focus on weight, skin, hair, or the shape or size of a certain body part. The way a person feels about their body can be influenced by many different factors. According to 10 the National Eating Disorder Association (NEDA), a range of beliefs, experiences, and generalizations contribute to body image.

Throughout history, people have given importance to the beauty of the human body. Society, media, 15 social media, and popular culture often shape these views, and this can affect how a person sees their own body.

However, popular standards are not always helpful.

Play: seven methods of killing kylie jenner

Constant bombardment by media images and social pressure can cause people to feel uncomfortable about their body, leading to distress and ill health. It can also affect work, social life, and other aspects of life. [...]

What does body image mean?

Body image refers to a person's emotional attitudes, beliefs, and perceptions of their own body. Experts describe it as a complex emotional experience.

Body image relates to:
- what a person believes about their appearance
- how they feel about their body, height, weight, and shape
- how they sense and experience their body

Positive body image is related to body satisfaction and acceptance, while negative body image is related to dissatisfaction and wanting one's body to be different.

A negative body image can contribute to body dysmorphic disorder (BDD), eating disorders, and other conditions. [...]

"[...] and even Miss Fitzgerald always said how pretty your hair was, and the only time she came remotely close to commenting on how nice my hair was, was when my Mum straightened it for the Year 5 pictures." (p. 35)

---

25 Pair work

Now take a look at the photo of a woman in front of a mirror by Carrie Mae Weems. **Webcode DSW-73698-11** What does she want to show the viewer about black body image / ethnic identity? Explain.

"I keep a scrapbook with pictures for everything that I write. The main image is currently [art by Carrie Mae Weems] of a black woman looking in the mirror saying "Mirror, mirror on the wall, who's the fairest of them all?" and the mirror's response is "Snow White, you black bitch." That's very much this play."
— *Jasmine Lee-Jones*

Elements and structure of a play

26 → **S11:** How to work with drama

a) Label the following elements of a play script.

> stage directions | scene | characters | title | setting | playwright | text | cast

---

seven methods of killing kylie jenner ← 1. _____

by Jasmine Lee-Jones ← 2. _____

← 3. _____

Cleo a.k.a @INCOGNEGRO   Leanne Henlon
Kara   Tia Bannon ← 4. _____

1.
← 5. _____

5th March 2019. 4:01AM. ← 6. _____
The bird expands and suddenly we are on Twitter.

[...]

Suddenly a figure enters lurking. She creeps on CLEO; touches her. CLEO jumps. ← 7. _____

KARA: (*In a roadman lilt.*) Fuck are you on blad! ← 8. _____

b) The development of the plot of a play usually follows a certain structure as shown below.
- Does Jasmine Lee-Jones's play meet this scheme?
- Where can you see contemporary elements?

> **Tip** You can find an explanation of the different terms in your textbook *Camden Town Oberstufe* on page 350.

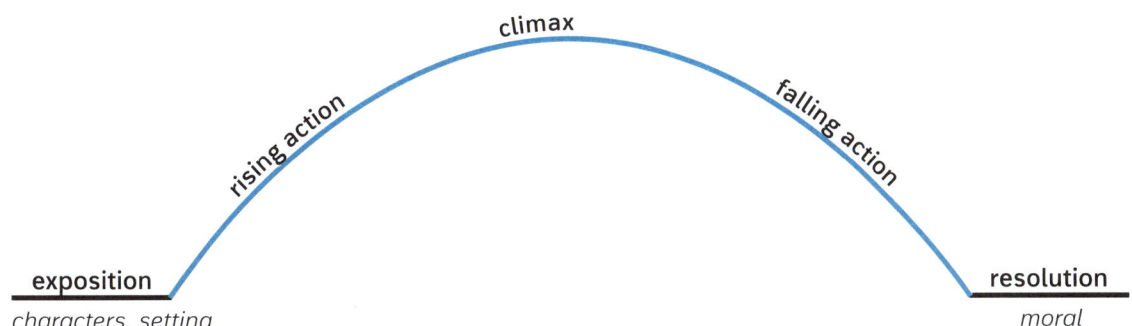

Identities

27

a) Cleo is a black woman having an identity in real life and in the world of Twitter (@INCOGNEGRO). For both identities, her ethnic identity seems to play a role.
How are these identities connected?

b) Choose one of the quotes below and explain it in the context of the conversation between Cleo and Kara.

"You don't own blackness just because you're dark-skinned!" (p. 37)

"You're a lightie." (p. 33)

"All the BW considered universally beautiful are lighties." (p. 34)

Stating your opinion

28 → **S6:** How to write a discussion/comment → **S9:** How to structure a text → **S8:** How to improve your text

Cleo shows her anger by creating hypothetical death threats against Kylie Jenner.

a) **CHOOSE**
Write a comment on the question of whether you think social media is a good channel to state your opinion.
OR
Pair work Write a digital text together with a partner in a collaborative document.

> **Help** Alternative options to state your opinion and make it public:
> - taking part in a demonstration
> - talking to people face-to-face
> - sending emails or letters to the government or to a newspaper
> - starting a petition

b) Why did the playwright choose to include Twitter in her play?

3 Play — seven methods of killing kylie jenner

Reviews

29

a) Jasmine Lee-Jones created a contemporary theatre play that has been widely reviewed. Compare the two extracts of reviews by Kate Wyver and Natasher Beecher.

> [...] Although the physicalisation of the internet is imaginative, the Twitter-interlude structure feels a little trapped towards the end, as if it's stopped inventing. The arguments begin to circle and the finale can't quite hold the weight of history it attempts to. Nevertheless, Henlon[1] and Bannon[2] are gripping throughout. Jones is a brilliant, dynamic writer, and this is a striking debut.
>
> _____
>
> Kate Wyver: "Seven Methods of Killing Kylie Jenner review – sharp, furious and funny." In: *The Guardian*, 23.06.2021

Annotations
[1] **Leanne Henlon** acted Cleo's part in *seven methods of killing kylie jenner* at the Royal Court Theatre.
[2] **Tia Bannon** acted Kara's part in *seven methods of killing kylie jenner* at the Royal Court Theatre.

> [...] For us black women '*seven methods of killing kylie jenner*' with its blend of nostalgia and heart, is us being seen and being heard in a way that's *almost* too difficult to watch, our collective trauma laid bare.
>
> For anyone who isn't black, and white people, in particular, this play will resonate with you in a magical way that you won't quite understand. But one thing is for sure, this poignant play that goes beyond just the zeitgeist is for everyone. It's a play for now and for after – a cultural marker of the way the world is changing and needs to change. Everyone should go see it.
>
> _____
>
> Natasher Beecher: "seven methods of killing kylie jenner review: 'This is one of the best plays I've ever seen'." In: Sophia A Jackson (ed.): *Afridiziak Theatre News*, 23.06.2021

b) **CHOOSE**
Write a review as a tweet.
OR
Write a review for a broadsheet newspaper.

_____
_____
_____
_____
_____
_____
_____
_____

c) Discuss the potential of the play to capture new audiences. Refer back to the article on p. 74. The following questions might give you some inspiration:

- Are you emotionally attached to the play?
- For what reasons would/wouldn't you watch the play?
- Does this play reach all audiences?
- What does it need to attract audiences to the theatre?

The changing media landscape: traditional and modern media

1
Read the short extract from *The Cambridge Introduction to Theatre Studies* and look at the cartoons. What challenges does the theatre face today? Refer to the material given below.

Theatre and media
by Christopher B. Balme

As one of the oldest media, theatre has survived several epochal shifts in media technology. Whether it was the invention of the printing press or the challenges posed by the invention of cinema, radio or television, the theatre met these innovations with openness and accommodation rather than with rejection. Very often, the new medium took the theatre as its model (with respect to presenting entertainment, especially of the fictional kind (dramatic stories)) before developing other forms and conventions. The theatre always reciprocated by integrating certain elements of the new medium into its own aesthetic and even organizational forms.

[...] the theatre has been exposed to competition from other media since the beginning of the twentieth century, and has certainly lost its previous dominant position as the main purveyor of fictionalized entertainment, [...].

2
Have a look at the website of the Royal Court Theatre in London. **Webcode** DSW-73698-12
Summarize the purpose of the theatre and the goals that are named.

Topic: seven methods of killing kylie jenner

The impact of the media on the individual and society

3

a) **Pair work** Brainstorming: List advantages and disadvantages of using social media.
b) Explain the chart. → **S18:** How to analyse statistics

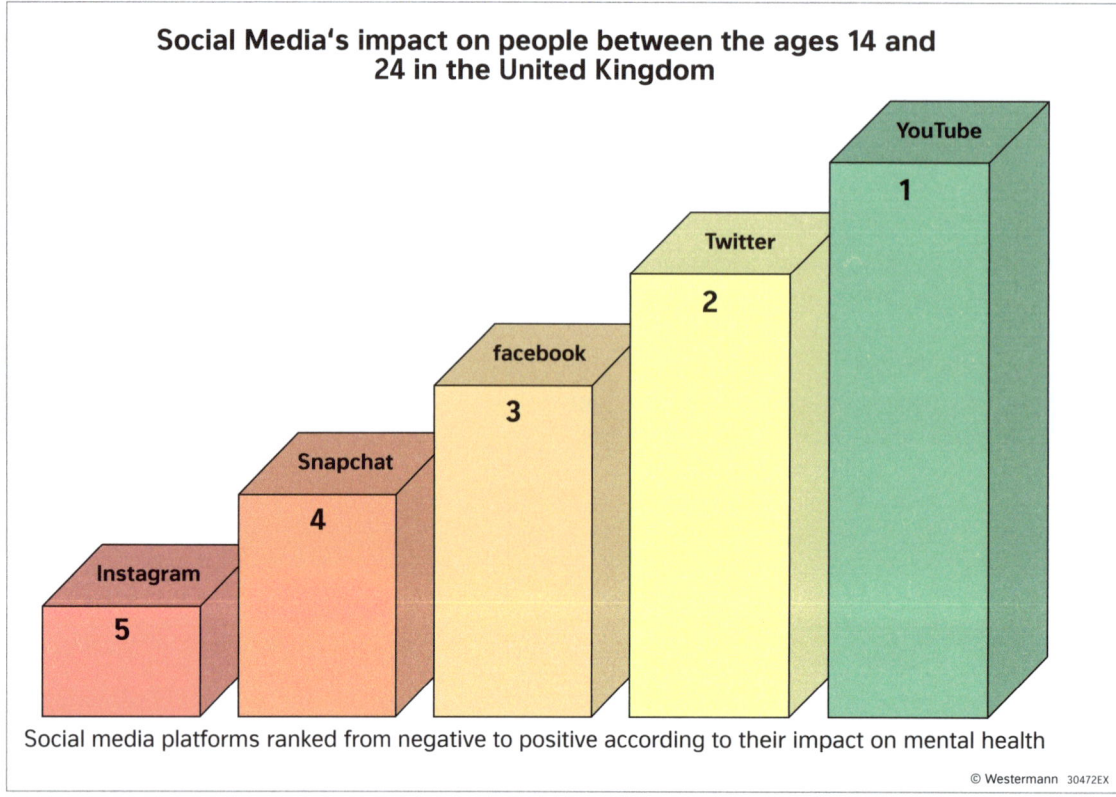

c) **Pair work** Discuss: Would you take part in a school challenge for a social media free week?

4

Tweets play a major role in *seven methods of killing kylie jenner* and are responsible for the development of the play.

a) Examine to what extent the comments on Twitter change over the course of the play. Use key words to fill in the table.

Content of the Twitterludes	Who is writing?	Scale of factual information (1 true to 9 false)	Scale of humour (1 little to 9 the most)	Scale of hatred (1 little to 9 the most)
1				
2				

seven methods of killing kylie jenner — Topic 3

Content of the Twitterludes	Who is writing?	Scale of factual information (1 true to 9 false)	Scale of humour (1 little to 9 the most)	Scale of hatred (1 little to 9 the most)
3				
4				
5				
6				
7				
8				
9				
10				
11				

Topic: seven methods of killing kylie jenner

b) Choose adjectives from the box to describe the development and use a timeline/graph/colour scheme to illustrate it.

> accusing | amused | conspirational | funny | homophobic | inflammatory | international | irritated | misogynist | racist | sexist | shocked | surprised

c) With the increasing usage of digital technologies, a new form of bullying has emerged: "cyberbullying". Have you or your friends ever experienced cyberbullying? Describe your experiences (topics, feelings, consequences).

d) **Pair work** At what point in the development of the Twitterludes do you think cyberbullying starts? Give reasons.

5

Cleo and Kara are having a discussion about possible reactions to the death threats against Cleo that are announced on the TL (pp. 43–44).

a) List their arguments. Give your opinion.
b) Cleo describes the following humiliating incident. What is happening?

> "[…] Camera's flashing without my consent
> Over and over
> Images posted all over socials
> Me a meme
> A silent, unconsenting gif
> Like I was some sort of spectacle
> Or a fucking freak
> I've never felt so ugly in my life […]." (p. 48)

c) Taking photos – now and fifty years ago: What has changed? What role does social media play today?
d) Internet research: Find out about the rules of taking photographs in public and private areas in Germany. Present your findings to the class.

Mediation

6 → **S19:** How to improve your mediation skills

a) Read the 2021 article from *Deutschlandfunk*.
b) Write an email to the playwright Jasmine Lee-Jones in which you describe the latest development in Germany concerning the influence of social media on politics. Refer to her play by pointing out parallels.

Anfeindungen gegen Sarah-Lee Heinrich
Medienexpertin: Koordinierte Twitter-Kampagnen als Methode

Immer häufiger werden Akteure aus Politik und Medien im Netz mit fragwürdigen Aussagen aus ihrer Vergangenheit konfrontiert. Dabei gerate aus dem Blick, aus welchen Kreisen diese Enthüllungen stammen, sagte Tajana Graovac vom „No Hate Speech Movement" im Dlf.

Sarah-Lee Heinrich

Ein paar Tweets können reichen, damit bei Twitter und darüber hinaus innerhalb weniger Stunden eine große Debatte in Gang kommt. So war das zuletzt zum Beispiel im Fall der neuen Bundessprecherin der Grünen Jugend.

seven methods of killing kylie jenner

Sarah-Lee Heinrich geriet in den Fokus wegen mehrerer alter Nachrichten, in denen sie im Jahr 2015 zum Beispiel „Heil" unter einen Tweet mit Hakenkreuz geschrieben hatte. Die heute 20-Jährige schrieb, sie könne sich nicht daran erinnern, als Jugendliche jemals einen solchen Tweet abgesetzt zu haben.

„Das war maximal dumm und unangebracht", schrieb Heinrich. Die Sozialwissenschafts-Studentin betonte aber auch, dass sie sich „jetzt nicht zu allem erklären" wolle, „was ich mal so mit 14 gedacht und gesagt habe".

Erst Tweets, dann Morddrohungen

Heinrich beklagte außerdem, seit ihrer Wahl versuchten Rechte, Shitstorms gegen sie hochzuziehen: „Haben wohl Bammel vor einer schwarzen, linken Frau", schrieb Heinrich.

Nach diesen Tweets zog sich Heinrich vorerst aus der Öffentlichkeit zurück. Der Grünen-Jugendorganisation zufolge hatte sie Mord- und Gewaltandrohungen erhalten. Es gehe „jetzt erst einmal darum, alles für ihre Sicherheit zu tun", sagte der scheidende Bundessprecher der Grünen Jugend, Georg Kurz.

„Das ist koordiniert"

Dass der Fall eine solche Entwicklung genommen hat, sei typisch, sagte Tajana Graovac vom „No Hate Speech Movement" im Deutschlandfunk. „Was wir feststellen können, dass es große Accounts sind, die meistens eher in der rechten Ecke zu finden sind, die große Reichweite haben", sagte Graovac.

Accounts aus rechten und rechtsextremen Kreisen würden dann dafür sorgen, dass sich die entsprechenden Nachrichten weit verbreiten. „Das ist koordiniert. Und es ist tatsächlich auch immer das gleiche Schema und das geht fast immer nach der gleichen Dynamik", so Graovac weiter.

Manipulierte Kampagnen erkennen

Zudem würden zum Teil Screenshots verbreitet, die nachträglich manipuliert worden seien. „Man schneidet die Zeit und das Datum ab, damit die irgendwie auch aktuell aussehen. Es werden teilweise Wörter weggelassen, damit die Tweets noch schlimmer klingen. Und das zieht dann wirklich Kreise." Aufgabe von Journalistinnen und Journalisten sei es, dies zu erkennen und nicht auf eine Kampagne hereinzufallen. Sie müssten offenlegen, „dass es eine gezielte, koordinierte Attacke ist gegen eine schwarze Person".

Stereotypes and images of black female identity

7 → **S17:** How to work with cartoons

a) Study the depiction of the woman carefully. Then describe the cartoon.

Topic: seven methods of killing kylie jenner

Language support

index finger | megaphone | speech bubble

b) Explain the message of the cartoon by referring to its individual elements.
c) Come up with a possible title and give reasons for your decision.
d) Black women have often been depicted in the media and society as 'angry', 'aggressive' and 'sassy'. Think of situations in which black women could be seen as behaving in an "angry" way.
e) Read an article about this stereotype from an online encyclopedia.
   Webcode DSW-73698-13
   Use key words to sum up the text. Compare your result with a partner.

f) Discuss how it is possible for black women to escape the vicious circle of being referred to as an "angry black woman" when they show anger about being called this term.
   You may refer to Michelle Obama's reactions described in the following extract from a 2012 article from the *BBC*.

Michelle Obama: 'I'm no angry black woman'

US First Lady Michelle Obama has challenged a new book's account of her role in the White House, saying critics have long attempted to portray her as "some kind of angry black woman".

The Obamas, by New York Times reporter Jodi Kantor, portrays her as a behind-the-scenes force in the White House. [...]
While she pushed back against the notion she
5 sits in political meetings, Mrs Obama did not deny being an important voice to her husband.
"I am his biggest ally," Mrs Obama said. "I am one of his biggest confidants. But he has dozens of really smart people who surround him. That's
10 not to say that we don't have discussions and conversations.

"I guess it's more interesting to imagine this conflicted situation here and a strong woman. But that's been an image that people have tried to
15 paint of me since the day Barack announced [he would run for president] – that I'm some angry black woman," she said.
"I just try to be me. And my hope is that over time people get to know me," she told CBS. "And they
20 get to judge me for me." [...]

8
Read the 2018 article from the *BBC*.
Outline the views on the stereotype of the "angry black woman" as presented in this article.

Serena Williams and the trope of the 'angry black woman'

By Ritu Prasad *11 September 2018*

Mammies, jezebels, Sapphires. Black women in America have long been dogged by negative stereotypes, rooted in a history of racism and slavery. In the aftermath of Serena Williams' controversial US Open loss, it's the trope[1] of the "angry black woman" that has once again re-emerged.

During the US Open final, Williams received a code violation for coaching[2], a penalty point for breaking her racquet and a game penalty for calling the umpire a "thief". And later, a fine of $17,000 (£13,000). Her reactions to the referee's calls – which the Women's Tennis Association has since decried as "sexist" – were no different from how many top players react in the heat of a championship game. But it was the way she was punished for her anger that has sparked further outrage.

"As it was unfolding I could tell this was not going to turn out well," says law professor Trina Jones. "I knew it was going to be a trainwreck."
In addition to being a long-time tennis fan, Prof Jones has studied racial stereotyping and how it plays into the lives of African-American women.
"Black women are not supposed to push back and when they do, they're deemed to be domineering. Aggressive. Threatening. Loud."
Similar words have been levelled[3] at Serena Williams more than once, as well as former First Lady Michelle Obama and top Democrat Maxine Waters in recent years.
Williams has been docked before for her behaviour on the court – in 2009, she was fined $82,500 for an angry outburst – though she is far from the only player to face punishment for similar conduct.
Prof Jones says some have compared the referee's calls to speeding tickets: many people speed and sometimes a few are caught.
But that analogy, she says, misses the point that African Americans are disproportionately pulled aside. In the case of Williams, she was first dinged[4] on a coaching violation that happens often but is rarely called out as the player's fault.
"Why would a black woman in a championship match therefore be called on it?" Prof Jones says, adding that an attack on one's integrity is only natural to be angry about.
"[Williams] is outraged because she knows the context."

The myth of the 'angry black woman'

The "angry black woman" trope has its roots in 19th Century America, when minstrel shows, which involved comic skits[5] and variety acts, mocking African Americans became popular.
Blair Kelley, associate professor of history at North Carolina State University, says black women were often played by overweight white men who painted their faces black and donned fat suits "to make them look less than human, unfeminine, ugly".
"Their main way of interacting with the men around them was to scream and fight and come off angry, irrationally so, in response to the circumstances around them," she says.
The 1930s programme *Amos 'n' Andy* was one of the first modern media portrayals to cement this stereotype through the character of Mrs Sapphire Stevens.
"The real problem in their everyday life was not the structural things that black people faced, but the mouth of the black woman – her tone, her irrationality and her anger," Prof Kelley says of Sapphire's role.
As segregation laws known as Jim Crow laws saw black Americans assaulted, jailed and killed, popular culture pushed ideas of "sassy[6] mammies" and "Sapphires" – an archetype depicting black women with iron-fists, yelling at everyone from children to white men.
This trope of the "angry black woman" has endured, and has been pervasive[7] in modern media even without more overtly racist portrayals, says Brandi Collins, senior campaign director at

---

Annotations

[1] **trope** = *Tropus, bildlicher Ausdruck*
[2] **coaching** = Players aren't allowed to be coached in Grand Slam matches. Violations lead to warnings or penalties.
[3] **to be levelled at** = to be aimed or directed at sb or sth
[4] **to ding** = to make a ringing sound (like a bell); to criticize sb
[5] **comic skit** = a short, funny play
[6] **sassy** = *frech*
[7] **pervasive** = present, noticeable, widespread

Topic: seven methods of killing kylie jenner

the racial justice organisation Color of Change.
On screen, it is easy to push sass for laughs.
But black women in America see these depictions
translate differently in real life.
For Ms Collins, the picture of the "hyperemotional" black woman has become more commonplace as Americans grapple[8] with issues of polarised politics and civility.

Black women, she says, are often faced with people responding to their emotions "from a place of perceived fear".

"There's almost a paranoia around it. A feeling that you have to go above and beyond to make people feel comfortable around you."

In a 2016 interview with Oprah Winfrey, former First Lady Michelle Obama echoed the same sentiment. "You think, that is so not me! But then you sort of think, well, this isn't about me," she said of being labelled as an "angry black woman".

"This is about the person or the people who write it ... We are so afraid of each other, you know?"

Robin Boylorn, an intercultural communications professor at the University of Alabama told the BBC it seems impossible to be a black woman and not be angry, after "generations of oppression, discrimination and erasure".

"Black women should be celebrated for not being completely consumed by anger," she says.

"Men are allowed to be angry as a performance of masculinity. White women are allowed to be angry as a clarion call[9]. So black women should be encouraged to express their anger as well, particularly in the face of injustice."

For Serena Williams, Prof Boylorn says the issue is compounded by the fact that "she cannot separate her blackness from her womanhood, from her class or social status".

But it's the double standard with men in particular that has come up in the ongoing debate of Williams' US Open performance.

In a cartoon that went viral after the final, Williams is drawn as a petulant, mannish figure while the referee tells her opponent, "Can you just let her win?"

"It's indicative of the way in which Serena has been, throughout her career, treated both by media and within US tennis as angry, unhinged, really aggressive," says Ms Collins of Color of Change.

"When you see her be degraded or treated in that way, it really can lead young black girls and girls in general to question whether or not they should be the full range of what it means to be a woman."

But Ms Collins notes that fixing the problem is not just about eliminating the "angry black woman" trope.

"For every type of white man you can imagine, there's a movie about his story and his experience and his journey. Black women in media aren't afforded that diversity of experience," she says. Instead, understanding the diversity of a black woman's experience – and not just her anger – is key.

For Williams, that's a lesson she hopes her fans will learn from her US Open upset.

"I'm here to fight for women's rights and women's equality. The fact that I have to go through this is an example," she told reporters after the match.

"Maybe it didn't work out for me, but it's going to work out for the next person."

Annotations
[8] to **grapple** = to try to deal with sth
[9] **clarion call** = *Weckruf*

9
Explain why it is inadequate to refer to an African-American woman as an "angry black woman".

Looking back at the play
10 Pair work

Cleo is being criticized for her behaviour on the TL, e.g. "I for one can't believe @INCOGNEGRO acting like dis. U ain't the next civil rights activist!" (p. 19).
Are there any more parallels between Serena Williams' depiction as an "angry black woman" and the comments on Twitter that describe Cleo as hysterical and overreacting?

11 Group work

Your school is planning a project week with the topic "school for the future" and is asking students to send in podcasts, videos, posters, etc. with ideas about how schools can address and eliminate racism. What would be your contribution?

A Midsummer Night's Dream — Play

Pre-reading

1

A Midsummer Night's Dream is one of William Shakespeare's most popular plays. The comedy was written around 1594–1596 and is set in Athens.
To get an idea of the setting and atmosphere of the play, carefully study the photos below.
Then choose the adjectives from the box that best describe the atmosphere the photos convey.
Give reasons for your choice.

> convivial | dreamlike | eccentric | electric | emotional | happy | heady | illusory | irrational | lively | romantic | stifling | strange | tense | unreal

1

2

3

4

2

a) As you have gained some insight into the setting, find out about the characters in *A Midsummer Night's Dream*. Read the short descriptions of the characters. Then start a character map in which you show the relationships between them. Add additional information to your map while you read the play.

Theseus	Hippolyta
Duke of Athens; he has conquered the Amazons	the conquered Queen of the Amazons; she is about to get married to Theseus

Egeus	Philostrate
father of Hermia, who wants his daughter to get married to Demetrius	Master of the Revels at Theseus's court

4 Play — A Midsummer Night's Dream

Hermia	Lysander
daughter of Egeus, who is in love with Lysander	a young man who is in love with Hermia

Helena	Demetrius
Hermia's friend, who is in love with Demetrius	a young man who courts Hermia

Oberon	Titania
King of the fairies	Queen of the fairies

Puck	Peaseblossom, Cobweb, Mote and Mustardseed
a mischievous sprite who serves Oberon	fairies

Quince, Bottom, Flute, Snout, Snug and Starveling
a group of workmen who want to rehearse a play in the woods for the wedding of Theseus and Hippolyta

b) Having caught a first glimpse at the characters involved, outline what you expect from the play.

Language support

I expect the play to be full of emotional entanglements / confusion / mischief-making / lovesickness / …
I think that … will try to win (back) … / avenge … / make mischief / …
From what I have read, I assume the play will be fast-paced / action-packed / a love story / a comedy / …

c) Watch a video by the Royal Shakespeare Company and check if your assumptions from the previous tasks were correct. Add new information to your character map from a). **Webcode** DSW-73698-14

3

Shakespeare seems to have taken some of his ideas for the play from various literary sources. Among these are Ovid's *Metamorphoses*, Plutarch's *Parallel Lives*, and Geoffrey Chaucer's *The Canterbury Tales*.

a) **Group work (3)**
Research the following works of literature and share the information with your group members.
- Ovid, *Metamorphoses: Pyramus and Thisbe*
- Plutarch, *Parallel Lives: Theseus*
- Geoffrey Chaucer, *The Canterbury Tales: The Knight's Tale*

b) Use the charts on the next page to illustrate the plots of these works of literature.

A Midsummer Night's Dream — Play — 4

Ovid: Pyramus and Thisbe

Pyramus   Thisbe

                    mulberry tree

     lioness   cloak

                        sword

                  metamorphosis:
                   mulberry tree

Plutarch: Theseus

            Phaedra   Theseus

                                    Athens
                    Amazons
      Hippolytus   Hippolyta

Chaucer: The Knight's Tale

   Theseus   Hippolyta

              Palamon   Arcite

                    Emily

                 tournament

                 three prayers:

       Arcite   Emily   Palamon

4 Play — A Midsummer Night's Dream

While reading: Act I

SCENE 1

The play opens with Theseus and Hippolyta entering the stage. They have been at war with each other, but now prepare to get married. The setting is Athens, Theseus's palace.
Read the opening scene of the play and try to understand as much as possible. You don't need to understand every single word.

Extract 1 (Act I, Scene 1)

Athens, the palace of THESEUS:
Enter THESEUS, HIPPOLYTA, PHILOSTRATE, *with others*
THESEUS. Now, fair Hippolyta, our nuptial hour
Draws on apace; four happy days bring in
Another moon – but O, methinks, how slow
This old moon wanes! She lingers my desires,
5 Like to a step-dame or a dowager
Long withering out a young man's revenue.
HIPPOLYTA. Four days will quickly steep themselves in night;
Four nights will quickly dream away the time;
And then the moon, like to a silver bow
10 New bent in heaven, shall behold the night
Of our solemnities.
THESEUS. Go, Philostrate,
Stir up the Athenian youth to merriments,
Awake the pert and nimble spirit of mirth;
Turn melancholy forth to funerals;
15 The pale companion is not for our pomp.
  Exit PHILOSTRATE
Hippolyta, I woo'd thee with my sword,
And won thy love doing thee injuries;
But I will wed thee in another key,
With pomp, with triumph, and with revelling.

> **Tip** Don't get confused by the line numbers. Sometimes a single verse line is divided up between two characters (for example, the verse in line 11:
> HIPPOLYTA: "Of our solemnities." –
> THESEUS: "Go, Philostrate,").

Annotations
l. 1   **our nuptial hour** = the time of our wedding
l. 2   **apace** = quickly
ll. 2–3 **four ... moon** = there will be a full moon in four days
l. 3   **methinks** = I think
l. 4   to **wane** = to fade
       to **linger** = *here:* to make me wait for
l. 5   **step-dame** = step-mother
       dowager = widow
l. 6   **long withering ... revenue** = growing old and spending a young man's inheritance (which he can only claim when she dies)
l. 7   to **steep** = to drown
l. 11 **solemnities** = wedding ceremonies
l. 12 **youth** = young people
l. 13 **pert** = lively, cheeky
       nimble = moving quickly and easily
l. 14 to **turn ... forth** = to send away
l. 15 **the pale ... pomp** = we can't have miserable guests at our celebrations
ll. 16–17 **I woo'd thee ... injuries** = In Greek mythology, Theseus was a legendary ruler of Athens who defeated an invasion of the Amazons and married their Queen, Hippolyta, afterwards.
l. 18 **in another key** = *here:* in a different way
l. 19 **triumph** = public festivities
       revelling = noisy celebrations

a) Tick (✓) the summary that fits best. Explain your choice.
  ☐ 1. Whereas Theseus complains that time is passing so slowly, Hippolyta seems rather relaxed about their wedding day. Theseus promises that he will make up for the suffering Hippolyta has had to endure by providing public festivities on their wedding day.
  ☐ 2. Theseus can't wait to get married to Hippolyta and instructs his master of the revels to see to the wedding preparations. He discloses that he will now make amends to her for having won her by force.
  ☐ 3. Theseus is impatient to get married to Hippolyta and tells his master of the revels to make sure the celebration will be a success.

b) Describe your first impression of the relationship between Theseus and Hippolyta. Give evidence from the text.

> **Language support**
> Their relationship can be described as ...
> caring | close | cold | formal | fragile | harmonious | intimate | love-hate | loving | stormy | troubled | violent | ...

c) Speculate why Shakespeare opens his play with two prominent figures from a classical myth that was well-known in Shakespeare's days.

A Midsummer Night's Dream — Play

5
Egeus enters with Hermia and her two suitors, Lysander and Demetrius, to see Theseus about a legal matter. Read the following extract.

Extract 2 (Act I, Scene 1)

EGEUS. Happy be Theseus, our renowned duke!
THESEUS. Thanks, good Egeus. What's the news with thee?
EGEUS. Full of vexation come I, with complaint
Against my child, my daughter Hermia.
5 Stand forth, Demetrius! – My noble lord,
This man hath my consent to marry her.
Stand forth, Lysander! – And, my gracious duke,
This man hath bewitch'd the bosom of my child.
Thou, thou, Lysander, thou hast given her rhymes,
10 And interchang'd love-tokens with my child.
Thou hast by moonlight at her window sung
With feigning voice verses of feigning love,
And stolen the impression of her fantasy,
With bracelets of thy hair, rings, gauds, conceits,
15 Knacks, trifles, nosegays, sweetmeats – messengers
Of strong prevailment in unharden'd youth;
With cunning hast thou filch'd my daughter's heart,
Turn'd her obedience, which is due to me,
To stubborn harshness. And, my gracious duke,
20 Be it so she will not here, before your grace,
Consent to marry with Demetrius,
I beg the ancient privilege of Athens;
As she is mine, I may dispose of her;
Which shall be either to this gentleman
25 Or to her death, according to our law
Immediately provided in that case.
THESEUS. What say you, Hermia? Be advis'd, fair maid.
To you your father should be as a god,
One that compos'd your beauties; yea, and one
30 To whom you are but as a form in wax
By him imprinted, and within his power
To leave the figure, or disfigure it.
Demetrius is a worthy gentleman.
HERMIA. So is Lysander.
THESEUS.   In himself he is;
35 But in this kind, wanting your father's voice,
The other must be held the worthier.
HERMIA. I would my father look'd but with my eyes.
THESEUS. Rather your eyes must with his judgement look.
HERMIA. I do entreat your grace to pardon me.
40 I know not by what power I am made bold,
Nor how it may concern my modesty
In such a presence here to plead my thoughts;
But I beseech your grace that I may know
The worst that may befall me in this case,
45 If I refuse to wed Demetrius.
THESEUS. Either to die the death, or to abjure
For ever the society of men.
Therefore, fair Hermia, question your desires,
Know of your youth, examine well your blood,

Annotations
- l. 3 **vexation** = worry or anger
- l. 8 **bosom** = *here:* heart
- l. 10 **token** = sign, symbol
- l. 12 **feigning** = pretending to be sincere
- l. 14 **gauds** = silly toys
  conceits = fancy things
- l. 15 **knacks** = knick-knacks, useless little things
  nosegays = bunches of flowers
  sweetmeats = sweets
- l. 16 **prevailment** = power
  unharden'd = inexperienced
- l. 17 to **filch** = to steal
- l. 18 **due** = owed
- l. 20 **be it so** = if
- l. 22 **privilege** = *here:* special right
- l. 23 **I may dispose of her** = I may have her at my command; I may get rid of her
- l. 29 **compos'd your beauties** = made you beautiful
- l. 32 to **disfigure** = to destroy
- l. 35 **kind** = *here:* matter
  wanting = *here:* lacking
  voice = *here:* approval
- l. 37 **I would** = *here:* I wish
- l. 39 to **entreat** = to beg
- l. 42 to **plead** = *here:* to express
- l. 43 to **beseech** = to beg
- l. 46 to **abjure** = to give up officially
- l. 49 to **know of** = *here:* to think of

Play — A Midsummer Night's Dream

50 Whether, if you yield not to your father's choice,
You can endure the livery of a nun,
For aye to be in shady cloister mew'd,
To live a barren sister all your life,
Chanting faint hymns to the cold fruitless moon.
55 Thrice blessed they that master so their blood
To undergo such maiden pilgrimage;
But earthlier happy is the rose distill'd
Than that which, withering on the virgin thorn,
Grows, lives, and dies in single blessedness.
60 **HERMIA.** So will I grow, so live, so die, my lord,
Ere I will yield my virgin patent up
Unto his lordship, whose unwished yoke
My soul consents not to give sovereignty.
THESEUS. Take time to pause, and by the next new moon,
65 The sealing-day betwixt my love and me
For everlasting bond of fellowship,
Upon that day either prepare to die
For disobedience to your father's will,
Or else to wed Demetrius, as he would,
70 Or on Diana's altar to protest
For aye austerity and single life.
DEMETRIUS. Relent, sweet Hermia; and, Lysander, yield
Thy crazed title to my certain right.
LYSANDER. You have her father's love, Demetrius;
75 Let me have Hermia's – do you marry him.
EGEUS. Scornful Lysander, true, he hath my love,
And what is mine my love shall render him;
And she is mine, and all my right of her
I do estate unto Demetrius.

Annotations
l. 50 **to yield** = to give in, to surrender
l. 51 **livery** = habit (a special piece of long clothing worn by nuns)
l. 52 **aye** = ever
mew'd = shut up
l. 54 **fruitless moon** = reference to Diana, goddess of the moon and of chastity
l. 55 **to master** = to discipline
blood = *here*: passions
l. 56 **maiden pilgrimage** = *here*: a life of celibacy
l. 57 **earthlier happy** = happier on earth
the rose distill'd = the rose that is plucked and whose scent is distilled to make perfume
l. 61 **ere** = before
yield my virgin patent up = give up my right to remain a virgin
l. 62 **his lordship** = the domination of this man
yoke = Joch
l. 65 **sealing-day** = the day on which they will seal their vows
betwixt = between
l. 70 **to protest** = *here*: to vow
l. 71 **aye** = ever
austerity = strict simplicity (i.e. the life of a nun)
l. 73 **crazed title** = uncertain claim
l. 79 **I do estate unto** = I give to (as a legal act)

a) Tick (✓) the correct answers. Give evidence from the text.

1. Egeus wants …
   ❑ a) Hermia to get married to Demetrius.
   ❑ b) Hermia to get married to Lysander.
   ❑ c) Lysander to court Hermia.

2. According to Egeus, Lysander …
   ❑ a) only pretends to be in love with her.
   ❑ b) is sincere in his wooing.
   ❑ c) is a good-for-nothing.

3. Lysander has given Hermia …
   ❑ a) books and jewellery.
   ❑ b) flowers and a strand of his hair.
   ❑ c) toys and pets.

4. Egeus complains about Hermia's …
   ❑ a) insolence.
   ❑ b) disloyalty.
   ❑ c) disobedience.

5. According to the Athenian law, Hermia must …
   ❑ a) either obey her father or die.
   ❑ b) leave Athens with Demetrius.
   ❑ c) stay unmarried until her death.

6. Theseus tries to …
   ❑ a) find out what Hermia really wants.
   ❑ b) understand Hermia's wish.
   ❑ c) convince Hermia to obey her father.

7. Hermia …
   ❑ a) rather wants to die or become a nun than obey her father.
   ❑ b) wants to reconsider Theseus's proposal.
   ❑ c) happily accepts Theseus's decision.

8. Lysander suggests that …
   ❑ a) Demetrius courts Helena.
   ❑ b) Demetrius marries Egeus.
   ❑ c) Hermia should obey her father.

b) Outline Egeus's and Hermia's conflict.

A Midsummer Night's Dream — Play

c) Collect information on how the women are presented in the scene. Start a table like the one below. Add new information as you read on.

Women in the play	
Quotation	Analysis/Interpretation
"I woo'd thee with my sword" (extract 1, l. 16) …	the Queen of the Amazons, Hippolyta, is defeated → "subjected" …

6

a) First impressions: Explain how Theseus, Egeus and Hermia come across. Give evidence from the text.

Language support

appeasing | conciliatory | domineering | gentle | headstrong | irreconcilable | meek | peace-making | relentless | remorseless | strong-minded | submissive | uncompromising | …

b) **Group work (4)**
Show their relationship in a tableau: Each student slips into the role of one character: Theseus, Egeus and Hermia. The fourth student serves as the director and presenter.
- First discuss a typical pose, mood or gesture of the characters.
- Then display in a still a particular gesture, expression or movement that shows each character's attitude towards the other characters.
- The fourth student invites other students to interpret the still and leads the talk.

Info

Tableau

In a tableau, still images of characters from a play are presented. This method can be used to show the relationship between characters or to point out important moments in a scene.

c) Step into the shoes of one of the characters – Theseus, Egeus or Hermia – and write a soliloquy, in which you reflect upon the meeting.

Info

Soliloquy

Soliloquy is the act of talking to oneself. This can be done silently or aloud. In drama, the term describes the practice by which a character, alone on stage, utters his or her thoughts for the audience to hear. Soliloquies serve as a dramatic device to let the audience know about the character's intentions and state of mind, and also to give additional information about the action of the play.

Soliloquies are often used to
- set the scene
- make the audience part of the play
- explicate the character's feelings
- clarify matters
- introduce further information.

Play — A Midsummer Night's Dream

7 Lysander and Hermia are alone hatching a plan. Read the following extract.

Extract 3 (Act I, Scene 1)

LYSANDER. How now, my love? Why is your cheek so pale?
How chance the roses there do fade so fast?
HERMIA. Belike for want of rain, which I could well
Beteem them from the tempest of my eyes.
5 **LYSANDER.** Ay me! For aught that I could ever read,
Could ever hear by tale or history,
The course of true love never did run smooth;
But either it was different in blood –
HERMIA. O cross! too high to be enthrall'd to low.
10 **LYSANDER.** Or else misgraffed in respect of years –
HERMIA. O spite! too old to be engag'd to young.
LYSANDER. Or else it stood upon the choice of friends –
HERMIA. O hell, to choose love by another's eyes!
LYSANDER. Or, if there were a sympathy in choice,
15 War, death, or sickness did lay siege to it,
Making it momentany as a sound,
Swift as a shadow, short as any dream,
Brief as the lightning in the collied night,
That in a spleen unfolds both heaven and earth,
20 And, ere a man hath power to say 'Behold!',
The jaws of darkness do devour it up.
So quick bright things come to confusion.
HERMIA. If then true lovers have been ever cross'd
It stands as an edict in destiny.
25 Then let us teach our trial patience,
Because it is a customary cross,
As due to love as thoughts, and dreams, and sighs,
Wishes, and tears – poor fancy's followers.
LYSANDER. A good persuasion. Therefore hear me, Hermia:
30 I have a widow aunt, a dowager,
Of great revenue, and she hath no child.
From Athens is her house remote seven leagues;
And she respects me as her only son.
There, gentle Hermia, may I marry thee;
35 And to that place the sharp Athenian law
Cannot pursue us. If thou lov'st me, then
Steal forth thy father's house tomorrow night,
And in the wood, a league without the town,
Where I did meet thee once with Helena
40 To do observance to a morn of May,
There will I stay for thee.
HERMIA. My good Lysander,
I swear to thee by Cupid's strongest bow,
By his best arrow with the golden head,
By the simplicity of Venus' doves,
45 By that which knitteth souls and prospers loves,
And by that fire which burn'd the Carthage queen
When the false Trojan under sail was seen,
By all the vows that ever men have broke –
In number more than ever women spoke –
50 In that same place thou hast appointed me,
Tomorrow truly will I meet with thee.
LYSANDER. Keep promise, love. Look, here comes Helena.

Annotations

- l. 2 **how chance** = why
- l. 3 **belike** = probably
  for want of = for lack of
- l. 4 to **beteem** = to allow
- l. 5 **aught** = anything
- l. 8 **blood** = *here:* social class
- l. 9 **enthrall'd** = fascinated
- l. 10 **misgraffed** = badly matched
- l. 11 **spite** = the desire to upset or hurt sb
- l. 12 to **stand upon** = *here:* to depend on
- l. 14 **sympathy** = *here:* agreement
- l. 15 to **lay siege to** = to make war on
- l. 18 **collied** = blackened
- l. 19 **spleen** = sudden impulse of anger
  to **unfold** = *here:* to light up
- l. 20 **ere** = before
  to **behold** = to see or look at
- l. 23 **cross'd** = *here:* annoyed, frustrated
- l. 24 **edict** = *Erlass, Anordnung*
- l. 25 **trial** = test
- l. 26 **customary** = usual, traditional
- l. 27 **due to** = belonging to
- l. 28 **fancy** = *here:* love
- l. 29 **persuasion** = *here:* advice
- l. 30 **dowager** = widow
- l. 31 **revenue** = income, money
- l. 32 **remote** = far away
  league = a unit of distance (usually about 3 miles)
- l. 36 to **pursue** = to follow and try to catch
- l. 38 **without** = *here:* outside
- l. 40 **observance** = a ritual or ceremony to celebrate a religious event
  morn = morning
- l. 41 to **stay** = *here:* to wait
- l. 42 **Cupid** = In classical mythology, Cupid (also known as Amor) is the god of love and desire. He is often depicted with a bow and two arrows.
- l. 44 **the simplicity of Venus' doves** = Venus is the Roman goddess of love. Her chariot used to be drawn by white doves, a symbol of the innocence of pure love.
- l. 45 to **knit** = *stricken, verknüpfen*
- l. 46 **the Carthage queen** = Dido was the legendary Queen of Carthage. According to the story in Virgil's *Aeneid*, she fell in love with the Trojan Aeneas and was so heartbroken when he sailed away from her that she killed herself.

A Midsummer Night's Dream — Play

a) "The course of true love never did run smooth; […]." (l. 7) Tick (✓) the obstacles lovers must overcome according to Lysander and Hermia.

	Possible obstacles	✓	Evidence
1	The lovers are from different social classes.	✓	*"different in blood"* (l. 8)
2	The lovers have a different financial background.		
3	The lovers differ in age.		
4	The lovers are advised against the relationship by family members, friends, guardians, etc.		
5	Other people fancy them.		
6	War tears them apart.		
7	They are from different ethnic groups.		
8	One lover dies or becomes ill.		
9	One lover changes his/her mind.		

b) Outline Lysander's plan.
c) In class, talk about the obstacles that lovers might need to overcome today.

8
Helena enters and pours out her heart to Hermia. Read the following extract.

Extract 4 (Act I, Scene 1)

HERMIA. God speed, fair Helena! Whither away?
HELENA. Call you me fair? That 'fair' again unsay.
Demetrius loves your fair: O happy fair!
Your eyes are lodestars, and your tongue's sweet air
5 More tuneable than lark to shepherd's ear
When wheat is green, when hawthorn buds appear.
Sickness is catching. O, were favour so,
Yours would I catch, fair Hermia, ere I go;
My ear should catch your voice, my eye your eye,
10 My tongue should catch your tongue's sweet melody.
Were the world mine, Demetrius being bated,
The rest I'd give to be to you translated.
O, teach me how you look, and with what art
You sway the motion of Demetrius' heart.
15 **HERMIA.** I frown upon him; yet he loves me still.
HELENA. O that your frowns would teach my smiles such skill!
HERMIA. I give him curses; yet he gives me love.
HELENA. O that my prayers could such affection move!
HERMIA. The more I hate, the more he follows me.

Annotations
l. 1 **God speed** = may God be with you
  fair = *here:* beautiful, lovely
  Whither away? = Where are you going?
l. 3 **your fair** = your beauty
l. 4 **lodestar** = guiding star
  air = *here:* sound, song, melody
l. 5 **tuneable** = melodious, with a pleasant tune
l. 6 **hawthorn** = Weißdorn
l. 7 **catching** = infectious, able to be given to sb else
  favour = *here:* beauty, charm
l. 8 **ere** = before
l. 11 **bated** = *here:* excepted
l. 12 **translated** = *here:* transferred
l. 14 to **sway** = to cause sth to move or change, to influence

4 Play — A Midsummer Night's Dream

20 **HELENA.** The more I love, the more he hateth me.
HERMIA. His folly, Helena, is no fault of mine.
HELENA. None but your beauty; would that fault were mine!
HERMIA. Take comfort: he no more shall see my face;
Lysander and myself will fly this place.
25 Before the time I did Lysander see,
Seem'd Athens as a paradise to me.
O then, what graces in my love do dwell,
That he hath turn'd a heaven unto a hell?
LYSANDER. Helen, to you our minds we will unfold:
30 [...]

Annotations
l. 21 **folly** = stupidity, foolishness
l. 22 **would** = *here:* I wish
l. 24 to **fly** = *here:* to leave, to escape from
l. 27 **grace** = *here:* quality
to **dwell** = to live or stay
l. 29 **mind** = *here:* thought, plan

a) Describe Helena's problem and Hermia's reaction.
b) Analyse the language Shakespeare uses to show the complications of love.
→ **Workshop:** Analysing a Shakespearean sonnet
c) **Pair work** Dramatic reading: Read out the dialogue. One student takes Hermia's role, the other student Helena's role. Try several different ways of delivering Helena's lines. How does she come across? You can find some ideas in the box.
d) Describe your first impression of Helena.

Literary devices: alliteration | anaphora | antithesis | epiphora | inversion | parallelism

Language support

admiring | desperate | infatuated | intimidated | respectful | servile | timid | ...

9

Hermia and Lysander have disclosed their plan to Helena: They want to elope and meet in the woods the following night. Then Helena is left alone on stage. Read the following extract.

Extract 5 (Act I, Scene 1)

HELENA. How happy some o'er other some can be!
Through Athens I am thought as fair as she.
But what of that? Demetrius thinks not so;
He will not know what all but he do know.
5 And as he errs, doting on Hermia's eyes,
So I, admiring of his qualities.
Things base and vile, holding no quantity,
Love can transpose to form and dignity.
Love looks not with the eyes, but with the mind,
10 And therefore is wing'd Cupid painted blind.
Nor hath love's mind of any judgement taste;
Wings, and no eyes, figure unheedy haste;
And therefore is love said to be a child
Because in choice he is so oft beguil'd.
15 As waggish boys in game themselves forswear,
So the boy Love is perjur'd everywhere;
For, ere Demetrius looked on Hermia's eyne,
He hail'd down oaths that he was only mine,
And when this hail some heat from Hermia felt,
20 So he dissolv'd, and showers of oaths did melt.
I will go tell him of fair Hermia's flight:
Then to the wood will he, tomorrow night,
Pursue her; and for this intelligence,
If I have thanks it is a dear expense;
25 But herein mean I to enrich my pain,
To have his sight thither, and back again.

Annotations
l. 1 **o'er** = over
l. 2 **fair** = *here:* beautiful, lovely
l. 5 to **dote on** = to love very much, to admire
l. 7 **base** = *here:* having no honour or morals
vile = bad, evil
quantity = *here:* value
l. 8 to **transpose** = to transform
l. 12 to **figure** = to cause
unheedy = thoughtless
haste = speed, the act of hurrying
l. 14 **beguil'd** = deceived
l. 15 **waggish** = playful, mischievous
themselves forswear = break promises
l. 16 **perjur'd** = *eidbrüchig, meineidig*
l. 17 **ere** = until
eyne = eyes
l. 18 to **hail down** = *niederhageln, niederprasseln*
l. 19 **hail** = small balls of ice that fall from the sky
l. 21 **flight** = *here:* escape
l. 23 **intelligence** = *here:* information
l. 24 **dear** = beloved; precious; highly priced
expense = cost
l. 26 **sight** = view
thither = to that place, there

A Midsummer Night's Dream — Play

4

What ideas does Helena express? Match the correct sentence halves.

1. It's a surprise
2. It's of no use that
3. Demetrius refuses to accept
4. Demetrius is as wrong about adoring Hermia
5. Love can make worthless things
6. When we are in love,
7. Before Demetrius fell in love with Hermia,
8. I'm going to tell him about Hermia and Lysander's elopement so that
9. I will pay a high price
10. At least I will be able to

a) as I am wrong about loving him.
b) we don't use our eyes, but our mind.
c) he courted me and promised he was mine.
d) for making him grateful for this information.
e) how much happier some people can be than others.
f) he will follow them into the forest.
g) see him come and go.
h) people think I am as beautiful as Hermia.
i) what other people know.
j) look beautiful.

1	2	3	4	5	6	7	8	9	10

10

a) Helena refers to the Roman god of love, Cupid, when she explains what she thinks about love. Describe how Cupid is portrayed in the painting and find references in Helena's passage that match the description.

Piero della Francesca: Cupid Blindfolded (1452–66)

b) Explain to what extent the message of the portrayal is true.

11

a) **Group work (3)** Should Helena disclose her friends' plan to elope? Collect arguments for and against disclosing Hermia and Lysander's plan to Demetrius. Then have one student (Helena) sit on a chair. Two other students (her conscience) stand behind her and take turns to tell her why she should or shouldn't disclose her friends' plan.

b) Comment on Helena's plan. Do you think it will work out? Explain why you think or don't think so.

Play — A Midsummer Night's Dream

SCENE 2

12

The craftsmen have gathered at the house of Peter Quince, the carpenter, to prepare a play, which they want to perform at the Duke's wedding. Read the following extract.

Extract 6 (Act I, Scene 2)

QUINCE. Is all our company here?
BOTTOM. You were best to call them generally, man by man, according to the scrip.
QUINCE. Here is the scroll of every man's name, which is thought fit
5 through all Athens to play in our interlude before the duke and the duchess on his wedding day at night.
BOTTOM. First, good Peter Quince, say what the play treats on; then read the names of the actors; and so grow to a point.
QUINCE. Marry, our play is 'The most lamentable comedy and most
10 cruel death of Pyramus and Thisbe'.
BOTTOM. A very good piece of work, I assure you, and a merry. Now, good Peter Quince, call forth your actors by the scroll. Masters, spread yourselves.
QUINCE. Answer as I call you. Nick Bottom, the weaver?
15 BOTTOM. Ready. Name what part I am for, and proceed.
QUINCE. You, Nick Bottom, are set down for Pyramus.
BOTTOM. What is Pyramus? A lover or a tyrant?
QUINCE. A lover that kills himself, most gallant, for love.
BOTTOM. That will ask some tears in the true performing of it. If I do
20 it, let the audience look to their eyes: I will move storms, I will condole, in some measure. To the rest – yet my chief humour is for a tyrant. […]
QUINCE. Francis Flute, the bellows-mender?
FLUTE. Here, Peter Quince.
QUINCE. Flute, you must take Thisbe on you.
25 FLUTE. What is Thisbe? A wandering knight?
QUINCE. It is the lady that Pyramus must love.
FLUTE. Nay, faith, let not me play a woman: I have a beard coming.
QUINCE. That's all one: you shall play it in a mask, and you may speak as small as you will.
30 BOTTOM. And I may hide my face, let me play Thisbe too. I'll speak in a monstrous little voice: 'Thisne, Thisne!' – 'Ah, Pyramus, my lover dear; thy Thisbe dear, and lady dear.'
QUINCE. No, no; you must play Pyramus; and Flute, you Thisbe.
BOTTOM. Well, proceed.
35 QUINCE. Robin Starveling, the tailor?
STARVELING. Here, Peter Quince.
QUINCE. Robin Starveling, you must play Thisbe's mother. Tom Snout, the tinker?
SNOUT. Here, Peter Quince.
40 QUINCE. You, Pyramus' father; myself, Thisbe's father; Snug, the joiner, you the lion's part; and I hope here is a play fitted.
SNUG. Have you the lion's part written? Pray you, if it be, give it me; for I am slow of study.
QUINCE. You may do it extempore; for it is nothing but roaring.
45 BOTTOM. Let me play the lion too. I will roar that I will do any man's heart good to hear me. I will roar that I will make the duke say 'Let him roar again, let him roar again!'
QUINCE. And you should do it too terribly, you would fright the duchess and the ladies that they would shriek; and that were enough to hang us
50 all.

Annotations

- l. 2 **generally** = Bottom sometimes confuses similar sounding words. Here he means 'separately'.
- l. 3 **scrip** = list
- l. 4 **scroll** = list
- l. 5 **interlude** = play
- l. 8 **grow to a point** = reach a conclusion
- l. 9 **marry** = *here:* an exclamation used for emphasis or to express an emotion
- ll. 12–13 **spread yourselves** = sit down
- l. 14 **weaver** = *Weber*
- l. 18 **gallant** = brave
- l. 20 to **condole** = to lament
- l. 21 **my chief humour is for …** = I would prefer …, I am best suited for …
- l. 22 **bellows-mender** = *Blasebalgflicker*
- l. 28 **that's all one** = that doesn't matter
- l. 29 **small** = *here:* high-pitched (like a woman's voice)
- l. 31 **monstrous** = *here:* unnatural
- l. 35 **tailor** = *Schneider*
- l. 38 **tinker** = *Kesselflicker*
- l. 40 **joiner** = *Tischler*
- l. 41 **fitted** = cast
- l. 44 **extempore** = spontaneously
- l. 48 **and** = *here:* if
  fright = frighten

A Midsummer Night's Dream — Play 4

ALL. That would hang us, every mother's son.

BOTTOM. I grant you, friends, if you should fright the ladies out of their wits they would have no more discretion but to hang us; but I will aggravate my voice so that I will roar you as gently as any sucking dove.
55 I will roar you and 'twere any nightingale.

QUINCE. You can play no part but Pyramus; for Pyramus is a sweet-faced man, a proper man as one shall see in a summer's day, a most lovely, gentlemanlike man: therefore you must needs play Pyramus.

BOTTOM. Well, I will undertake it. What beard were I best to play it in?

60 QUINCE. Why, what you will. [...] But, masters, here are your parts, and I am to entreat you, request you, and desire you to con them by tomorrow night, and meet me in the palace wood, a mile without the town, by moonlight; there will we rehearse, for if we meet in the city we shall be dogged with company, and our devices known. In the meantime I will
65 draw a bill of properties, such as our play wants. I pray you, fail me not.

BOTTOM. We will meet, and there we may rehearse most obscenely and courageously. Take pains, be perfect: adieu!

QUINCE. At the duke's oak we meet.

BOTTOM. Enough; hold, or cut bowstrings.

Annotations
- l. 52 **fright** = frighten
- l. 53 **no more discretion** = Here Bottom means 'no other choice'.
- l. 54 to **aggravate** = to intensify
  sucking dove = Here Bottom mixes up two expressions of gentleness, 'sucking lamb' and 'sitting dove'.
- l. 55 **and 'twere** = as though it were
  nightingale = Nachtigall
- ll. 56–57 **sweet-faced** = good-looking
- l. 58 **needs** = here: certainly
- l. 61 to **entreat** = to beg
  to **con** = to learn
- l. 62 **without** = here: outside
- l. 64 **dogged** = here: followed
  device = here: plan
- l. 65 **bill of properties** = list of stage equipment
- l. 66 **obscenely** = Here Bottom probably means 'unseen' or 'properly'.
- l. 67 **take pains** = work hard
- l. 69 **hold, or cut bowstrings** = The exact meaning of this phrase is unknown. Bottom probably means that the actors must keep their promises so as not to be disgraced.

a) Match the different roles to the characters. Use the middle column in the grid below.

b) Collect information about the craftsmen: character traits, outer appearance, etc. Use the right-hand column of the grid for your notes.

c) The title of the craftsmen's play is "The most lamentable comedy and most cruel death of Pyramus and Thisbe" (ll. 9–10). Comment on this title.

Character	Role	Information
Peter Quince		
Nick Bottom		
Francis Flute		
Robin Starveling		
Tom Snout		
Snug		

Play — A Midsummer Night's Dream

13 Group work (6)

a) The craftsmen provide a striking contrast to the mythical world of Theseus and Hippolyta. In your group, discuss why Shakespeare might have chosen the group of craftsmen.

b) Identify humorous lines in the scene. Talk about how you would speak the lines to make the most of the humorous situations. Example:
"The most lamentable comedy …" (ll. 9–10) → to emphasize the paradox: stress the two words

c) Each group member chooses a craftsman and establishes a role card for him. Present your character to the other group members. Then act out the scene together.

LOOKING BACK AT ACT I

14

a) Who is in love with whom? Create a diagram to show the love entanglements and the problems that the following characters have.
- Demetrius • Egeus • Helena • Hermia • Hippolyta • Lysander • Theseus

b) **Pair work** Stage an interview: Partner A takes on the role of one of these characters. Partner B is an interviewer, who wants to find out what the character thinks about love, his or her relationship, the problems love can cause and possible solutions.

c) Present your interview to the class.

15

a) Read the information about verse and prose in Shakespeare's time.

Info

Verse and prose in Shakespeare's time

In the 16th century, playwrights often used verse, rhymed or unrhymed, in their plays. This style was particularly suitable for characters such as kings, or important topics such as war and peace or tragic events. Characters spoke in prose, too, but this often mirrored their social position or petty matters. Therefore, noble characters often spoke in verse whereas their subjects or comic characters used prose.

It was a stage convention to use **blank verse**, an unrhymed verse with a five-beat rhythm (**iambic pentameter**). Each line has five feet (= pentameter) which consist of one unstressed (x) syllable and one stressed (/) syllable. Example:

x / x / x /x / x /
"The course of true love never did run smooth"

As stage technology such as curtains or light did not exist in Shakespeare's time, a lot of scenes and acts as well as long speeches in blank verse often end with a **rhyming couplet** (two lines) to mark their end. Shakespeare also made use of four-stress lines (= tetrameter). For example, the lines spoken by the fairies are mostly written in catalectic (= incomplete) **trochaic tetrameter**. A trochee consists of a stressed (/) syllable followed by an unstressed (x) syllable. Example:

/ x /x / x /
"Through the forest have I gone"

b) Find examples of
- blank verse (unrhymed) • rhyme in verse • rhyming couplets • prose

in the play and analyse the use: Who uses verse (rhymed or unrhymed)? Who uses prose? What is the context?

While reading: Act II

SCENE 1

16

Act II of the play is set in a forest near Athens. Read the following extract.

Extract 7 (Act II, Scene 1)

A wood near Athens:
Enter a FAIRY *at one door, and* PUCK *at another*
PUCK. How now, spirit; whither wander you?
FAIRY. Over hill, over dale,
   Thorough bush, thorough briar,
   Over park, over pale,
5   Thorough flood, thorough fire;
   I do wander everywhere
   Swifter than the moon's sphere;
   And I serve the Fairy Queen,
   To dew her orbs upon the green.
10 [...]
Farewell, thou lob of spirits; I'll be gone.
Our queen and all her elves come here anon.
PUCK. The king doth keep his revels here tonight.
Take heed the queen come not within his sight,
15 For Oberon is passing fell and wrath,
Because that she as her attendant hath
A lovely boy stol'n from an Indian king;
She never had so sweet a changeling,
And jealous Oberon would have the child
20 Knight of his train, to trace the forests wild.
But she perforce withholds the loved boy,
Crowns him with flowers, and makes him all her joy.
And now they never meet in grove or green,
By fountain clear or spangl'd starlight sheen,
25 But they do square, that all their elves for fear
Creep into acorn cups and hide them there.
FAIRY. Either I mistake your shape and making quite,
Or else you are that shrewd and knavish sprite
Called Robin Goodfellow. Are not you he
30 That frights the maidens of the villagery,
Skim milk, and sometimes labour in the quern,
And bootless make the breathless housewife churn,
And sometime make the drink to bear no barm,
Mislead night-wanderers, laughing at their harm?
35 Those that 'Hobgoblin' call you, and 'Sweet Puck',
You do their work, and they shall have good luck.
Are not you he?
PUCK.   Thou speakest aright;
I am that merry wanderer of the night.
I jest to Oberon, and make him smile
40 [...].
But room, fairy: here comes Oberon.
FAIRY. And here my mistress. Would that he were gone!

Annotations
l. 2 **dale** = valley
l. 3 **thorough** = *here:* through
    briar = thorn
l. 4 **pale** = gated bit of land
l. 5 **flood** = *here:* water
l. 7 **swifter** = quicker
    sphere = orbit
l. 9 **dew her orbs** = place the dew
    green = *here:* grass
l. 11 **lob** = unsophisticated peasant
l. 12 **anon** = soon
l. 13 **doth keep his revels** = is having a party
l. 14 **take heed** = be careful
l. 15 **is passing fell and wrath** = is extremely angry
l. 16 **attendant** = servant
l. 18 **changeling** = human child
l. 20 **to trace** = to wander
l. 21 **perforce withholds** = refuses to give over
l. 23 **in grove or green** = in the forests or the fields
l. 24 **fountain clear** = clear river
    spangl'd starlight sheen = under the stars
l. 25 **to square** = to argue
l. 27 **I mistake ... quite** = I am totally wrong
l. 28 **shrewd** = mischievous
    knavish = naughty
l. 31 **to skim** = to take the cream from milk
    labour in the quern = block up the flour mill
l. 32 **bootless ... churn** = prevent the milk from becoming butter, so that they are exhausted from the effort
l. 33 **make the drink to bear no barm** = make the beer flat
l. 38 **merry** – *here:* mischievous
l. 39 **to jest** = to joke
l. 41 **room** = *here:* make some space
l. 42 **would that** = if only

Put the sentences below into the correct order and give line references.

4 Play — A Midsummer Night's Dream

No.	Contents	References
	Titania refuses to hand the boy over to Oberon.	
	Puck admits his identity and describes himself.	
	Oberon is angry about Titania having taken a little boy from India.	
	The fairy describes some of the mischievous tricks Puck plays on people.	
	Puck announces the arrival of Oberon in the forest and warns the fairy to make Titania stay away from Oberon.	
	The fairy recognizes Oberon's attendant as Robin Goodfellow, better known as Puck.	
1	Two fairies meet by chance: one belongs to Titania's train, the other is Oberon's attendant, Puck.	ll. 1, 8, 39
	He is so beautiful that Oberon wants to make him his knight.	

17

a) The fairy and Puck create vivid images of things that happen in the fairy world in the audience's mind. Collect examples that illustrate the world of the fairies. Use a grid like the one on the right.

The fairy	Puck
The fairy flies quickly through the landscape. (ll. 2–7)	…

b) Some of the examples you have listed might be difficult to put on stage. In class, talk about how you would stage the scene. Consider the following aspects:
- costumes
- props
- scenery
- masks
- light

18

Oberon and Titania enter the stage from opposite sides with their royal trains and immediately start to quarrel. Read the following extract.

Extract 8 (Act II, Scene 1)

OBERON. Ill met by moonlight, proud Titania!
TITANIA. What, jealous Oberon? Fairies, skip hence.
I have forsworn his bed and company.
OBERON. Tarry, rash wanton! Am not I thy lord?
5 **TITANIA.** Then I must be thy lady. But I know
When thou hast stol'n away from Fairyland,
And in the shape of Corin sat all day
Playing on pipes of corn, and versing love
To amorous Phillida. Why art thou here
10 Come from the farthest step of India? –
But that, forsooth, the bouncing Amazon,
Your buskin'd mistress and your warrior love,
To Theseus must be wedded; and you come
To give their bed joy and prosperity.
15 **OBERON.** How canst thou thus, for shame, Titania,
Glance at my credit with Hippolyta,
Knowing I know thy love to Theseus?

Annotations
l. 1 **ill met by moonlight** = I am unhappy to see you tonight
l. 2 **skip hence** = let's go
l. 3 **forsworn** = promised to give up
l. 4 **to tarry** = to wait
rash wanton = impulsive creature
lord = *here:* husband
l. 5 **lady** = *here:* wife
l. 6 **stol'n away** = sneaked away
l. 7 **shape of Corin** = disguised as a shepherd (Corin is a shepherd from a famous story)
l. 8 **versing love** = reciting love poetry
l. 9 **to amorous Phillida** = to a loving shepherdess
l. 10 **step** = *here:* hill
l. 11 **forsooth** = of course
the bouncing Amazon = reference to Hippolyta
l. 12 **buskin'd** = wearing a type of high boots
l. 14 **bed** = *here:* marriage
l. 16 **to glance at** = *here:* to scorn
credit = relationship

Didst not thou lead him through the glimmering night
From Perigenia, whom he ravished,
20 And make him with fair Aegles break his faith,
With Ariadne, and Antiopa?
TITANIA. These are the forgeries of jealousy:
And never since the middle summer's spring
Met we on hill, in dale, forest, or mead,
25 By paved fountain or by rushy brook,
Or in the beached margent of the sea
To dance our ringlets to the whistling wind,
But with thy brawls thou hast disturb'd our sport.
Therefore the winds, piping to us in vain,
30 As in revenge have suck'd up from the sea
Contagious fogs; which, falling in the land,
Hath every pelting river made so proud
That they have overborne their continents.
The ox hath therefore stretch'd his yoke in vain,
35 The ploughman lost his sweat, and the green corn
Hath rotted ere his youth attain'd a beard.
The fold stands empty in the drowned field,
[…]
And thorough this distemperature we see
40 The seasons alter; hoary-headed frosts
Fall in the fresh lap of the crimson rose,
And on old Hiems' thin and icy crown
An odorous chaplet of sweet summer buds
Is, as in mockery, set. The spring, the summer,
45 The childing autumn, angry winter change
Their wonted liveries, and the mazed world
By their increase now knows not which is which.
And this same progeny of evils comes
From our debate, from our dissension.
50 We are their parents and original.
OBERON. Do you amend it, then: it lies in you.
Why should Titania cross her Oberon?
I do but beg a little changeling boy
To be my henchman.
TITANIA. Set your heart at rest.
55 The fairy land buys not the child of me.
His mother was a votress of my order,
And in the spiced Indian air by night
Full often hath she gossip'd by my side,
[…].
60 But she, being mortal, of that boy did die,
And for her sake do I rear up her boy;
And for her sake I will not part with him.
OBERON. How long within this wood intend you stay?
TITANIA. Perchance till after Theseus' wedding day.
65 If you will patiently dance in our round,
And see our moonlight revels, go with us:
If not, shun me, and I will spare your haunts.
OBERON. Give me that boy, and I will go with thee.
TITANIA. Not for thy fairy kingdom! Fairies, away.
70 We shall chide downright if I longer stay.
 Exeunt TITANIA *and her train*
OBERON. Well, go thy way. Thou shalt not from this grove
Till I torment thee for this injury.

Annotations
l. 19 **to ravish** = to abduct and rape
l. 22 **forgeries** = lies
l. 23 **middle summer's spring** = beginning of midsummer
l. 24 **dale** = valley
 mead = meadow, field
l. 25 **paved fountain** = spring surrounded by rocks
 rushy = rushing, flowing
l. 26 **beached margent** = beach next to
l. 28 **brawls** = quarrels, arguing
 sport = *here:* fun
l. 29 **piping** = calling
 in vain = without response
l. 31 **contagious** = disease-carrying
l. 32 **pelting** = measly, inferior
 proud = *here:* powerful
l. 33 **overborne their continents** = flooded over into the fields
l. 34 **the ox … in vain** = there was no point in ploughing the fields
l. 35 **lost his sweat** = wasted his efforts
l. 36 **ere … beard** = before it grew ripe
l. 37 **fold** = animal enclosure
l. 39 **distemperature** = disturbance
l. 40 **to alter** = to change
 hoary-headed = bitter, extreme
l. 41 **fall in the fresh lap of** = descend upon
l. 42 **old Hiems** = a personification of winter and the cold
l. 43 **odorous chaplet** = scented decorative crown
l. 44 **as in mockery** = like some sort of prank
l. 45 **childing** = fruitful
l. 46 **wonted liveries** = usual uniforms
 mazed = confused
l. 47 **by … which** = cannot use the produce that grows to know what season they are in
l. 48 **progeny of evils** = set of bad outcomes
l. 49 **dissension** = arguing
l. 50 **original** = *here:* origin
l. 51 **Do you amend it, then** = So are you going to fix it?
 it lies in you = it is up to you
l. 52 **to cross** = to disobey
l. 54 **henchman** = assistant
 set your heart at rest = calm down
l. 56 **votress** = priestess
l. 60 **of that boy** = when giving birth to that boy
l. 61 **to rear up** = to raise
l. 62 **to part with** = to be separated from
l. 64 **perchance** = maybe
l. 65 **dance in our round** = dance in a circle with us
l. 66 **moonlight revels** = midnight celebrations
l. 67 **to shun** = to stay away from
 spare your haunts = keep out of your lands
l. 70 **chide downright** = fight for real
l. 72 **torment thee for this injury** = make you suffer for this behaviour

4 Play — A Midsummer Night's Dream

a) Tick (✓) the summary that fits best. Explain your choice.

☐ 1. Titania and Oberon blame each other for the havoc in the world of the mortals and fight over an Indian boy.
☐ 2. Titania and Oberon are jealous of each other and begrudge each other's happiness with the mortals.
☐ 3. Titania and Oberon accuse each other of feeling attracted to the mortals: Titania blames Oberon for loving Hippolyta. Oberon accuses Titania of showing an interest in Theseus. Titania then claims that her conflict with Oberon has changed the climate in the world of the mortals.

b) Describe what – according to Titania – has changed in nature as well as in the seasons.
c) Explain what reasons Titania gives why she will not hand over the Indian boy.

19

Titania hints at the disorder the world of the mortals is in. What did the Elizabethans think about disordered states? Read the information below to find out what the Elizabethans believed in. Explain how this relates to the situation in *A Midsummer Night's Dream*.

Info

The Elizabethan world picture

Most people believed that everything, from the lowest grain of sand to the highest angel, had its set position in a great hierarchy. This concept was called "the great chain of being". When things were in their proper place, harmony was the result. When order was violated, the entire structure was shaken.
Any break in the chain, such as a marriage across social classes, was believed to result in chaos. Accordingly, marriage was usually arranged to bring wealth and prestige to the family – regardless of the feelings of the bride. In fact, women were quite powerless under the law.
Many Elizabethans were convinced that analogous relations existed in the universe and the political world. They believed, for example, that the king was as important to the state as the sun was to the sky. As the chosen representative of God on earth, the king had a supreme position. It was his responsibility to enforce and uphold the order in the world. Any violation of his position would destroy the perfect order of the universe and lead to intense problems, conflicts and chaos on earth. Therefore, any act of treachery against the king was considered to be a mortal sin against God and thus was punished severely.
The concept of microcosm and macrocosm rests upon the idea that there is a corresponding similarity between human beings and the universe: Man is seen as a smaller representation of the universe.

20

Analyse Titania and Oberon's relationship. Choose adjectives that best describe their relationship. Then give evidence from the text to explain your choice.

> electric | emotional | gloomy | heady | heated | highly charged | hostile | lively | oppressive | passionate | …

21

Oberon tells Puck about his plan and sends him to get a magic flower. Read the following extract.

Extract 9 (Act II, Scene 1)

OBERON. […]
My gentle Puck, come hither. […]
Fetch me that flower, the herb I show'd thee once;
The juice of it on sleeping eyelids laid
5 Will make or man or woman madly dote
Upon the next live creature that it sees.
Fetch me this herb, and be thou here again
Ere the leviathan can swim a league.

Annotations
l. 2 **hither** = here
l. 4 **laid** = put on (passive)
ll. 5–6 **to dote upon** = to be in love with
l. 8 **ere … league** = as quick as you can

PUCK. I'll put a girdle round about the earth
10 In forty minutes!
    Exit
OBERON.   Having once this juice
I'll watch Titania when she is asleep,
And drop the liquor of it in her eyes:
The next thing then she, waking, looks upon –
Be it on lion, bear, or wolf, or bull,
15 On meddling monkey, or on busy ape –
She shall pursue it with the soul of love.
And ere I take this charm from off her sight –
As I can take it with another herb –
I'll make her render up her page to me.
20 But who comes here? I am invisible,
And I will overhear their conference.

Annotations
l. 9 **put a girdle round** = circle
l. 10 **having once** = once I have
l. 16 **pursue it with the soul of love** = fall in love with it
l. 19 **render her page** = give the boy
l. 21 **conference** = *here:* conversation

a) Describe Oberon's plan in your own words.
b) **Pair work** What does his plan reveal about his character? Share your view with a partner.
c) Create an additional scene after Puck has left, in which Oberon reflects his plan. Write Oberon's soliloquy. (You can find more information about soliloquies in the box on p. 103.)

22
Oberon is listening in on the conversation between Demetrius and Helena. Read the following extract.

Extract 10 (Act II, Scene 1)

DEMETRIUS. I love thee not, therefore pursue me not.
Where is Lysander and fair Hermia?
The one I'll slay, the other slayeth me.
Thou told'st me they were stol'n unto this wood,
5 And here am I, and wood within this wood
Because I cannot meet my Hermia.
Hence, get thee gone, and follow me no more.
HELENA. You draw me, you hard-hearted adamant!
But yet you draw not iron, for my heart
10 Is true as steel. Leave you your power to draw,
And I shall have no power to follow you.
DEMETRIUS. Do I entice you? Do I speak you fair?
Or rather do I not in plainest truth
Tell you I do not, nor I cannot love you?
15 **HELENA.** And even for that do I love you the more.
I am your spaniel; and, Demetrius,
The more you beat me I will fawn on you.
Use me but as your spaniel: spurn me, strike me,
Neglect me, lose me; only give me leave,
20 Unworthy as I am, to follow you.
What worser place can I beg in your love –
And yet a place of high respect with me –
Than to be used as you use your dog?
DEMETRIUS. Tempt not too much the hatred of my spirit;
25 For I am sick when I do look on thee.
HELENA. And I am sick when I look not on you.
DEMETRIUS. You do impeach your modesty too much,
To leave the city and commit yourself
Into the hands of one that loves you not;
30 To trust the opportunity of night,

Annotations
l. 1 to **pursue** = to follow
l. 3 **the one ... slayeth me** = I will kill Lysander, but Hermia's beauty is killing me
l. 4 **were stol'n unto** = sneaked off to
l. 5 **wood within** = far in
l. 7 **got thee gone** = go away
l. 8 to **draw** = to attract
    adamant = magnet
l. 10 **leave ... draw** = if you give up your powers to attract me
l. 12 **speak you fair** = speak kindly to you
l. 13 **in plainest truth** = very clearly
l. 16 **spaniel** = notoriously loyal dog breed
l. 17 to **fawn on** = to love
l. 18 **use me but as your spaniel** = treat me like a dog
    to **spurn** = to kick
l. 19 **give me leave** = allow me
l. 21 to **beg** = to ask for
    in your love = *here:* in your heart
l. 22 **and yet ... with me** = but I would consider it an honour
l. 23 **used** = *here:* treated
l. 24 to **tempt** = to encourage
l. 27 **impeach your modesty** = call your modesty (chastity) into question

4 Play — A Midsummer Night's Dream

And the ill counsel of a desert place,
With the rich worth of your virginity.
HELENA. Your virtue is my privilege: for that
It is not night when I do see your face,
35 Therefore I think I am not in the night;
Nor doth this wood lack worlds of company,
For you, in my respect, are all the world.
Then how can it be said I am alone
When all the world is here to look on me?
40 **DEMETRIUS.** I'll run from thee and hide me in the brakes,
And leave thee to the mercy of wild beasts.
[…] I will not stay thy questions. Let me go;
Or if thou follow me, do not believe
But I shall do thee mischief in the wood.
45 **HELENA.** Ay, in the temple, in the town, the field,
You do me mischief. Fie, Demetrius,
Your wrongs do set a scandal on my sex!
We cannot fight for love, as men may do;
We should be woo'd, and were not made to woo.
   Exit DEMETRIUS
50 I'll follow thee, and make a heaven of hell,
To die upon the hand I love so well.
   Exit
OBERON. Fare thee well, nymph. Ere he do leave this grove
Thou shalt fly him, and he shall seek thy love.
   Enter PUCK
Hast thou the flower there? Welcome, wanderer.
55 **PUCK.** Ay, there it is.
OBERON.   I pray thee, give it me.
[…]
There sleeps Titania sometime of the night,
Lull'd in these flowers with dances and delight;
And there the snake throws her enamell'd skin,
60 Weed wide enough to wrap a fairy in;
And with the juice of this I'll streak her eyes,
And make her full of hateful fantasies.
Take thou some of it, and seek through this grove:
A sweet Athenian lady is in love
65 With a disdainful youth; anoint his eyes,
But do it when the next thing he espies
May be the lady. Thou shalt know the man
By the Athenian garments he hath on.
Effect it with some care, that he may prove
70 More fond on her than she upon her love.
And look thou meet me ere the first cock crow.
PUCK. Fear not, my lord; your servant shall do so.

Annotations
l. 31 **ill counsel** = bad ideas
    desert = deserted
l. 33 **your virtue is my privilege** = your good nature will protect me
l. 37 **in my respect** = to me
l. 40 **brakes** = bushes
l. 41 **beasts** = *here:* animals
l. 42 to **stay** = *here:* to stay and listen to
    thy questions = *here:* your arguments
l. 45 **ay** = just like, as
l. 46 **fie** = curse you
l. 47 **set a scandal on** = insult
    sex = *here:* gender, i.e. all women
l. 49 to **woo** = to pursue romantically
l. 52 **fare thee well** = goodbye
    grove = forest
l. 53 to **fly** = *here:* to run away from
l. 58 **lull'd** = soothed to sleep
l. 59 to **throw** = *here:* to shed
    enamell'd = shiny
l. 60 **weed wide enough** = a piece of clothing wide enough
l. 61 to **streak** = to wet
l. 62 **hateful** = *here:* pathetic
l. 63 to **seek through** = to search
l. 65 **disdainful youth** = rude boy
l. 69 to **effect** = *here:* to do
l. 71 **ere the first cock crow** = before dawn

a) Match the correct sentence halves.

1. Demetrius does not want
2. He is looking for
3. Helena compares herself to
4. Demetrius chides Helena
5. Helena persists in
6. Demetrius wants to
7. Helena is determined to

a) Hermia in the forest.
b) follow him.
c) wooing Demetrius.
d) Helena to follow him any further.
e) run off and leave Helena to the wild beasts.
f) a faithful spaniel.
g) for putting her reputation at risk.

1	
2	
3	
4	
5	
6	
7	

b) Analyse the atmosphere between Demetrius and Helena. Choose adjectives that best describe it, find evidence from the text, and interpret it.

> calm | desperate | emotional | hostile | intimate | romantic | stifling | strained | tense | …

c) Use your results from b) to write the analysis.

d) **Pair work** What are Demetrius and Helena thinking? Write thought bubbles for Demetrius and Helena and present them to the class.

23

Oberon has watched Demetrius and Helena and makes plans.

a) Sum up the plots Oberon has hatched for Titania and Helena.

b) Imagine you are a fortune-teller. Write Titania's or Helena's horoscope.

SCENE 2

24

While Titania is asleep, Oberon sprinkles Titania's eyes with the magic juice of his flower and leaves. Then Lysander and Hermia enter the stage. They have eloped into the forest and have got lost. Read the following extract.

Extract 11 (Act II, Scene 2)

LYSANDER. Fair love, you faint with wandering in the wood,
And, to speak truth, I have forgot our way.
We'll rest us, Hermia, if you think it good,
And tarry for the comfort of the day.
5 **HERMIA.** Be it so, Lysander; find you out a bed,
For I upon this bank will rest my head.
LYSANDER. One turf shall serve as pillow for us both;
One heart, one bed, two bosoms, and one troth.
HERMIA. Nay, good Lysander, for my sake, my dear,
10 Lie further off yet; do not lie so near.
LYSANDER. O take the sense, sweet, of my innocence!
Love takes the meaning in love's conference;
I mean that my heart unto yours is knit,
So that but one heart we can make of it:
15 Two bosoms interchained with an oath,
So then two bosoms and a single troth.
Then by your side no bed-room me deny,
For lying so, Hermia, I do not lie.
HERMIA. Lysander riddles very prettily.
20 Now much beshrew my manners and my pride
If Hermia meant to say Lysander lied.
But, gentle friend, for love and courtesy
Lie further off, in human modesty;
Such separation as may well be said
25 Becomes a virtuous bachelor and a maid,
So far be distant, and good night, sweet friend;
Thy love ne'er alter till thy sweet life end!
LYSANDER. Amen, amen, to that fair prayer say I,
And then end life when I end loyalty!
30 Here is my bed; sleep give thee all his rest.
HERMIA. With half that wish the wisher's eyes be press'd.
They sleep
Enter PUCK

Annotations
l. 1 to **faint** = to get weaker
l. 2 **I have forgot our way** = I am lost
l. 4 to **tarry** = to wait
l. 6 **bank** = small lump in ground
l. 7 **turf** = ground
l. 8 **bosoms** = *here:* bodies
troth = truth; vow, promise
l. 10 **off** = *here:* away
l. 11 **take … my innocence** = understand I meant it innocently
l. 12 **love … conference** = there is room for interpretation of what lovers say to one another
l. 13 **knit** = joined
l. 14 **but one** = only one
l. 15 **interchained** = joined
oath = vow, promise
l. 17 **no bed-room me deny** = let me sleep here
l. 19 to **riddle** = to play with words
prettily = *here:* cleverly
l. 20 **beshrew** = curse, a curse upon
l. 22 **for** = *here:* for the sake of
l. 25 **becomes** = it is suitable for them
maid = young girl
l. 26 **so far** = for now
l. 29 **end life … loyalty** = may I die should I ever be disloyal to you

4 Play — A Midsummer Night's Dream

PUCK. Through the forest have I gone,
But Athenian found I none
On whose eyes I might approve
35 This flower's force in stirring love.
Night and silence – Who is here?
Weeds of Athens he doth wear:
This is he my master said
Despised the Athenian maid;
40 And here the maiden, sleeping sound
On the dank and dirty ground.
Pretty soul, she durst not lie
Near this lack-love, this kill-courtesy.
Churl, upon thy eyes I throw
45 All the power this charm doth owe.
   He drops the juice on LYSANDER's *eyelids*
When thou wak'st let love forbid
Sleep his seat on thy eyelid.
So, awake when I am gone;
For I must now to Oberon.

Annotations
l. 34 to **approve** = to deem worthy
l. 36 **night and silence** = (*exclamation*) whoa!
l. 37 **weeds** = garments, clothing
l. 41 **dank** = moist
l. 43 **lack-love** = hard-hearted
     kill-courtesy = rude
l. 44 **churl** = villain
l. 45 to **owe** = *here:* to have, to possess
l. 46 to **forbid** = to prevent
l. 47 **sleep ... eyelid** = you falling asleep

a) Outline Hermia and Lysander's conversation.
b) Shakespeare is a master of word play. Identify the pun in ll. 13–21 and explain its meaning. In class, discuss why Shakespeare uses that word pun there.
c) Contrast Hermia and Lysander's attitude towards spending the night together in each other's company.
d) **Pair work** Partner A takes Lysander's role, Partner B takes Hermia's role. Write down their thoughts when they are falling asleep. Consider the following aspects:
 - what has happened so far
 - the feelings they have for one another
 - the different attitudes towards spending the night together.

> **Info**
> **Pun – A play on words**
> A pun is the humorous use of a word that either has more than one meaning or sounds like another word with a different meaning.

25
Puck has wandered through the forest and has finally come across Lysander and Hermia.

a) Reread Puck's words and explain his thoughts.
b) Read the information about dramatic irony and examine how Shakespeare succeeds in creating suspense at this moment.
c) Discuss in class how you view Puck in this scene.
 Is he ... mischievous, naive, serious, or well-intentioned?

> **Info**
> **Dramatic irony**
> This literary device is used when the audience knows more than the characters in the play, thus being able to foresee an outcome different to the characters' expectations.

26
While Helena is following Demetrius into the woods, she stumbles across Lysander. Read the following extract.

Extract 12 (Act II, Scene 2)

HELENA. [...] But who is here? – Lysander, on the ground?
Dead, or asleep? I see no blood, no wound.
Lysander, if you live, good sir, awake!
LYSANDER. (*Waking*) And run through fire I will for thy sweet sake!
5 Transparent Helena, nature shows art
That through thy bosom makes me see thy heart.
Where is Demetrius? O, how fit a word
Is that vile name to perish on my sword!

Annotations
l. 2 **wound** = injuries
l. 4 **and run ... sake** = I would run through fire for you
l. 5 **transparent** = *here:* beautiful
    art = *here:* magic

HELENA. Do not say so, Lysander, say not so.
10 What though he love your Hermia? Lord, what though?
Yet Hermia still loves you; then be content.
LYSANDER. Content with Hermia? No; I do repent
The tedious minutes I with her have spent.
Not Hermia, but Helena I love.
15 Who will not change a raven for a dove?
The will of man is by his reason sway'd,
And reason says you are the worthier maid.
Things growing are not ripe until their season;
So I, being young, till now ripe not to reason.
20 And touching now the point of human skill,
Reason becomes the marshal to my will.
And leads me to your eyes, where I o'erlook
Love's stories written in love's richest book.
HELENA. Wherefore was I to this keen mockery born?
25 When at your hands did I deserve this scorn?
Is't not enough, is't not enough, young man,
That I did never, no, nor never can
Deserve a sweet look from Demetrius' eye
But you must flout my insufficiency?
30 Good troth, you do me wrong, good sooth, you do,
In such disdainful manner me to woo!
But fare you well: perforce I must confess
I thought you lord of more true gentleness.
O, that a lady of one man refus'd
35 Should of another therefore be abus'd!
   Exit
LYSANDER. She sees not Hermia. Hermia, sleep thou there,
And never mayst thou come Lysander near.
For, as a surfeit of the sweetest things
The deepest loathing to the stomach brings,
40 Or as the heresies that men do leave
Are hated most of those they did deceive,
So thou, my surfeit and my heresy,
Of all be hated, but the most of me!
And, all my powers, address your love and might
45 To honour Helen, and to be her knight.
   Exit
HERMIA. (*Waking*) Help me, Lysander, help me! Do thy best
To pluck this crawling serpent from my breast!
Ay me, for pity! What a dream was here!
Lysander, look how I do quake with fear –
50 Methought a serpent ate my heart away,
And you sat smiling at his cruel prey.
Lysander! What, remov'd? Lysander, lord!
What, out of hearing? Gone? No sound, no word?
Alack, where are you? Speak and if you hear,
55 Speak, of all loves! I swoon almost with fear.
No? Then I well perceive you are not nigh.
Either death or you I'll find immediately.

Annotations
l. 10 **what though** = what does it matter
l. 12 **to repent** = to regret
l. 16 **will** = desires
   sway'd = controlled
l. 18 **things growing** = fruits and vegetables
l. 19 **ripe to reason** = be mature in judgement
l. 20 **touching** = *here:* reaching
   human skill = making good judgements
l. 21 **marshal** = director
l. 22 **to o'erlook** = to read over
l. 24 **wherefore** = why
   keen = cruel
   born = *here:* subjected to
l. 25 **when ... scorn** = what did I do to deserve this mockery
l. 28 **sweet** = *here:* loving
l. 29 **to flout** = to make fun of
   insufficiency = not being good enough
l. 30 **good troth** = honestly
   good sooth = really
l. 32 **perforce** = indeed
l. 33 **gentleness** = courtesy, kindness
l. 35 **abus'd** = mocked
l. 38 **surfeit** = excess
l. 39 **loathing** = *here:* sickness
l. 40 **heresies** = false beliefs
l. 43 **of** = *here:* by
l. 44 **might** = strength
l. 45 **knight** = loyal man
l. 47 **to pluck** = to remove
   serpent = snake
l. 48 **Ay me, for pity!** = Oh my goodness!
l. 49 **to quake** = to shake, to tremble
l. 50 **methought** = I thought
l. 52 **What, remov'd?** = Where have you gone?
l. 53 **What, out of hearing?** = Are you too far away to hear me?
l. 54 **alack** = alas
l. 55 **to swoon** = to faint
l. 56 **to perceive** = *here:* to guess
   nigh = nearby

a) Decide whether the statements below are right or wrong. Correct them if necessary.

4 Play — A Midsummer Night's Dream

Statement		Right	Wrong	Correction
1	Helena finds Lysander dead on the ground.			
2	Lysander compares Helena to a raven.			
3	Helena thinks that Lysander makes fun of her.			
4	Lysander explains how his feelings for Hermia have changed.			
5	After Hermia wakes up from a nightmare, she finds that Lysander is gone.			

b) Hermia wakes up from a nightmare. Describe the nightmare and interpret its meaning.

c) Discuss to what extent the dream reveals some subconscious fears of hers.

LOOKING BACK AT ACT II

27

a) Read the information about the world of the fairies. Then examine to what extent the fairy world mirrors the world of the mortals in the play. Consider the following aspects:
- characters
- conflicts
- power and control
- language

b) **Group work** Discuss how the fairy world and the world of the mortals reflect the Elizabethan world picture.

Info

The world of the fairies

Before Shakespeare's time, fairies were considered evil or mischievous spirits that made people's lives difficult. It was mainly a rural belief, but Elizabethan playgoers would know the stories about fairies: They played tricks on servants and old women, they stole things, they pinched maids and caused them to drop things, or they led travellers astray. For example, Puck, or Robin Goodfellow, is also a character in English folklore. Despite the many treatises about anti-superstition, the fairy world fascinated the Elizabethans, which is why many authors of the 16th and 17th centuries made use of the fairy world in their works – such as William Shakespeare, John Lyly and Edmund Spenser.

28

a) Study the quotations about Puck. Conclude what they tell the audience about him.

1. "I am that merry wanderer of the night."
   (Puck, Act II, Scene 1)

2. "I jest to Oberon, and make him smile [...]."
   (Puck, Act II, Scene 1)

3. "My gentle Puck, come hither. [...]"
   (Oberon, Act II, Scene 1)

4. "Fear not, my lord; your servant shall do so."
   (Puck, Act II, Scene 1)

5. "[...] you are that shrewd and knavish sprite Called Robin Goodfellow."
   (Fairy, Act II, Scene 1)

6. "[...] Are not you he
   That frights the maidens of the villagery,
   Skim milk, and sometimes labour in the quern,
   And bootless make the breathless housewife churn,
   And sometime make the drink to bear no barm,
   Mislead night-wanderers, laughing at their harm?"
   (Fairy, Act II, Scene 1)

b) Analyse how Shakespeare refashions Puck's role.
c) Look at some photos of different actors playing the role of Puck. What do you think? Which portrayal captures him best? Explain your choice.

1 2 3

d) In class, discuss why Shakespeare makes use of the fairy world.

While reading: Act III

SCENE 1

29

While Titania is asleep, the craftsmen meet in the forest to talk about some staging problems and rehearse the play of *Pyramus and Thisbe*. Puck, who is watching, decides to play a prank on them: He puts a donkey's head on Bottom. Read the following extract.

Extract 13 (Act III, Scene 1)

Enter PUCK, *and* BOTTOM *with the ass head on*
BOTTOM. (*as Pyramus*) If I were fair, fair Thisbe, I were only thine.
QUINCE. O monstrous! O strange! We are haunted! Pray, masters, fly, masters! Help!
　Exeunt QUINCE, SNUG, FLUTE, SNOUT, *and* STARVELING
[…]
5 **BOTTOM.** Why do they run away? This is a knavery of them to make me afeard.
　Enter SNOUT
SNOUT. O Bottom, thou art changed. What do I see on thee?
BOTTOM. What do you see? You see an ass head of your own, do you?
　Exit SNOUT
　Enter QUINCE
QUINCE. Bless thee, Bottom, bless thee! Thou art translated!
　Exit
10 **BOTTOM.** I see their knavery. This is to make an ass of me, to fright me, if they could; but I will not stir from this place, do what they can. I will walk up and down here, and I will sing, that they shall hear I am not afraid.

Annotations
l. 1　**fair** = handsome
　　　I were = I would be
l. 2　**monstrous** = *here:* a monster
　　　to fly = *here:* to run away
l. 5　**knavery** = trick, practical joke
l. 6　**afeard** = scared, afraid
l. 7　**on thee** = on your head
l. 8　**ass** = donkey
l. 9　**translated** = transformed

4 Play — A Midsummer Night's Dream

(*Sings*) The ousel cock so black of hue,
15 With orange-tawny bill,
   The throstle with his note so true,
   The wren with little quill –
TITANIA. (*Waking*) What angel wakes me from my flowery bed?
BOTTOM. (*Sings*) The finch, the sparrow, and the lark,
20 The plainsong cuckoo grey,
   Whose note full many a man doth mark
   And dares not answer nay –
for indeed, who would set his wit to so foolish a bird? Who would give a bird the lie, though he cry 'cuckoo' never so?
25 **TITANIA.** I pray thee, gentle mortal, sing again;
Mine ear is much enamour'd of thy note.
So is mine eye enthralled to thy shape,
And thy fair virtue's force perforce doth move me
On the first view to say, to swear, I love thee.
30 **BOTTOM.** Methinks, mistress, you should have little reason for that. And yet, to say the truth, reason and love keep little company together nowadays; the more the pity that some honest neighbours will not make them friends. Nay, I can gleek upon occasion.
TITANIA. Thou art as wise as thou art beautiful.
35 **BOTTOM.** Not so neither; but if I had wit enough to get out of this wood, I have enough to serve mine own turn.
TITANIA. Out of this wood do not desire to go:
Thou shalt remain here, whether thou wilt or no.
I am a spirit of no common rate;
40 The summer still doth tend upon my state,
And I do love thee. Therefore go with me.
I'll give thee fairies to attend on thee,
And they shall fetch thee jewels from the deep,
And sing, while thou on pressed flowers dost sleep;
45 And I will purge thy mortal grossness so
That thou shalt like an airy spirit go.
Peaseblossom, Cobweb, Moth, and Mustardseed!
   Enter four FAIRIES

Annotations
- l. 14 **ousel cock** = male blackbird
  hue = colour
- l. 15 **tawny** = tan-coloured
  bill = beak
- l. 16 **throstle** = *Drossel*
  note so true = beautiful singing voice
- l. 17 **wren** = *Zaunkönig*
  quill = high-pitched voice
- l. 20 **plainsong** = song that never changes
- l. 21 **many a man doth mark** = heard by many men
- l. 23 **set his wit to** = argue with
- ll. 23–24 **give a lie** = say it was lying
- l. 25 **gentle mortal** = noble human
- l. 27 **shape** = *here*: looks, appearance
- l. 28 **thy fair virtue's force** = the power of your beauty
  perforce = indeed
  to **move** = *here*: to cause
- l. 31 **keep little company together** = have no link
- l. 32 **the more the pity** = it is a shame
- l. 33 to **gleek** = to tell a joke
- l. 35 **not so neither** = also untrue
  to **have wit** = to be smart
- l. 36 **turn** = *here*: needs
- l. 39 **no common rate** = no ordinary rank
- l. 40 **tend upon my state** = serve me
- l. 42 to **attend on** = to serve
- l. 45 to **purge** = *here*: to remove
  mortal grossness = human body
- l. 46 **airy** = light

a) Explain the situation Bottom finds himself in.
b) Is this a funny or sad scene? Discuss this question in class.

30
a) While the craftsmen rehearse their play, Titania is sleeping on stage. If you were the director, where would you make her sleep on stage? Give reasons for your answer.
b) Titania is woken up by Bottom's singing. Describe Titania's reaction.
c) Examine how reason and love are presented in this extract.

31
a) Describe how Bottom reacts to Titania. Is he … intimidated, flattered, surprised, baffled, or courteous? Explain your choice.
b) Write Bottom's inner monologue after he has met Titania and the fairies.

SCENE 2
32
Puck informs Oberon of his successful deeds. Read the following extract.

Extract 14 (Act III, Scene 2)

PUCK. [...] When in that moment, so it came to pass,
Titania wak'd, and straightway loved an ass.
OBERON. This falls out better than I could devise.
But hast thou yet latch'd the Athenian's eyes
5 With the love juice, as I did bid thee do?
PUCK. I took him sleeping – that is finished too –
And the Athenian woman by his side,
That when he wak'd, of force she must be ey'd.
    Enter DEMETRIUS *and* HERMIA
OBERON. Stand close: this is the same Athenian.
10 PUCK. This is the woman, but not this the man.
DEMETRIUS. O, why rebuke you him that loves you so?
Lay breath so bitter on your bitter foe.
HERMIA. Now I but chide; but I should use thee worse,
For thou, I fear, hast given me cause to curse.
15 If thou hast slain Lysander in his sleep,
Being o'er shoes in blood, plunge in the deep,
And kill me too.
The sun was not so true unto the day
As he to me. Would he have stol'n away
20 From sleeping Hermia? I'll believe as soon
This whole earth may be bor'd, and that the moon
May through the centre creep, and so displease
Her brother's noontide with th'Antipodes.
It cannot be but thou hast murder'd him:
25 So should a murderer look; so dead, so grim.
DEMETRIUS. So should the murder'd look, and so should I,
Pierc'd through the heart with your stern cruelty;
Yet you, the murderer, look as bright, as clear,
As yonder Venus in her glimmering sphere.
30 HERMIA. What's this to my Lysander? Where is he?
Ah, good Demetrius, wilt thou give him me?
DEMETRIUS. I had rather give his carcass to my hounds.
HERMIA. Out, dog! Out, cur! Thou driv'st me past the bounds
Of maiden's patience. Hast thou slain him then?
35 Henceforth be never number'd among men.
O, once tell true; tell true, even for my sake:
Durst thou have look'd upon him being awake?
And hast thou kill'd him sleeping? O, brave touch!
Could not a worm, an adder do so much?
40 An adder did it; for with doubler tongue
Than thine, thou serpent, never adder stung.
DEMETRIUS. You spend your passion on a mispris'd mood.
I am not guilty of Lysander's blood,
Nor is he dead, for aught that I can tell.
45 HERMIA. I pray thee, tell me then that he is well.
DEMETRIUS. And if I could, what should I get therefor?
HERMIA. A privilege, never to see me more;
And from thy hated presence part I so.
See me no more, whether he be dead or no.
    Exit
50 DEMETRIUS. There is no following her in this fierce vein;
Here therefore for a while I will remain. [...]
    He lies down and sleeps

Annotations

l. 1 **to come to pass** = to happen
l. 3 **this ... devise** = this turned out better than I could have hoped
l. 4 **latch'd** = captured
l. 5 **to bid** = to instruct
l. 8 **of force** = certainly
    ey'd = seen
l. 11 **to rebuke** = to be cruel to
l. 12 **breath** = *here:* words
    bitter foe = worst enemy
l. 13 **to chide** = to scold
l. 15 **slain** = killed
l. 16 **o'er shoes in blood** = knee-deep in blood (i.e. guilty)
    plunge in the deep = go all the way
ll. 18–19 **the sun ... to me** = he is more faithful to me than the sun is to the daytime
l. 19 **stol'n** = sneaked
l. 21 **bor'd** = *durchbohrt*
l. 23 **her brother** = reference to the sun
    with th'Antipodes = at the other side of the planet
l. 27 **stern** = harsh
l. 29 **yonder** = over there
    Venus = reference to the evening star and the goddess of love
    sphere = orbit
l. 30 **what's this to** = what does this have to do with
l. 32 **carcass** = dead body
l. 33 **cur** = dog
    past the bounds = too far
l. 35 **number'd among** = counted as
l. 37 **durst** = dare
l. 39 **worm** = *here:* snake
ll. 40–41 **for with ... stung** = for there has never been such a fork-tongued snake as you
l. 42 **to spend passion** = to waste energy
    mispris'd mood = misunderstanding
l. 43 **blood** = *here:* murder
l. 46 **therefor** = for it
l. 50 **in this fierce vein** = when she is this angry

4 Play — A Midsummer Night's Dream

OBERON. What hast thou done? Thou hast mistaken quite,
And laid the love juice on some true love's sight.
Of thy misprision must perforce ensue
55 Some true love turn'd, and not a false turn'd true.
PUCK. Then fate o'errules, that, one man holding troth,
A million fail, confounding oath on oath.
OBERON. About the wood go swifter than the wind,
And Helena of Athens look thou find.
60 All fancy-sick she is and pale of cheer
With sighs of love, that costs the fresh blood dear.
By some illusion see thou bring her here;
I'll charm his eyes against she do appear.
PUCK. I go, I go, look how I go!
65 Swifter than arrow from the Tartar's bow.
Exit

Annotations
l. 52 **mistaken quite** = made a big mistake
l. 53 **on some true love's sight** = on someone who is really in love
l. 54 **of thy** = because of your
misprision = error, mistake
to **ensue** = consequently happen
l. 56 **o'errules** = *here:* ensures
holding troth = remaining faithful
l. 57 **confounding oath on oath** = making many promises to many lovers
l. 58 **swifter** = faster
l. 60 **fancy-sick** = heartbroken
cheer = *here:* complexion
l. 63 **against** = *here:* ready for when
l. 65 **Tartar** = The Tartars (from central Asia) were skilled archers.

a) Decide whether the statements below are right or wrong. Give evidence or correct them if necessary.

Statement		Right	Wrong	Evidence / Correction
1	Puck has used the magic spell on the right couple.			
2	Hermia thinks that Demetrius has killed Lysander.			
3	Demetrius has fed Lysander to his dogs.			
4	According to Demetrius, Hermia is mistaken in her belief that he has killed Lysander.			
5	Hermia wants to see Demetrius again if he tells her where to find Lysander.			

b) Analyse how the language Hermia uses reflects her state of mind.
c) Describe Oberon's reaction. Is he angry or amused?
d) Reread ll. 52–55. Explain what Oberon means when he says these lines.

33

While Demetrius is asleep, Oberon sprinkles his eyes with the magic juice of the flower. Then the other young Athenians arrive one by one and start to quarrel. This is a rather long scene, full of emotions and with a lot of back and forth. Read the following extract.

Extract 15 (Act III, Scene 2)

LYSANDER. Why should you think that I should woo in scorn?
Scorn and derision never come in tears.
Look when I vow, I weep; and vows so born,
In their nativity all truth appears.
5 How can these things in me seem scorn to you,
Bearing the badge of faith to prove them true?
HELENA. You do advance your cunning more and more.
When truth kills truth, O devilish-holy fray!
[…]

Annotations
l. 1 to **woo** = to pursue romantically
in scorn = as a cruel joke
l. 2 **derision** = mockery
in tears = with tears
l. 3 to **vow** = to swear love to
l. 4 **nativity** = origin
l. 7 **advance your cunning** = get sneakier and sneakier
l. 8 **truth kills truth** = one true love kills another true love
O devilish-holy fray! = What a fight it will be!

DEMETRIUS. (*Waking*)
10 O Helen, goddess, nymph, perfect, divine!
To what, my love, shall I compare thine eyne?
Crystal is muddy! O, how ripe in show
Thy lips, those kissing cherries, tempting grow!
[…]   O, let me kiss
15 This princess of pure white, this seal of bliss!
HELENA. O spite! O hell! I see you all are bent
To set against me for your merriment.
If you were civil, and knew courtesy,
You would not do me thus much injury.
20 Can you not hate me, as I know you do,
But you must join in souls to mock me too?
If you were men, as men you are in show,
You would not use a gentle lady so,
To vow, and swear, and superpraise my parts,
25 When I am sure you hate me with your hearts.
You both are rivals, and love Hermia;
And now both rivals to mock Helena.
A trim exploit, a manly enterprise,
To conjure tears up in a poor maid's eyes
30 With your derision! None of noble sort
Would so offend a virgin, and extort
A poor soul's patience, all to make you sport.
LYSANDER. You are unkind, Demetrius: be not so,
For you love Hermia – this you know I know –
35 And here with all good will, with all my heart,
In Hermia's love I yield you up my part;
And yours of Helena to me bequeath,
Whom I do love, and will do till my death.
HELENA. Never did mockers waste more idle breath.
40 **DEMETRIUS.** Lysander, keep thy Hermia; I will none.
If e'er I lov'd her, all that love is gone.
My heart to her but as guest-wise sojourn'd,
And now to Helen is it home return'd,
There to remain.
LYSANDER.   Helen, it is not so. […]
        Enter HERMIA
45 **HERMIA.** Dark night, that from the eye his function takes,
The ear more quick of apprehension makes;
Wherein it doth impair the seeing sense
It pays the hearing double recompense.
Thou art not by mine eye, Lysander, found;
50 Mine ear, I thank it, brought me to thy sound.
But why unkindly didst thou leave me so?
LYSANDER. Why should he stay whom love doth press to go?
HERMIA. What love could press Lysander from my side?
LYSANDER. Lysander's love, that would not let him bide,
55 Fair Helena – who more engilds the night
Than all yon fiery oes and eyes of light.
(*To Hermia*) Why seek'st thou me? Could not this make thee know
The hate I bare thee made me leave thee so?
HERMIA. You speak not as you think; it cannot be.
60 **HELENA.** Lo, she is one of this confederacy!
Now I perceive they have conjoin'd all three
To fashion this false sport in spite of me.

Annotations
l. 11 **eyne** = eyes
l. 12 **muddy** = unclear (in comparison)
     in show = in appearance
l. 15 **seal of bliss** = happiness if he were to marry her
l. 16 **you all are bent** = you have all decided
l. 17 **merriment** = amusement
l. 21 **in souls** = all together
l. 22 **as you are in show** = as you pretend to be
l. 23 **to use** = *here:* to treat
l. 24 **to superpraise** = to praise over the top
     my parts = my appearance
l. 28 **trim exploit** = impressive achievement
     manly enterprise = a manly thing to do
l. 29 **to conjure tears up** = to make cry
l. 30 **derision** = mockery
     of noble sort = noble people
l. 31 **virgin** = *here:* innocent girl
     to extort = to manipulate
l. 32 **make you sport** = entertain you
l. 36 **yield … my part** = give over
l. 37 **to bequeath** = *here:* to give
l. 39 **mockers** = bullies
     waste idle breath = waste their effort
l. 40 **I will none** = I don't want her
l. 42 **but as guest-wise sojourn'd** = was only visiting her as a guest
l. 47 **to impair** = to block
l. 48 **pays … double recompense** = makes … twice as good
l. 52 **Why … go?** = Why should I stay when love told me to go?
l. 53 **to press** = *here:* to take
     from my side = away from me
l. 54 **to bide** = to stay, to wait
l. 55 **to engild** = to light up
l. 56 **yon fiery … light** = the stars
l. 57 **make thee know** = show you
l. 58 **I bare thee** = I have for you
l. 59 **you speak not as you think** = you don't mean what you are saying
l. 60 **confederacy** = *here:* group mocking Helena
l. 61 **conjoin'd** = joined together
l. 62 **to fashion** = to create
     false sport = game of lies
     in spite of = in scorn of

Injurious Hermia, most ungrateful maid,
Have you conspir'd, have you with these contriv'd
65 To bait me with this foul derision?
Is all the counsel that we two have shar'd,
The sisters' vows, the hours that we have spent
When we have chid the hasty-footed time
For parting us – O, is all forgot?
70 All schooldays' friendship, childhood innocence?
[…] And will you rent our ancient love asunder,
To join with men in scorning your poor friend?
It is not friendly, 'tis not maidenly.
Our sex, as well as I, may chide you for it,
75 Though I alone do feel the injury.
HERMIA. I am amazed at your passionate words.
I scorn you not; it seems that you scorn me.
HELENA. Have you not set Lysander, as in scorn,
To follow me, and praise my eyes and face?
80 And made your other love, Demetrius,
Who even but now did spurn me with his foot,
To call me goddess, nymph, divine and rare,
Precious, celestial? Wherefore speaks he this
To her he hates? And wherefore doth Lysander
85 Deny your love, so rich within his soul,
And tender me, forsooth, affection,
But by your setting on, by your consent?
What though I be not so in grace as you,
So hung upon with love, so fortunate,
90 But miserable most, to love unlov'd:
This you should pity rather than despise.
HERMIA. I understand not what you mean by this.
[…]
LYSANDER. Stay, gentle Helena: hear my excuse,
95 My love, my life, my soul, fair Helena!
HELENA. O, excellent!
HERMIA. (*To Lysander*) Sweet, do not scorn her so.
DEMETRIUS. If she cannot entreat, I can compel.
LYSANDER. Thou canst compel no more than she entreat;
Thy threats have no more strength than her weak prayers.
100 Helen, I love thee, by my life, I do:
I swear by that which I will lose for thee
To prove him false that says I love thee not.
DEMETRIUS. I say I love thee more than he can do.
LYSANDER. If thou say so, withdraw, and prove it too.
105 **DEMETRIUS.** Quick, come.
HERMIA. Lysander, whereto tends all this?
LYSANDER. Away, you Ethiop!
DEMETRIUS. No, no, sir,
Seem to break loose, take on as you would follow,
But yet come not. You are a tame man, go.
LYSANDER. Hang off, thou cat, thou burr! Vile thing, let loose,
110 Or I will shake thee from me like a serpent.
HERMIA. Why are you grown so rude? What change is this,
Sweet love?
LYSANDER. Thy love? – out, tawny Tartar, out;
Out, loath'd medicine! O hated potion, hence!
HERMIA. Do you not jest?

Annotations
l. 63 **injurious** = hurtful
l. 64 **contriv'd** = schemed
l. 65 to **bait** = to torment
 foul = awful
l. 66 **counsel** = secret conversations
l. 67 **sisters' vows** = promises to each other
l. 68 **chid** = cursed
 hasty-footed time = quickness of time
l. 71 to **rent asunder** = to tear apart
l. 73 **maidenly** = ladylike
l. 74 **sex** = *here:* gender
l. 78 to **set** = *here:* to instruct
l. 81 to **spurn** = to kick
l. 83 **wherefore** = why
l. 85 **your love** = *here:* his love for you
l. 86 to **tender** = to offer
 forsooth = indeed
l. 87 **but by … consent** = unless you told him to
l. 88 **in grace** = lucky
l. 89 **hung upon with love** = loved
l. 94 **hear my excuse** = let me explain
l. 96 **sweet** = my love
l. 97 **If she cannot entreat, I can compel.** = If she can't make you stop, I will.
l. 98 **thou … entreat** = you can't force me to stop anymore than she can beg me to
l. 99 **prayers** = *here:* begging
l. 104 **withdraw** = get out your sword
l. 105 **whereto … this** = What does all this mean?
l. 106 **Ethiop** = blackamoor *(racist)*
l. 107 to **seem** = *here:* to pretend
 to **take on** = to act like
l. 108 **tame man** = coward
l. 109 **hang off** = let go
 burr = *Klette*
l. 112 **out** = *here:* go away
 tawny = dark-skinned
 Tartar = person from the Tartar region
l. 113 **loath'd medicine** = disgusting poison
l. 114 to **jest** = to joke

A Midsummer Night's Dream — Play 4

HELENA. Yes, sooth, and so do you.
115 **LYSANDER.** Demetrius, I will keep my word with thee.
DEMETRIUS. I would I had your bond, for I perceive
A weak bond holds you. I'll not trust your word.
LYSANDER. What? Should I hurt her, strike her, kill her dead?
Although I hate her, I'll not harm her so.
120 **HERMIA.** What? Can you do me greater harm than hate?
Hate me? Wherefore? O me, what news, my love?
Am not I Hermia? Are not you Lysander?
I am as fair now as I was erewhile.
Since night you loved me; yet since night you left me.
125 Why then, you left me – O, the gods forbid! –
In earnest, shall I say?
LYSANDER. Ay, by my life;
And never did desire to see thee more.
Therefore be out of hope, of question, of doubt;
Be certain, nothing truer – 'tis no jest
130 That I do hate thee and love Helena.
HERMIA. (*To Helena*) O me, you juggler, you canker-blossom,
You thief of love! What, have you come by night
And stol'n my love's heart from him?
HELENA. Fine, i'faith!
Have you no modesty, no maiden shame,
135 No touch of bashfulness? What, will you tear
Impatient answers from my gentle tongue?
Fie, fie, you counterfeit, you puppet, you!
[…]

Annotations
l. 114 **sooth** = of course
l. 116 **bond** = *here:* written promise
l. 117 **bond** = *here:* the grasp of Hermia's arms
l. 118 **to strike** = to hit
l. 121 **O me** = poor me
    what news = what is going on
l. 123 **erewhile** = before
l. 126 **in earnest** = actually
l. 129 **'tis** = it's
l. 131 **juggler** = trickster
    canker-blossom = worm-eaten flower
l. 134 **maiden shame** = decency
l. 135 **bashfulness** = shame, embarrassment
l. 137 **fie** = damn you
    counterfeit = *here:* liar

Put the sentences below into the correct order and give line references.

No.	Contents	References
	Hermia wants to know from Lysander why he has left her alone in the forest.	
	The young men take turns in expressing their love to Helena, leaving Hermia completely baffled.	
	Demetrius attempts to woo Helena by praising her beauty.	
	Hermia turns against Helena and accuses her of plotting against her.	
	Helena recounts the change of moods of the young men.	
	Demetrius's love for Hermia was only short-termed.	
	Helena thinks that Hermia has conspired with Lysander and Demetrius against her and reminds Hermia of their happy childhood.	
	Lysander wants to give way for Demetrius's love to Hermia.	
	Helena despises the young men as she thinks they both make fun of her.	
1	Helena thinks that Lysander mocks her in his wooing.	ll. 7-8

Play — A Midsummer Night's Dream

34
Describe the overall atmosphere of this scene. Choose adjectives that you find the most appropriate.

> heady | sad | confusing | explosive | …

35
Read the information about stichomythia. Identify examples of stichomythia in ll. 94–119 and analyse the effect on the audience.

> **Info**
>
> ## Stichomythia
>
> Stichomythia is a dialogue of rapidly alternating lines, a device often used in a play when two characters have a vigorous exchange of words or when the emotional intensity of a scene is emphasized. Characters may take turns stating antithetical opinions, take up the other character's words or use puns on them.

36
Use your results from tasks 33–35 to write an analysis of how the language Shakespeare uses contributes to the atmosphere in this scene.

37
After the four young Athenians have left, Oberon and Puck come forward. Read the following extract.

Extract 16 (Act III, Scene 2)

OBERON. This is thy negligence. Still thou mistak'st,
Or else committ'st thy knaveries wilfully.
PUCK. Believe me, King of Shadows, I mistook.
Did not you tell me I should know the man
5 By the Athenian garments he had on?
And so far blameless proves my enterprise
That I have 'nointed an Athenian's eyes;
And so far am I glad it so did sort,
As this their jangling I esteem a sport.
10 OBERON. Thou seest these lovers seek a place to fight:
Hie therefore, Robin, overcast the night;
The starry welkin cover thou anon
With drooping fog as black as Acheron,
And lead these testy rivals so astray
15 As one come not within another's way.
Like to Lysander sometime frame thy tongue,
Then stir Demetrius up with bitter wrong,
And sometime rail thou like Demetrius;
And from each other look thou lead them thus,
20 Till o'er their brows death-counterfeiting sleep
With leaden legs and batty wings doth creep.
Then crush this herb into Lysander's eye,
Whose liquor hath this virtuous property,
To take from thence all error with his might,
25 And make his eyeballs roll with wonted sight.
When they next wake, all this derision
Shall seem a dream and fruitless vision,
And back to Athens shall the lovers wend
With league whose date till death shall never end.
30 Whiles I in this affair do thee employ
I'll to my queen and beg her Indian boy;
And then I will her charmed eye release
From monster's view, and all things shall be peace.
[…]

Annotations
l. 1 **negligence** = fault
still = *here:* continually, always
l. 2 **knavery** = trick, practical joke
wilfully = on purpose
l. 6 **blameless … enterprise** = I can't be blamed for what I did
l. 7 **'nointed** = *here:* put love juice in
l. 8 to **sort** = to turn out that way
l. 9 **jangling** = arguing
to **esteem** = to find, to see as
sport = *here:* fun
l. 11 to **hie** = to go quickly
to **overcast** = to make cloudy
l. 12 **welkin** = sky
anon = at once
l. 13 **drooping** = heavy
Acheron = black river in the underworld
l. 14 **testy** = angry
to **lead astray** = to make sb get lost
l. 16 **frame thy tongue** = imitate
l. 17 to **stir up** = to taunt, to provoke
bitter wrong = false accusation
l. 18 to **rail** = to insult
l. 19 **from each other look** = away from each other
l. 20 **death-counterfeiting sleep** = really deep sleep
l. 21 **batty** = bat-like (i.e. silent)
l. 23 **virtuous property** = healing power
l. 25 **eyeballs roll with wonted sight** = see as he used to
l. 26 **derision** = mockery
l. 27 **fruitless** = insignificant
l. 28 to **wend** = to go
l. 29 **league** = union
l. 30 **affair** = task
l. 31 **to** = *here:* go to
to **beg** = to ask for
l. 32 **her charmed eye release** = reverse the spell
l. 33 **from monster's view** = from loving Bottom

35 **PUCK.** On the ground sleep sound.
　　I'll apply to your eye,
　　Gentle lover, remedy.
　　He drops the juice on LYSANDER's *eyelids*
　　When thou wak'st, thou tak'st
　　True delight in the sight
40　Of thy former lady's eye;
　　And the country proverb known,
　　That every man should take his own,
　　In your waking shall be shown.
　　Jack shall have Jill,
45　Naught shall go ill:
　The man shall have his mare again, and all shall be well.
　　Exit PUCK; *the lovers remain on stage, asleep*

Annotations
l. 41 **proverb** = *Sprichwort*
l. 44 **Jack shall have Jill** = the man will get the woman he wants
l. 45 **naught** = nothing
l. 46 **mare** = female horse

a) Explain how Puck justifies his actions in front of Oberon.
b) Compare Puck's attitude towards his deeds with your impressions of him from what you have read so far.
c) Describe the contents of the plan Oberon wants Puck to carry out.

LOOKING BACK AT ACT III

38

a) Read the information about the use of language in Shakespeare's day.

Info

The use of second-person pronouns in Shakespeare's time

In modern-day English the pronouns 'you' and 'your' may refer to one person or several people. However, in Shakespeare's time the use of the pronouns 'thou', 'thee', 'thy' and 'thine' was very common alongside 'you' and 'your' – and people were very sensitive to the different implications these pronouns had.
- 'Thou' might be friendly and familiar, but it could also show contempt for someone socially inferior and even express an insult.
- 'You' was used for a polite, more formal, respectful or distant form of address.

Depending on the social context, speakers would switch from one pronoun to the other. A character in a play might switch from one register to the other to express a change of mood or attitude towards another character.

b) Identify the second-person pronouns that the four young lovers use in extract 15 when the characters address each other. Explain what feelings the use of the pronouns reveal. The words and phrases from the box below might help you.

Language support

(to) show contempt / hatred / anger for sb | (to) look down on sb | (to) scorn sb | (to) mock sb | (to) loathe sb | (to) abhor sth | (to) express one's aggression towards | (to) treat sb harshly / respectfully / leniently | (to) accuse sb of sth | (to) chide sb for sth | (to) be bewildered and confused | (to) be honest with sb | (to) dote on sb | (to) be head over heels in love with sb | (to) create intimacy with sb | …

c) **Group work (4)** Dramatic reading: Take parts as Helena, Hermia, Demetrius and Lysander and read out extract 15. Try to emphasize the characters' use of second-person pronouns to express their feelings for each other. Present your dialogue to the class.

Play 4 — A Midsummer Night's Dream

While reading: Act IV

SCENE 1

39

Titania and the fairies are attending to Bottom. Read the following extract.

Extract 17 (Act IV, Scene 1)

TITANIA. What, wilt thou hear some music, my sweet love?
BOTTOM. I have a reasonable good ear in music. Let's have the tongs and the bones.
TITANIA. Or say, sweet love, what thou desir'st to eat.
5 **BOTTOM.** Truly, a peck of provender, I could munch your good dry oats. Methinks I have a great desire to a bottle of hay. Good hay, sweet hay, hath no fellow.
TITANIA. I have a venturous fairy that shall seek
The squirrel's hoard, and fetch thee new nuts.
10 **BOTTOM.** I had rather have a handful or two of dried peas. But, I pray you, let none of your people stir me; I have an exposition of sleep come upon me.
TITANIA. Sleep thou, and I will wind thee in my arms.
Fairies, be gone, and be all ways away.
    Exeunt FAIRIES
15 So doth the woodbine the sweet honeysuckle
Gently entwist; the female ivy so
Enrings the barky fingers of the elm.
O, how I love thee! How I dote on thee!
    They sleep
    Enter PUCK
OBERON. (*Coming forward*)
Welcome, good Robin. Seest thou this sweet sight?
20 Her dotage now I do begin to pity;
For, meeting her of late behind the wood
Seeking sweet favours for this hateful fool,
I did upbraid her and fall out with her,
For she his hairy temples then had rounded
25 With a coronet of fresh and fragrant flowers;
And that same dew, which sometime on the buds
Was wont to swell like round and orient pearls,
Stood now within the pretty flowerets' eyes
Like tears that did their own disgrace bewail.
30 When I had at my pleasure taunted her,
And she in mild terms begg'd my patience,
I then did ask of her her changeling child,
Which straight she gave me, and her fairy sent
To bear him to my bower in Fairyland.
35 And now I have the boy, I will undo
This hateful imperfection of her eyes.
And, gentle Puck, take this transformed scalp
From off the head of this Athenian swain,
That, he awaking when the other do,
40 May all to Athens back again repair,
And think no more of this night's accidents
But as the fierce vexation of a dream.
But first I will release the fairy queen.
    He drops the juice on TITANIA's *eyelids*

Annotations
l. 2 **reasonable** = quite
    tongs = triangle (instrument)
l. 3 **bones** = sticks hit together for percussion
l. 5 **peck** = bundle
    provender = animal feed
    to **munch** = to eat
l. 6 **bottle** = *here:* small bundle
l. 7 **hath no fellow** = nothing is as good as it
l. 8 **venturous** = adventurous
l. 9 **hoard** = pile of food
    to **fetch** = to get
ll. 10–11 **I pray you** = please
l. 11 to **stir** = to disturb
    exposition = Here Bottom means 'disposition, or desire to'.
l. 13 **wind ... in my arms** = cuddle
l. 15 **woodbine** = a climbing plant
    honeysuckle = a climbing plant
l. 16 to **entwist** = to wrap around
l. 17 to **enring** = to curl around
    barky fingers = branches
    elm = *Ulme*
l. 18 to **dote on** = to love very much
l. 20 **dotage** = obsessive love
l. 21 **meeting her of late** = having met her recently
l. 22 **sweet favours** = pretty flowers
    hateful = intolerable
l. 23 to **upbraid** = to scold
    to **fall out** = to have an argument or disagreement
l. 24 **temple** = *Schläfe*
    to **round** = to circle, to put around
l. 25 **coronet** = crown
l. 26 **sometime** = *here:* formerly
    bud = *Knospe*
l. 27 **was wont ... pearls** = decorated like shining pearls
l. 28 **floweret** = small flower
l. 29 **disgrace** = source of shame
    to **bewail** = to express great sadness
l. 30 to **taunt** = to provoke with insulting remarks
l. 31 **in mild terms** = gently
l. 33 **straight** = immediately
l. 34 to **bear** = to carry, to take
    bower = chambers
l. 36 **hateful imperfection** = bad spell
l. 37 **transformed scalp** = (Bottom's) changed head
l. 38 **swain** = common man
l. 39 **other** = *here:* others
l. 40 to **repair** = to return
l. 41 **accidents** = *here:* strange events
l. 42 **the fierce vexation of a dream** = *here:* a nightmare

A Midsummer Night's Dream — Play

> Be as thou wast wont to be;
> See as thou wast wont to see.
> Dian's bud o'er Cupid's flower
> Hath such force and blessed power.
> Now, my Titania, wake you, my sweet queen!
>
> **TITANIA.** (*Starting up*) My Oberon, what visions have I seen!
> Methought I was enamour'd of an ass.
>
> **OBERON.** There lies your love.
>
> **TITANIA.** How came these things to pass?
> O, how mine eyes do loathe his visage now!
>
> **OBERON.** Silence awhile: Robin, take off this head.
> Titania, music call, and strike more dead
> Than common sleep of all these five the sense.
>
> **TITANIA.** Music, ho, music such as charmeth sleep!
>
> *Soft music plays*
>
> **PUCK.** (*To Bottom, removing the ass's head*)
> Now, when thou wak'st, with thine own fool's eyes peep.
>
> **OBERON.** Sound, music! Come, my queen, take hands with me,
> And rock the ground whereon these sleepers be.
>
> *They dance*
>
> Now thou and I are new in amity,
> And will tomorrow midnight solemnly
> Dance in Duke Theseus' house triumphantly,
> And bless it to all fair prosperity.
> There shall the pairs of faithful lovers be
> Wedded, with Theseus, all in jollity.
> [...]
>
> **TITANIA.** Come, my lord, and in our flight
> Tell me how it came this night
> That I sleeping here was found
> With these mortals on the ground.

Annotations
l. 44 **wont** = used
l. 50 **enamour'd of** = in love with
l. 52 to **loathe** = to hate
l. 54 to **strike** = *here:* to charm
l. 57 to **peep** = to look
l. 60 **amity** = friendship
l. 65 **jollity** = happiness

a) Answer the following questions.
1. How does Oberon feel about Titania's obsession with Bottom?
2. How has nature reacted to Titania's love for Bottom?
3. What is Titania's reaction when Oberon reproaches her?
4. How does Oberon take advantage of Titania?
5. What does Oberon wish for Bottom and the other mortals?
6. How does Titania react when Oberon wakes her up and she sees Bottom?
7. What is Oberon and Titania's relationship like after Titania has woken up?
8. What will happen at Theseus's court according to Oberon?

b) **Pair work**

Partner A: Analyse how Oberon's attitude towards Titania has developed in the course of the play. Consider his language and his behaviour towards Titania.

Partner B: Compare Titania's attitude towards Bottom before and after Oberon has used the magic potion on her the second time.

Then share your results.

40 Group work

Discuss how you would present Bottom in this scene. Consider the following aspects:
- Is Bottom aware of his outer appearance?
- What does his language reveal about his attitude towards the fairies?
- How does he like the situation he is in?

Play — A Midsummer Night's Dream

41

Titania asks Oberon to tell her how she came to sleep with Bottom on the ground. Write Oberon's version of the story.

42

After Puck, Oberon and Titania have left, Theseus, Hippolyta and Egeus arrive in the woods with their attendants and find the young couples sleeping. Read the following extract.

Extract 18 (Act IV, Scene 1)

    EGEUS. My lord, this is my daughter here asleep,
    And this Lysander; this Demetrius is,
    This Helena, old Nedar's Helena.
    I wonder of their being here together.
5 **THESEUS.** No doubt they rose up early to observe
    The rite of May, and hearing our intent
    Came here in grace of our solemnity.
    But speak, Egeus; is not this the day
    That Hermia should give answer of her choice?
10 **EGEUS.** It is, my lord.
    THESEUS. Go, bid the huntsmen wake them with their horns.
      Shout within; wind horns; the lovers all start up
    Good morrow, friends. Saint Valentine is past;
    Begin these wood-birds but to couple now?
    LYSANDER. Pardon, my lord.
    THESEUS.   I pray you all, stand up.
15 I know you two are rival enemies:
    How comes this gentle concord in the world,
    That hatred is so far from jealousy
    To sleep by hate, and fear no enmity?
    LYSANDER. My lord, I shall reply amazedly,
20 Half sleep, half waking; but as yet, I swear,
    I cannot truly say how I came here.
    But as I think – for truly would I speak,
    And now I do bethink me, so it is –
    I came with Hermia hither. Our intent
25 Was to be gone from Athens, where we might
    Without the peril of the Athenian law –
    EGEUS. Enough, enough, my lord; you have enough –
    I beg the law, the law upon his head!
    They would have stol'n away, they would, Demetrius,
30 Thereby to have defeated you and me,
    You of your wife, and me of my consent,
    Of my consent that she should be your wife.
    DEMETRIUS. My lord, fair Helen told me of their stealth,
    Of this their purpose hither to this wood;
35 And I in fury hither follow'd them,
    Fair Helena in fancy following me.
    But, my good lord, I wot not by what power –
    But by some power it is – my love to Hermia,
    Melted as the snow, seems to me now
40 As the remembrance of an idle gaud
    Which in my childhood I did dote upon;
    And all the faith, the virtue of my heart,
    The object and the pleasure of mine eye,
    Is only Helena. To her, my lord,
45 Was I betroth'd ere I saw Hermia;

Annotations
l. 3 **old Nedar** = Helena's father
l. 4 to **wonder** = *here:* to be surprised
l. 6 the **rite of May** = May Day festival
l. 7 in **grace of our solemnity** = to honour our wedding ceremony
l. 11 to **bid** = to tell them to
l. 12 **morrow** = morning
     Saint Valentine = Valentine's Day (14 February)
l. 13 **wood-birds** = lovebirds, lovers
     to **couple** = to form pairs
l. 14 **I pray you** = please
l. 16 **gentle concord** = peacefulness
l. 17 **jealousy** = suspicion
l. 18 **by hate** = by the side of one who hates you
l. 19 **amazedly** = *here:* that I am confused
l. 23 **bethink me** = think about it
l. 24 **hither** = here
l. 26 **peril** = threat
l. 28 **upon his head** = brought down on him
l. 29 **stol'n away** = sneaked off
l. 30 **defeated** = *here:* tricked
l. 33 **stealth** = sneaky plans, secret escape
l. 34 **purpose hither** = reason for going here
l. 35 **fury** = anger
l. 36 **in fancy** = in her love
l. 37 **wot** = know
l. 40 **remembrance** = memory
     idle gaud = worthless toy
l. 41 to **dote upon** = to love very much
l. 43 **object** = focus
     mine = my
l. 45 **betroth'd** = engaged
     ere = before

But like in sickness did I loathe this food.
But, as in health come to my natural taste,
Now I do wish it, love it, long for it,
And will for evermore be true to it.
50 **THESEUS.** Fair lovers, you are fortunately met.
Of this discourse we more will hear anon.
Egeus, I will overbear your will;
For in the temple, by and by, with us
These couples shall eternally be knit.
55 And, for the morning now is something worn,
Our purpos'd hunting shall be set aside.
Away with us to Athens. Three and three,
We'll hold a feast in great solemnity.
Come, Hippolyta.
    Exit THESEUS *with* HIPPOLYTA, EGEUS, *and his train*
60 **DEMETRIUS.** These things seem small and undistinguishable,
Like far-off mountains turned into clouds.
HERMIA. Methinks I see these things with parted eye,
When everything seems double.
HELENA.   So methinks;
And I have found Demetrius, like a jewel,
65 Mine own, and not mine own.
DEMETRIUS.   Are you sure
That we are awake? It seems to me
That yet we sleep, we dream. Do not you think
The duke was here, and bid us follow him?
HERMIA. Yea, and my father.
HELENA.   And Hippolyta.
70 **LYSANDER.** And he did bid us follow to the temple.
DEMETRIUS. Why, then, we are awake. Let's follow him,
And by the way let us recount our dreams.

Annotations
l. 46 **to loathe** = to hate
l. 47 **come** = returned
l. 49 **for evermore** = from now on forever
l. 50 **fortunately met** = lucky
l. 51 **discourse** = conversation
    anon = presently
l. 52 **to overbear** = to overrule
l. 54 **knit** = *here:* married
l. 55 **something worn** = almost over
l. 56 **purpos'd** = planned
    to set aside = to cancel
l. 58 **solemnity** = celebration
l. 60 **undistinguishable** = hard to understand
l. 62 **with parted eye** = with blurry vision
l. 63 **everything seems double** = I am seeing double
l. 67 **yet** = still
l. 68 **bid** = told
l. 71 **why** = *here:* well
l. 72 **by the way** = on the way
    to recount = to tell each other about

a) Outline what reasons the two young men give to Theseus for being in the woods.
b) Analyse the language Demetrius uses when he talks to Theseus. What does it reveal about Demetrius's attitude towards Hermia and Helena? Consider stylistic devices and his choice of words.
c) The audience already knows basically all the details about why the couples are in the woods. In class, talk about possible reasons why Shakespeare revises the plot here.

43
a) Compare Egeus's and Theseus's reactions to the news.
b) **Group work** What might the characters be thinking at this moment? Write thought bubbles for them and present your ideas to the class.

44 Group work (4)
a) The four young lovers reflect upon their situation. Sketch the ways each character describes their experience by either drawing or briefly outlining them.
b) Talk about which metaphor or simile the characters use you like best. Explain your choice.
c) Each group member chooses one character and writes a recount of his or her experience. Consider the following aspects:
- what the characters have experienced
- to what extent they have changed their attitudes towards other people
- what they have learned about themselves
- what they think about love.

d) Present their recounts to the class.

Play — A Midsummer Night's Dream

45

Bottom wakes up, alone on stage. Read the following extract.

Extract 19 (Act IV, Scene 1)

BOTTOM. When my cue comes, call me, and I will answer. My next is 'Most fair Pyramus'. Heigh-ho! Peter Quince? Flute the bellows-mender? Snout the tinker? Starveling? God's my life! Stolen hence and left me asleep! I have had a most rare vision. I have had a dream, past the wit
5 of man to say what dream it was. Man is but an ass if he go about to expound this dream. Methought I was – there is no man can tell what. Methought I was – and methought I had – but man is but a patched fool if he will offer to say what methought I had. The eye of man hath not heard, the ear of man hath not seen, man's hand is not able to taste, his
10 tongue to conceive, nor his heart to report what my dream was! I will get Peter Quince to write a ballad of this dream; it shall be called 'Bottom's Dream', because it hath no bottom; and I will sing it in the latter end of a play, before the duke. Peradventure, to make it the more gracious, I shall sing it at her death.

Annotations
- l. 1 **cue** = time to be on stage
  I will answer = *here:* I will say my lines
- l. 2 **Heigh-ho!** = Hey there!
- l. 3 **God's my life!** = Oh my god!
  stolen hence = all gone somewhere else
- l. 4 **rare vision** = weird dream
- ll. 4–5 **past the wit of man** = beyond explanation
- l. 5 **to go about to** = to try to
- l. 6 **to expound** = to explain
  no man can tell = no one can describe
- l. 7 **patched** = *here:* downright, total
- l. 8 **to offer to** = to try to
- l. 10 **to conceive** = *here:* to feel
  to report = to describe
- l. 12 **hath no bottom** = has no basis in reality
  in the latter end = at the end
- l. 13 **peradventure** = perhaps
  gracious = pleasing
- l. 14 **her** = i.e. Thisbe's

a) Choose the adjective that best describes Bottom. Is he … puzzled, bewildered, philosophical, or witty? Explain your choice.

b) Paraphrase Bottom's monologue in your own words.

c) Compare Bottom's version with that of the Bible:

d) In class, talk about possible reasons why Shakespeare makes Bottom refer to the Bible.

> However, as it is written:
> "What no eye has seen,
> what no ear has heard,
> and what no human mind has conceived" –
> the things God has prepared for those who love him –
> these are the things God has revealed to us by his Spirit.
> – 1 Corinthians 2:9–10

SCENE 2

46

The craftsmen are waiting for Bottom at Quince's house. Read the following extract.

Extract 20 (Act IV, Scene 2)

Enter BOTTOM
BOTTOM. Where are these lads? Where are these hearts?
QUINCE. Bottom! O most courageous day! O most happy hour!
BOTTOM. Masters, I am to discourse wonders – but ask me not what; for if I tell you, I am no true Athenian. I will tell you everything, right as
5 it fell out.
QUINCE. Let us hear, sweet Bottom.
BOTTOM. Not a word of me. All that I will tell you is – that the duke hath dined. Get your apparel together, good strings to your beards, new ribbons to your pumps: meet presently at the palace, every man look o'er
10 his part. For the short and the long is, our play is preferred. In any case, let Thisbe have clean linen; and let not him that plays the lion pare his nails, for they shall hang out for the lion's claws. And, most dear actors, eat no onions nor garlic; for we are to utter sweet breath, and I do not doubt but to hear them say it is a sweet comedy. No more words. Away!
15 Go, away!

Annotations
- l. 1 **lads** = my friends
  hearts = good people
- l. 2 **O most courageous day!** = What a great day!
- l. 3 **I am to discourse wonders** = I am going to tell you incredible stories
- l. 4 **right** = exactly
- l. 5 **to fall out** = to happen
- l. 8 **to dine** = to eat dinner
  apparel = costumes
  good strings to = i.e. fasten them on
- l. 9 **pumps** = dancing-shoes
  presently = immediately
- l. 10 **the short and the long is** = in sum, basically
  preferred = recommended
- l. 11 **linen** = underwear
  to pare = to cut down
- l. 12 **to hang out** = to stick out
- l. 13 **to utter sweet breath** = to have fresh breath and say pleasing words

a) List the pieces of advice and commands Bottom gives his fellow craftsmen for their play.
b) From what you have read so far, how do you expect the craftsmen's play to go? Give reasons.
c) Give further pieces of advice to the actors.

LOOKING BACK AT ACT IV

47

In plays, conflicts are usually resolved in Act V. But in *A Midsummer Night's Dream* this already happens in Act IV. So it's time to take stock. Use a grid like the one below: List the ideas or themes of the conflicts. Describe each conflict in detail, e.g. how it starts, how it develops, etc. Then explain how the conflict is resolved. Give evidence from the text.

Idea / Theme of the conflict	Description of the conflict	Resolution of the conflict
…	…	…

48

a) Identify the most crucial moments in Act IV.
b) **Pair work** Compare your ideas with a partner.

While reading: Act V

SCENE 1

49

The final scene is set at Theseus's palace. After the wedding ceremonies, the craftsmen perform their play in front of the newly-wed couples. Read the following extract.

Extract 21 (Act V, Scene 1)

Flourish of trumpets
Enter QUINCE *as Prologue*
[…]
Enter with a Trumpeter before them BOTTOM *as Pyramus,* FLUTE *as Thisbe,* SNOUT *as Wall,* STARVELING *as Moonshine and* SNUG *as Lion*
QUINCE. (*as Prologue*) Gentles, perchance you wonder at this show,
But wonder on, till truth make all things plain.
This man is Pyramus, if you would know;
This beauteous lady Thisbe is, certain.
5 This man with lime and rough-cast doth present
Wall, that vile Wall which did these lovers sunder;
And through Wall's chink, poor souls they are content
To whisper – at the which let no man wonder.
This man with lanthorn, dog, and bush of thorn,
10 Presenteth Moonshine; for, if you will know,
By moonshine did these lovers think no scorn
To meet at Ninus' tomb, there, there to woo.
This grisly beast, which Lion hight by name,
The trusty Thisbe, coming first by night,
15 Did scare away, or rather did affright;
And as she fled, her mantle she did fall,
Which Lion vile with bloody mouth did stain.
Anon comes Pyramus, sweet youth and tall,
And finds his trusty Thisbe's mantle slain;

Annotations
l. 1 **gentles** = ladies and gentlemen
perchance = maybe
l. 2 **plain** = clear, evident
l. 3 **would** = *here:* would like to
l. 4 **beauteous** = beautiful
l. 5 **rough-cast** = plaster (walls)
l. 6 **vile** = bad, nasty
to **sunder** = to separate
l. 7 **chink** = gap
l. 8 **let no man wonder** = which shouldn't surprise you
l. 9 **lanthorn** = lantern
l. 11 **think no scorn** = not find shameful
l. 13 **grisly** = scary
hight = is called
l. 14 **trusty** = faithful
l. 15 to **affright** = to frighten
l. 16 **mantle** = cloak
to **fall** = *here:* to drop
l. 17 **Lion vile** = the horrible Lion
l. 18 **anon** = then
l. 19 **slain** = *here:* covered in blood

Play — A Midsummer Night's Dream

20 Whereat with blade, with bloody, blameful blade,
He bravely broach'd his boiling bloody breast;
And Thisbe, tarrying in mulberry shade,
His dagger drew, and died. For all the rest,
Let Lion, Moonshine, Wall, and lovers twain
25 At large discourse, while here they do remain.
    Exeunt QUINCE, BOTTOM, FLUTE, SNUG *and* STARVELING
THESEUS. I wonder if the lion be to speak?
DEMETRIUS. No wonder, my lord; one lion may, when many asses do.
SNOUT. (*as Wall*) In this same interlude it doth befall
That I, one Snout by name, present a wall;
30 And such a wall as I would have you think
That had in it a crannied hole or chink,
Through which the lovers, Pyramus and Thisbe,
Did whisper often, very secretly.
This loam, this rough-cast, and this stone doth show
35 That I am that same wall; the truth is so.
And this the cranny is, right and sinister,
Through which the fearful lovers are to whisper.
THESEUS. Would you desire lime and hair to speak better?
DEMETRIUS. It is the wittiest partition that ever I heard discourse, my
40 lord.

    Enter BOTTOM *as Pyramus*
THESEUS. Pyramus draws near the wall; silence!
BOTTOM. (*as Pyramus*) O grim-look'd night, O night with hue so black,
O night which ever art when day is not!
O night, O night, alack, alack, alack,
45 I fear my Thisbe's promise is forgot!
And thou, O wall, O sweet, O lovely wall,
That stand'st between her father's ground and mine,
Thou wall, O wall, O sweet and lovely wall,
Show me thy chink, to blink through with mine eyne.
    Wall parts his fingers
50 Thanks, courteous wall; Jove shield thee well for this!
But what see I? No Thisbe do I see.
O wicked wall, through whom I see no bliss,
Curs'd be thy stones for thus deceiving me!
THESEUS. The wall, methinks, being sensible, should curse again.
55 **BOTTOM.** No, in truth, sir, he should not. 'Deceiving me' is Thisbe's cue.
She is to enter now, and I am to spy her through the wall. You shall see it
will fall pat as I told you. Yonder she comes.

    Enter FLUTE *as Thisbe*
FLUTE. (*as Thisbe*) O wall, full often hast thou heard my moans,
For parting my fair Pyramus and me.
60 My cherry lips have often kiss'd thy stones,
Thy stones with lime and hair knit up in thee.
BOTTOM. (*as Pyramus*) I see a voice; now will I to the chink,
To spy and I can hear my Thisbe's face.
Thisbe!
FLUTE. (*as Thisbe*) My love! Thou art my love, I think?
65 **BOTTOM.** (*as Pyramus*) Think what thou wilt, I am thy lover's grace,
[…].
O, kiss me through the hole of this vile wall!
FLUTE. (*as Thisbe*) I kiss the wall's hole, not your lips at all.

Annotations

- l. 20 **whereat** = because of this
  blade = sword
  bloody = *here:* bloodthirsty
- l. 21 **broach'd** = pierced
  boiling bloody breast = beating heart
- l. 22 **tarrying** = waiting
  in mulberry shade = under a mulberry bush
- l. 24 **twain** = both
- l. 25 **to discourse** = to explain
- l. 26 **be to** = will
- l. 27 **no wonder** = it wouldn't be a surprise
  ass = *here:* foolish person (wordplay)
- l. 28 **interlude** = short play
  to befall = to happen
- l. 31 **crannied** = cracked
- l. 34 **loam** = clay
- l. 36 **cranny** = crack
  right and sinister = running across from left to right
- l. 38 **lime and hair** = materials from which bricks were made
- l. 39 **wittiest** = cleverest
  partition = dividing wall, or division of a speech
- l. 42 **grim-look'd** = dark-looking
  hue = colour
- l. 43 **art** = *here:* exists
- l. 44 **alack** = alas
- l. 47 **ground** = *here:* property, land
- l. 49 **to blink** = *here:* to look
  eyne = eyes
- l. 50 **Jove** = Zeus (powerful god)
  to shield = to protect
- l. 52 **wicked** = evil
  bliss = happiness
- l. 54 **sensible** = *here:* sensitive, having thoughts and feelings
  again = *here:* back at him
- l. 55 **cue** = Stichwort
- l. 57 **to fall** = *here:* to happen
  pat = exactly
  yonder = there
- l. 59 **parting** = separating
- l. 61 **knit up** = made up of
- l. 65 **lover's grace** = gracious lover
- l. 67 **vile** = awful

BOTTOM. (*as Pyramus*) Wilt thou at Ninny's tomb meet me straightway?
70 FLUTE. (*as Thisbe*) Tide life, tide death, I come without delay.
Exeunt BOTTOM *and* FLUTE *in different directions*
SNOUT. (*as Wall*) Thus have I, Wall, my part discharged so;
And being done, thus Wall away doth go.
Exit
THESEUS. Now is the mural down between the two neighbours.
DEMETRIUS. No remedy, my lord, when walls are so wilful to hear
75 without warning.
HIPPOLYTA. This is the silliest stuff that ever I heard.
THESEUS. The best in this kind are but shadows; and the worst are no worse, if imagination amend them.
HIPPOLYTA. It must be your imagination then, and not theirs.
80 THESEUS. If we imagine no worse of them than they of themselves, they may pass for excellent men. Here come two noble beasts in, a man and a lion.

Enter SNUG *as Lion and* STARVELING *as Moonshine*
SNUG. (*as Lion*) You, ladies, you whose gentle hearts do fear
The smallest monstrous mouse that creeps on floor,
85 May now, perchance, both quake and tremble here,
When Lion rough in wildest rage doth roar.
Then know that I as Snug the joiner am
A lion fell, nor else no lion's dam;
For if I should as lion come in strife
90 Into this place, 'twere pity on my life.
THESEUS. A very gentle beast, and of a good conscience.
DEMETRIUS. The very best at a beast, my lord, that e'er I saw.
[…]
STARVELING. (*as Moonshine*) This lanthorn doth the horned moon present –
95 DEMETRIUS. He should have worn the horns on his head.
THESEUS. He is no crescent, and his horns are invisible within the circumference.
STARVELING. (*as Moonshine*) This lanthorn doth the horned moon present;
Myself the man i'th'moon do seem to be –
100 […]
HIPPOLYTA. I am aweary of this moon. Would he would change!
THESEUS. It appears by his small light of discretion that he is in the wane; but yet in courtesy, in all reason, we must stay the time.
LYSANDER. Proceed, Moon.
105 STARVELING. All that I have to say is to tell you that the lanthorn is the moon, I the man i'th'moon, this thorn bush my thorn bush, and this dog my dog.
DEMETRIUS. Why, all these should be in the lantern, for all these are in the moon. But silence: here comes Thisbe.

Enter FLUTE *as Thisbe*
110 FLUTE. (*as Thisbe*) This is old Ninny's tomb. Where is my love?
SNUG. (*as Lion*) O!
Lion roars. Thisbe drops her mantle and runs off
DEMETRIUS. Well roared, Lion!
THESEUS. Well run, Thisbe!
HIPPOLYTA. Well shone, Moon! Truly, the moon shines with a good
115 grace.

Annotations
l. 69 **straightway** = right now
l. 70 to **tide** = *here*: to come
l. 71 **discharged** = *here*: performed
l. 73 **mural** = wall
l. 74 **no remedy** = there's nothing we can do
l. 77 **the best in this kind** = even the best actors in this play
l. 78 **amend them** = make up for their lacking performance
l. 80 **than they of themselves** = than they think they are
l. 85 to **quake** = to shake
l. 88 **fell** = *here*: savage
      dam = mother
l. 89 **in strife** = looking for a fight
l. 90 **pity on my life** = cost my life
l. 92 **best at** = best at playing
l. 93 **horned moon** = crescent moon
ll. 96–97 **within the circumference** = inside the full circle
l. 99 **myself … be** = I am playing the man in the moon
l. 101 **aweary** = tired, bored
l. 102 **of discretion** = being produced
ll. 102–103 **in the wane** = going away
l. 103 **in courtesy** = to be polite
       stay the time = stay until the end
l. 106 **i'th'moon** = in the moon
l. 108 **why** = *here*: well
ll. 114–115 **with a good grace** = well

4 Play — A Midsummer Night's Dream

Lion worries Thisbe's mantle
THESEUS. Well moused, Lion!
DEMETRIUS. And then came Pyramus –
  Enter BOTTOM *as Pyramus*
LYSANDER. And so the lion vanished.
  Exit Lion
BOTTOM. (*as Pyramus*) Sweet moon, I thank thee for thy sunny beams;
120 I thank thee, moon, for shining now so bright;
For by thy gracious, golden, glittering gleams
I trust to take of truest Thisbe sight.
  But stay – O spite!
  But mark, poor knight,
125 What dreadful dole is here?
  Eyes, do you see?
  How can it be?
  O dainty duck, O dear!
  Thy mantle good –
130 What, stain'd with blood?
  Approach, ye Furies fell!
  O Fates, come, come,
  Cut thread and thrum,
  Quail, crush, conclude, and quell.
135 **THESEUS.** This passion, and the death of a dear friend, would go near to make a man look sad.
HIPPOLYTA. Beshrew my heart, but I pity the man.
BOTTOM. (*as Pyramus*) O wherefore, Nature, didst thou lions frame,
Since lion vile hath here deflower'd my dear?
140 Which is – no, no – which was the fairest dame
That liv'd, that lov'd, that lik'd, that look'd with cheer.
  Come tears, confound!
  Out sword, and wound
  The pap of Pyramus,
145 Ay, that left pap,
  Where heart doth hop:
  Thus die I, thus, thus, thus!
  He stabs himself
  Now am I dead,
  Now am I fled;
150 My soul is in the sky.
  Tongue, lose thy light;
  Moon, take thy flight.
  Exit Moonshine
  Now die, die, die, die, die.
  He dies
DEMETRIUS. No die, but an ace for him; for he is but one.
155 **LYSANDER.** Less than an ace, man; for he is dead, he is nothing.
THESEUS. With the help of a surgeon he might yet recover, and yet prove an ass.
HIPPOLYTA. How chance Moonshine is gone before Thisbe comes back and finds her lover?
160 **THESEUS.** She will find him by starlight.
  Enter FLUTE *as Thisbe*
Here she comes and her passion ends the play.
HIPPOLYTA. Methinks she should not use a long one for such a Pyramus; I hope she will be brief.
  [...]

Annotations
l. 116 **moused** = shaken as a cat would shake a mouse
l. 118 to **vanish** = to disappear
l. 121 **gleams** = beams of light
l. 122 **truest** = faithful
   to **take sight of** = to see
l. 123 **stay** = *here:* wait
   O spite! = Oh no!
l. 124 **mark** = look
l. 125 **dreadful dole** = awful sight
l. 128 **dainty duck** = *here:* my darling
l. 131 **Furies fell** = vengeance-seeking goddesses from Greek mythology
l. 133 **cut thread and thrum** = end my life
l. 134 to **quail** = to overpower
   to **conclude** = to finish
   to **quell** = to kill
l. 135 **go near to** = almost
l. 137 to **beshrew** = to curse
l. 138 **wherefore** = why
   to **frame** = to create
l. 139 **deflower'd** = ravished, carried off; maybe Bottom meant to say 'devoured' (eaten)
l. 141 **look'd with cheer** = smiled
l. 142 to **confound** = to destroy
l. 144 **pap** = chest
l. 145 **left pap** = left side of chest
l. 146 to **hop** = to beat
l. 151 **lose thy light** = stop being able to see
l. 152 **take thy flight** = leave
l. 154 **die** = *here:* one of a pair of dice
   ace = side of a die with one dot
   he is but one = he is an original
l. 156 **surgeon** = *here:* doctor
   to **prove** = *here:* to become
l. 157 **ass** = donkey
l. 158 **how chance** = how does it happen that
l. 161 **passion** = *here:* crying
l. 162 **use a long one** = cry for a long time
l. 163 **brief** = quick

165 **FLUTE.** (*as Thisbe*) Asleep, my love?
　　What, dead, my dove?
　　O Pyramus, arise.
　　Speak, speak! Quite dumb?
　　Dead, dead? A tomb
170　Must cover thy sweet eyes.
　　These lily lips,
　　This cherry nose,
　　These yellow cowslip cheeks
　　Are gone, are gone.
175　[…]
　　Tongue, not a word!
　　Come, trusty sword,
　　Come, blade, my breast imbrue!
　　She stabs herself
　　And farewell, friends.
180　Thus Thisbe ends –
　　Adieu, adieu, adieu!
　　She dies
THESEUS. Moonshine and Lion are left to bury the dead.
DEMETRIUS. Ay, and Wall, too.
BOTTOM. (*Starting up, as* FLUTE *does also*) No, I assure you, the wall is
185 down that parted their fathers. Will it please you to see the epilogue, or to hear a Bergomask dance between two of our company?
THESEUS. No epilogue, I pray you; for your play needs no excuse. Never excuse; for when the players are all dead, there need none to be blamed. Marry, if he that writ it had played Pyramus and hanged himself in
190 Thisbe's garter, it would have been a fine tragedy: and so it is, truly, and very notably discharged. But come, your Bergomask; let your epilogue alone.
　　The company return; two of them dance, then exeunt BOTTOM, FLUTE, *and their fellows*
　　The iron tongue of midnight hath told twelve.
　　Lovers, to bed; 'tis almost fairy time.
195　I fear we shall outsleep the coming morn
　　As much as we this night have overwatch'd.
　　This palpable-gross play hath well beguil'd
　　The heavy gait of night. Sweet friends, to bed.
　　A fortnight hold we this solemnity
200 In nightly revels and new jollity.
　　Exeunt

Annotations

l. 166 **my dove** = my darling
l. 167 to **arise** = to wake up
l. 168 **dumb** = mute, unable to talk
l. 173 **cowslip** = *Schlüsselblume*
l. 178 **blade** = sword
　　to **imbrue** = to stain with blood
l. 186 **Bergomask dance** = country dance
　　company = acting group
l. 187 **I pray you** = please
l. 189 **marry** = in fact
　　writ it = wrote the play
l. 190 **garter** = *Strumpfband*
l. 191 **notably discharged** = well performed
l. 193 **iron tongue** = clock hand
　　told twelve = struck midnight
l. 195 **outsleep the coming morn** = sleep in late
l. 196 **this night have overwatch'd** = have stayed up late
l. 197 **palpable-gross** = terribly bad
ll. 197–198 **beguil'd the heavy gait of night** = amused us and passed the time
l. 199 **fortnight** = two weeks
　　hold we this solemnity = we continue to celebrate
l. 200 **revels** = parties
　　jollity = happiness

4 Play — A Midsummer Night's Dream

Put the sentences below into the correct order.

No.	Contents
	Bottom suggests he can deliver an epilogue, which Theseus refuses.
	The audience makes funny remarks on Pyramus's death and Thisbe's reappearance.
	Theseus and Demetrius make fun of the talking wall.
	As soon as Thisbe notices the lion, she runs off leaving her coat behind.
	Pyramus and Thisbe express their love through a space in the wall and arrange a nightly meeting.
	Snout presents himself as Wall, through which the lovers keep in touch.
	Theseus, Hippolyta and Demetrius comment on the play.
	After Thisbe returns to their meeting place and finds Pyramus dead, she stabs herself, too.

No.	Contents
	When Bottom as Pyramus is looking for Thisbe, he happens to find her coat.
	Starveling presents himself as Moonshine and is interrupted by Theseus's and Demetrius's comments.
	Theseus expects to hear the wall speak again, but Bottom explains why this won't happen.
1	Quince as Prologue welcomes the audience and outlines the contents of the play.
	Snout as Wall takes his leave.
	Pyramus thinking that Thisbe was killed by a lion stabs himself.
	Snug introduces himself as Lion, so as not to scare the audience.
	Bottom as Pyramus tries to contact Thisbe through the wall.

50

a) Read the information below and examine the function of the play-within-the-play in *A Midsummer Night's Dream*.

--- Info ---

The play-within-the-play

The play-within-the-play is a dramatic convention very popular in Shakespeare's time: A character in a story or play becomes the narrator of or an actor in a second story. As the first permanent theatre in England had only been established some years before in 1576, Elizabethan authors liked to explore the new technical possibilities of the theatre and the nature of entertainment. Besides, the question of the kind of truth that can be told through plays was a point of interest for playwrights. Thus, it is not surprising that Shakespeare used the technique of the play-within-the-play to mirror the play's themes and present different perspectives of them. It also enables the female characters to assume the role of the audience and the critic of male-dominated themes such as male hegemony.

In general, the inset story or play may have various functions. It may simply offer entertainment, provide an example of what is told in the outer story, have symbolic or psychological significance to the characters of the outer story, or reveal the truth about something that has happened in the outer story. Finally, it may also deflect the audience's attention from a plot twist.

b) **Group work** Perform the play-within-the-play: Strip the craftsmen's play to its bare bones and make a two-minute play out of it. Then try to reduce more details and act it out in one minute. Can you do it in 30 seconds? Discuss the effect of this acting method.

51

Hippolyta says: "This is the silliest stuff that ever I heard." (l. 76)
Do you agree? Write a comment in which you express your opinion.

52

Reread ll. 77–81 and explain how Theseus sees the role of one's imagination.

A Midsummer Night's Dream — Play 4

53

Imagine you are a costume designer and must design the costumes for the play-within-the-play. Create the costumes for Pyramus, Thisbe, Wall, Moonshine and Lion. You can either draw or sketch the costumes for the actors, find magazine cuttings or look for pictures on the Internet.

54

After the mortals have gone to bed, Oberon, Titania, and their fairies appear to bless the newly-wed couples. Then Puck is left alone on stage to address the audience.

Extract 22 (Act V, Scene 1)

PUCK. (*To the audience*) If we shadows have offended,
Think but this, and all is mended:
That you have but slumber'd here
While these visions did appear;
5 And this weak and idle theme,
No more yielding but a dream,
Gentles, do not reprehend;
If you pardon, we will mend.
And, as I am an honest Puck,
10 If we have unearned luck
Now to 'scape the serpent's tongue,
We will make amends ere long,
Else the Puck a liar call.
So, good night unto you all.
15 Give me your hands, if we be friends,
And Robin shall restore amends.
    Exit

Annotations
- l. 1 **shadows** = *here:* fairies or actors
- l. 2 **mended** = fixed
- l. 3 **but** = *here:* only
       slumber'd = slept
- l. 5 **this weak and idle theme** = this silly and foolish plot
- l. 6 **no more yielding but** = producing no more than
- l. 7 **gentles** = ladies and gentlemen
       to **reprehend** = to blame
- l. 8 to **pardon** = to forgive
       to **mend** = to make better
- l. 10 **unearned luck** = luck we don't deserve
- l. 11 **'scape the serpent's tongue** = avoid being booed and hissed at (showing the audience's disapproval)
- l. 12 to **make amends** = to fix things
       ere long = soon
- l. 15 **your hands** = *here:* a round of applause
- l. 16 to **restore amends** = to make it up to you

a) **Pair work** Read out Puck's soliloquy by taking turns with your partner.
b) Sum up Puck's message in one or two sentences.
c) Speculate about the reason why Shakespeare makes Puck end the play.
d) Imagine a different character from the play would speak the final lines. Write his or her soliloquy and present it to the class.

Post-reading: Looking back at the play

AN OVERVIEW

55

Identify the main theme of each scene and explain its function. The first one is given as an example.

Act, Scene	What happens?	What is the function of the scene?
I, 1	wedding preparations; the characters unfold their problems: arranged marriage, elopement	introduction of characters; setting the scene and atmosphere
I, 2	…	…

Film: A Midsummer Night's Dream

THE STRUCTURE OF *A MIDSUMMER NIGHT'S DREAM*

56 → **S11:** How to work with drama

a) Look at the diagram. A classical play usually has the following structure:

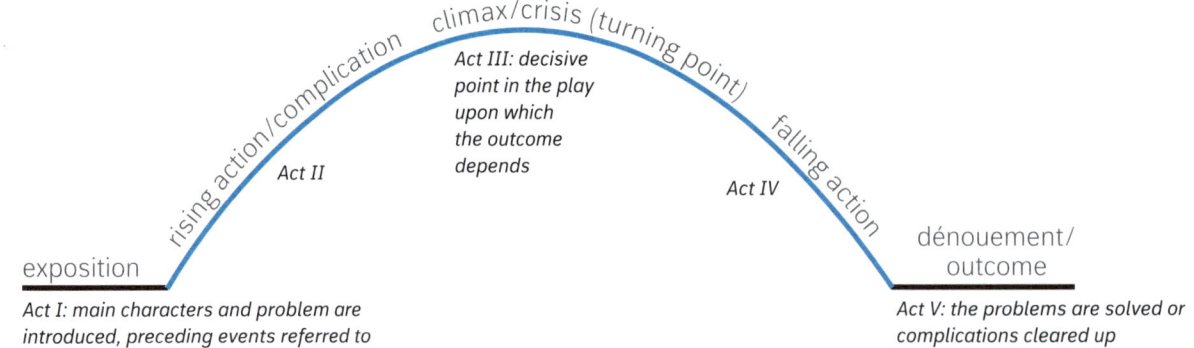

b) Identify the plot developments in *A Midsummer Night's Dream* and give examples from the play to show how they fit into the structure.

c) Group work (4–5) CHOOSE

Decide which are the most important passages in the play. Then act out the play in only three minutes (e.g. in a pantomime). One student is the timekeeper. Explain why you chose the passages you did.

OR

Work out a freeze-frame showing the most important moment in a scene. The others must guess what moment is shown in the freeze-frame.

A modern film adaptation: Michael Hoffman's *A Midsummer Night's Dream* (1999)

PRE-VIEWING

In this section, you are going to design your own modern film version of *A Midsummer Night's Dream* and pitch your idea to a production company.

1 Group work (3–4)

Create a poster about the most important scenes or events in the play. Use a symbol to indicate what each scene is about, headline the scene and summarize it in one sentence. Then present your ideas to the class.

2 Group work (4)

Discuss the relevance of the play for modern audiences.

Info

Placemat

Work in groups of four.
1. Fold a big piece of paper twice and draw a square or a rectangle in the middle (look at the example).
2. Each of you writes their ideas in one corner of the paper.
3. Turn the paper round until everyone has read and commented on their neighbours' ideas.
4. Decide on the most important ideas as a group and write them in the middle.
5. One of you presents the results to the class.

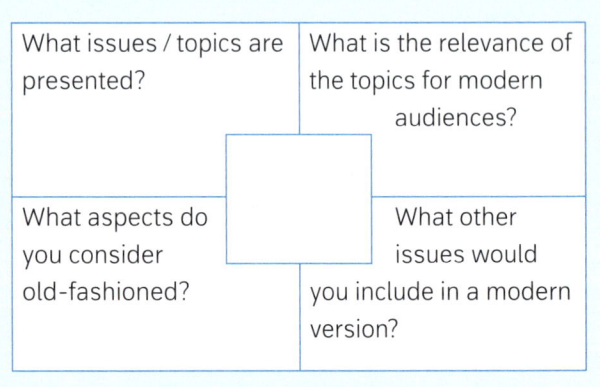

A Midsummer Night's Dream — Film

3
Imagine you are a film director and want to turn Shakespeare's *A Midsummer Night's Dream* into a modern film version.

a) Design your modern film version. Think about the following aspects and make notes.
- title
- genre (e.g. romance, sitcom, horror film, …)
- setting (Where and when does the story take place?)
- cast (actors for the main roles)

b) Present your ideas to the class.

4
a) **Pair work**

Prepare a pitch for your modern film version of *A Midsummer Night's Dream* to convince a production company to fund the project.
- Summarize the original plot.
- Present your reasons for making such a film.
- Talk about the relevance of the story for modern audiences.
- Outline the idea for your film version.

> **Info**
>
> **Pitch**
>
> A pitch is a short oral presentation of an idea. When you make a pitch, you try to persuade someone to support your idea. As time is money, a pitch must be concise and to the point.

b) Present your pitch to the class. The other students function as the board of film producers at the production company. At the end of the presentations, vote for the best pitch.

5 → **Workshop:** Analysing a feature film   → **S16:** Checklist: Analysis of a film scene

In 1999, a film version of *A Midsummer Night's Dream* by American director Michael Hoffman came out, with Rupert Everett, Calista Flockhart, Kevin Kline, Michelle Pfeiffer, Stanley Tucci, Christian Bale, Anna Friel and Dominic West playing the main roles.

a) Look at the film stills below and match them with the cinematic devices in the box. More than one term might fit.

> medium shot | blurry foreground | establishing shot | close-up | out of focus | blurry background | over-the-shoulder shot | long shot | bird's eye view | full shot | low-angle shot | high-angle shot | superimposed text | point-of-view shot | worm's eye view | eye-level shot | in focus

b) In class, talk about your first impressions that the film stills convey, e.g. the overall atmosphere, the setting and the characters.

4 Film — A Midsummer Night's Dream

WHILE VIEWING

The beginning of the film

6 → **Workshop:** Analysing a feature film → **S16:** Checklist: Analysis of a film scene

a) Read the opening scene of the play again (extract 1, p. 100). Then outline how you would turn it into a film scene if you were a director. Use the middle column in the grid below.
b) Now watch the beginning of Michael Hoffman's version of *A Midsummer Night's Dream* (0:00:00–0:04:59). Note down your first impressions. Compare them to your impressions from task 5b).
c) Watch the scene again and fill in the right-hand column of the grid.
d) **Pair work** Compare your notes with a partner.
e) Explain which version you prefer and give reasons for your choice.

	Your idea	Film version
The setting: Where and when does the story take place?		
Choice of actors for the roles of Theseus and Hippolyta: Describe their physical appearances and personalities.		
Events: What happens in the scene?		
Cinematic devices: field size, camera angle, special effects, music		

The relationship between father and daughter

7

a) Read extract 2 again (p. 101f.). Analyse the relationship between Egeus and his daughter Hermia as depicted by Shakespeare. Choose words from the box that best describe the relationship. Explain your choice and give line references to support it.

> cold-hearted | unloving | unemotional | indifferent | broken | intimate | difficult | love-hate | full of hatred | toxic

b) **Pair work** Choose the most important lines in this extract for Egeus and his daughter. Compare your choice with a partner.
c) Watch the film scene in which the conflict between Egeus and Hermia is presented (0:04:59–0:09:29). Note down your first impression of the father-daughter relationship in the film scene.
d) **Pair work** Watch the film scene again, this time focusing on the lines they speak. Compare your ideas from b) with the lines chosen for the film. If the lines differ, discuss possible reasons for the differences.
e) **EXTRA** Identify some of the cinematic devices the director uses to convey the nature of the father-daughter relationship. → **Workshop:** Analysing a feature film → **S16:** Checklist: Analysis of a film scene

A Midsummer Night's Dream — Film

The play-within-the-play

8 Group work

a) Reread the scene in which *Pyramus and Thisbe* is performed at the Duke's palace (extract 21, p. 135ff.). Then decide how you would adapt this scene for a film. Create a storyboard for your film scene, which includes the following elements:
- sketches of the different shots
- for each shot:
  → the lines to be spoken
  → a short description of the action
  → camera movements, music and sound effects
  → further directions

Kevin Kline (as Nick Bottom) and Michael Hoffman (director)

b) **EXTRA** Film the scene based on your ideas from a).
c) Watch the film scene (1:31:52–1:46:09) and compare it to your ideas.
d) Discuss possible reasons for Michael Hoffman's decision to film the scene in this way.

POST-VIEWING

9

a) **Group work** Read some reviews of the film on the Internet and outline the reviewers' opinions of Michael Hoffman's film version. Exchange the views with your group members.
b) Read what Roger Ebert, a famous American film critic and author, said about *A Midsummer Night's Dream*.

Reviews Roger Ebert   May 14, 1999

William Shakespeare's A Midsummer Night's Dream

[…] Michael Hoffman's new film of "William Shakespeare's a Midsummer Night's Dream" (who else's?) is updated to the 19th century, set in Italy and furnished with bicycles and operatic[1] interludes. But it is founded on Shakespeare's language and is faithful, by and large, to the original play. […]

Hoffman, whose wonderful "Restoration"[2] re-created a time of fire and plague, here conducts with a playful touch. There are small gems of stagecraft for all of the actors, including Snout, the village tinker, who plays a wall in the performance for the duke, and makes a circle with his thumb and finger to represent a chink in it. It's wonderful to behold Pfeiffer's infatuation with the donkey-eared Bottom, who she winds in her arms as "doth the woodbine the sweet honeysuckle gently twist"; her love is so real, we almost believe it. Kline's Bottom tactfully humors her mad infatuation, good natured and accepting. And Tucci's Puck suggests sometimes that he has a darker side, but it not so much malicious as incompetent. […]

Why is Shakespeare so popular with filmmakers when he contains so few car chases and explosions? Because he is the measuring stick by which actors and directors test themselves. His insights into human nature are so true that he has, as [Harold] Bloom argues in his book, actually created our modern idea of the human personality. Before Hamlet asked, "to be, or not to be?," dramatic characters just were. Ever since, they have known and questioned themselves. Even in a comedy like "Midsummer," there are quick flashes of brilliance that help us see ourselves. "What fools these mortals be," indeed.

Annotations
[1] **operatic** = characteristic of opera
[2] ***Restoration*** (1995) is another film directed by Michael Hoffman. It is a historical drama set in 17th century England, which is based on the 1989 novel by Rose Tremain

---

c) Describe Roger Ebert's explanation about Shakespeare's ongoing popularity in your own words.
d) What "quick flashes of brilliance" can you find in the play?
e) Write your own film review of Michael Hoffman's version of *A Midsummer Night's Dream*.

4 Topic — A Midsummer Night's Dream

Questions of identity

AMBITIONS AND OBSTACLES, CONFORMITY VS. INDIVIDUALISM

1 `CHOOSE`

First write down your name with each letter beginning a new line. Then write an acrostic with it. Think of words that form your personality.

OR

Create a 'me'-map, in which you show all the different sides of your personality, e.g. personal facts (gender, nationality, …), character traits, hobbies, etc.

> **Info**
>
> ### Acrostic
>
> An acrostic is a poem in which particular letters, for example the first letters of each line, make a new word or phrase.

ME

2 → **Workshop:** Analysing a cartoon → **S17:** How to work with cartoons

Choose one of the two cartoons and talk about it.

- Introduce the cartoon. (Name the cartoonist and the topic.)
- Describe the cartoon. (Give a detailed account of its pictorial elements and its caption/text.)
- Analyse the cartoon. (Explain the function of its elements and its message.)
- Evaluate the cartoon. (Do you agree with the message?)

"All these years and some people still mistake me for a bird or a plane."

3

Discuss in class what qualities form your identity and how they differ.

4 Pair work

Read the online article about two aspects of identity. Then test your partner's knowledge by asking them the questions on the next page.

Difference Between Conformity and Individuality

Both individuality and conformity are essential in society. They involve behaviors which are related with the expression of one's feelings and thoughts. Hence, these concepts are often associated with psychology, sociology, and philosophy. Specifically, conformity is a social influence which involves compliance[1] with group norms or laws while individuality refers to the quality that distinguishes a person from others. The following discussions further delve[2] into their differences.

What is Conformity?
"Conformity" came from the Latin word "conformare" which means "to form". It is matching one's behaviors to the majority's expectations or the compliance with group norms or laws. This type of social influence was first studied by Arthur Jenness (1932), who asked research participants to individually estimate how many beans does a bottle contain. The participants were then ushered into a room where they were asked to estimate the number of beans as a group. After the group discussion, Jenness asked the participants individually if they would like to change their initial estimate; almost all of them changed their original answers to be closer to the group's estimation. Ergo, people's judgements are significantly influenced by the majority's opinions, particularly in vague situations.

The following are the three types of conformity according to [Herbert C.] Kelman:

- Compliance
  It is a temporary[3] behavior change since the compliance stops when there is no group pressure. This happens when an individual accepts the influence even if he does not personally agree; he complies because he aims to receive a favorable response (such as approval) from the group. For example, a guest, who got invited to a birthday party, does not really like eating vegetables. However, he ate a lot of vegetable salad to please his vegan host and his family.

- Identification
  This occurs when an individual adjusts his behavior to be able to be a member of a certain group. This is stronger as compared to compliance since it involves public and private conformity; however, it may stop when the individual leaves the group. For example, a foreign student adopted a new way of life; however, he went back to his previous culture when he went back to his own country.

- Internalization
  This happens when an individual is intrinsically[4] motivated to accept the influence because he agrees with the ideas and actions involved. In this case, compliance is also both public and private. This is the deepest type since the behavior change is relatively permanent. For instance, someone who got invited to a church service by his friends eventually became a Christian and changed his lifestyle.

What is Individuality?
"Individuality" came from the medieval Latin word "individualitas" which refers to the quality that distinguishes a person from others. It emphasizes that a certain individual has his own beliefs, needs, desires, responsibilities, rights, etc. This concept is concerned with the forces which help us develop into distinct[5] beings. It is also associated with diversity since it values uniqueness and depth. Every human being has a certain level of individuality and its loss can significantly injure a society. For example, a workplace which does not value the employees' gender identities, religions, and socio-economic status will likely lead to a decrease in job satisfaction and performance. [...]

Annotations
[1] **compliance** = the act of obeying a law or rule, or doing everything that sb tells you to do
[2] to **delve into** sth = to examine sth
[3] **temporary** = not permanent
[4] **intrinsically** = coming from within; belonging naturally to sb or sth
[5] **distinct** = different, unique

4 Topic — A Midsummer Night's Dream

Now take turns and test your partner:
1. How is conformity defined?
2. How is individuality explained?
3. What was the experiment about?
4. Explain the three aspects of conformity.
5. What does individuality emphasize?
6. What happens when people lose their individuality?

5

a) Read the article from the American business magazine *Forbes* and outline its main ideas.
b) Analyse the language the author uses to show her attitude towards conformity and individuality.
c) **Group work** Discuss to what extent individuality and conformity matter at school.

Want To Fit In Or Stand Out? The Conformity Paradox

By Renee Goyeneche Jun 2, 2022

Maintaining an independent sense of identity within the professional world can be difficult for a number of reasons. One of the most significant hurdles comes from the idea of "falling in line" to meet professional expectations[1]. There are certain standards of conduct[2] in the workplace, and most people understand their careers can hinge[3] on the interpersonal relationships formed there. That knowledge means we censor ourselves to conform to written and unwritten rules, allowing us to fit in and gain what's known as social capital. Social capital is the value gained by forming positive connections with people, and it's particularly important in the workplace. Acceptance at work helps provide access to people who can facilitate[4] career success: networks and social groups, mentors and thought leaders. When we look at the dynamics and politics in our workplace, we consider a number of factors. Among them: how does leadership behave? What is the communication style? Who is rewarded, and for what?

We pay attention to norms, follow cues and adhere[5] to expectations because we understand that those labeled "other" are often left out of the conversations and activities that would help them build professional relationships. When we conform, we sacrifice a portion of our individuality. Still, it's a logical strategy, especially if we sense that a lack of conformity might result in exclusion, discrimination or judgment from our colleagues. That type of response from even one key player can undercut[6] our social capital and effectively stifle[7] our professional growth.

Two types of conformity are especially prevalent[8] in the workplace: informational and normative. Informational conformity is when we study others to help us gain information, form opinions, or assist us in decision-making. Normative conformity is when we behave in specific ways to gain acceptance.

There are benefits to fitting in at work, because harmonious relationships make everything easier. When you relate well to others, your colleagues lend support more readily and are more willing to speak up on your behalf. They're also more likely to help ensure a balanced workload and create a shared professional safety net.

However, while a certain degree of cohesiveness[9] between workmates is necessary to keep operations moving smoothly, it's essential to look at how often and to what degree we're censoring our authentic selves. Therein lies the paradox: conforming may make us more palatable[10] to others, but at what cost to our own sense of identity?

Some things to think about:
- **How dramatically do you change the way you present yourself?** We all do little things, especially at the surface level. Maybe you tone down makeup, cover up tattoos or avoid edgy clothing that is more your vibe in a personal setting. It's probably not a big deal, because while these things provide some context for your true character, they don't define it. Think now about what you choose (or don't

Annotations
[1] to **meet expectations** = to fulfil expectations
[2] **conduct** = behaviour
[3] to **hinge on** = to depend on
[4] to **facilitate** = to make sth easier or possible
[5] to **adhere to** = to stick to
[6] to **undercut** = to weaken
[7] to **stifle** = to suppress, to hold back
[8] **prevalent** = widespread, common
[9] **cohesiveness** = *here*: team spirit
[10] **palatable** = pleasant, acceptable

choose) to share about yourself and your core beliefs or values. Would someone who knows you well outside of work recognize you in a professional setting?

- **To what degree do you modify how you speak?** This question has many layers. The simplest interpretation is, how do you phrase what you say? You may choose your words more carefully, soften your comments or omit language you might have used in a more authentic interaction. These are reasonable and professional accommodations. However, consider next *what you feel comfortable saying*, and the idea becomes more nuanced. Do you stay silent when you know you should speak up? If you hold a dissenting view or opinion, do you express it or bite your tongue?

If you're leading a team, striking a balance regarding the concept of conformity becomes even more closely tied to success. A "wild west" atmosphere rarely serves a company's best interest. However, research proves that diverse teams have higher success rates, so creating a workplace that provides clear expectations but supports individualism and authenticity should always be a key corporate initiative. It's critical to understand that employees who feel constrained by their environment offer an edited version of themselves. They're less able to rely on their innate strengths, often resulting in diminished productivity and subpar[11] work.

How to cultivate a professional environment that focuses on cooperation, not conformity:

1. **Solicit[12] opinions privately and in advance of a discussion whenever possible.** You'll get more genuine feedback if people are not influenced or silenced by others. Starting a meeting with, "I've gotten some great suggestions on this topic, and I'd like to review them today" opens the floor to all ideas without preconceptions[13]. As your team workshops[14] the concepts, you'll be able to credit[15] people as appropriate. Another benefit: posing questions in advance allows people to develop their ideas more completely before the meeting.

2. **Manage the tone of communications.** One person's voice should not dominate the team. As a leader, you can prevent that by familiarizing yourself with each member's natural strengths. When you see the opportunity, you can call on those whose voices are softer, ensuring everyone is heard.

3. **Offer transparency in the decision-making process.** There are times when company leaders are not the foremost experts. Acknowledging this idea and laying out the options for a team decision-making process encourages weighing pros and cons in a "no-judgment zone." Showing respect for various solutions establishes the expectation that team members can debate ideas but not disparage them. The ideal work environment marries the ideas of conformity and individuality. The most effective teams establish a hybrid workplace that calls on people to foster a respectful, supportive atmosphere while celebrating diversity and independent thought.

Annotations
[11] **subpar** = below average, worse than expected
[12] to **solicit** = to ask for
[13] **preconception** = an opinion that is formed before you have enough information or experience
[14] to **workshop** = to develop sth by sharing knowledge, discussing ideas and working together
[15] to **credit** sb **as** = to believe that sb is of a particular quality

QUESTIONS OF IDENTITY IN *A MIDSUMMER NIGHT'S DREAM*

6

a) **Group work** (5) Find examples from the play where aspects of identity in general, ambitions, obstacles, individuality and conformity in particular become clear. Note them down in the grid below.

Ambitions	Obstacles
– The two lovers, Hermia and Lysander, want to escape into the woods. (Extract 3, l. 30ff.)	

Topic: A Midsummer Night's Dream

Questions of identity	
Individuality	**Conformity**

b) Examine how Shakespeare deals with questions of identity in his play. Use the information from a).

Language support

William Shakespeare explores questions of identity in various ways in his play to show …
In Act I, it becomes clear that Hermia and Lysander do not stand a chance against her father Egeus and the Athenian law, which is why …
In the fairy world, too, questions of identity play a role, when Puck mistakes the young Athenians and makes Lysander fall in love with Helena. Shakespeare demonstrates how …
Besides, …
In conclusion, one might say …

7 Pair work

a) Choose one of the characters from the play, whose identity you would like to explore further. Your partner is a psychiatrist who wants to find out about the identity, feelings, desires and ambitions of your character. Use the questions below to prepare a role play showing a meeting between your character and the psychiatrist.

- What is your character's situation like?
- How does your character feel about their situation?
- What is their social background?
- What role does their social background play for them?
- What troubles them?
- What is important for your character?
- How does your character envision their future life?
- What are your character's hopes and fears?

b) Act out the role play in front of the class.

8 → **S9:** How to structure a text → **S8:** How to improve your text

Write an essay on one of the following topics.
- Individuality and conformity in Shakespeare's time
- Mistaken identities in *A Midsummer Night's Dream*
- Questions of identity in *Pyramus and Thisbe*

Language support

Introduction:
This essay will be about … | In this essay I shall discuss / look at …

Main part:
first of all | next | then | furthermore | besides | finally | for example | for instance | such as | similarly | likewise | on the one hand …, on the other hand … | however | in contrast | …

Conclusion:
to sum up | all in all | in conclusion | …

9

Using the play and the painting below as a starting point, assess the importance of dealing with questions of identity at school.

Edwin Landseer: Scene from *A Midsummer Night's Dream*. Titania and Bottom (1848–51)

| Topic | A Midsummer Night's Dream |

Chances and challenges for society: gender issues

1

a) **Pair work** How do you explain the term "gender role"? Write a definition with your partner.
b) Look up the term on the Internet. Choose the definition you think is the most appropriate.
c) Compare your definition from a) with the one you have found on the Internet.

2

a) Look at the adjectives in the box. Decide which adjectives are typically attributed to women and which ones to men. Sort them into the grid below.
b) **Pair work** Compare your results with a partner.

> active | aggressive | analytical | blunt | competitive | cruel | dependent | dominant | easily influenced | emotional | gentle | graceful | home-oriented | independent | innocent | logical | obedient | self-confident | submissive | talkative | tough

Traditional gender stereotypes	
feminine	masculine

3

Read about the campaign *Look Beyond* by UN Women and UNFPA (United Nations Population Fund) on the organisation's website. **Webcode** DSW-73698-15

a) Answer the following questions.
  1. How has the COVID-19 pandemic affected the field of work?
  2. How are women affected in particular?
  3. What is the aim of the campaign?
  4. Why is the pandemic seen as an opportunity to change the situation for women?
  5. Why is unpaid care work important for communities?
  6. What results have surveys shown?
  7. What chores are usually attributed to women?
  8. How does the reshaping of gender roles relate to domestic violence?
  9. How does the campaign try to bring about the changes?

b) **Group work** Discuss the importance of such campaigns for gender equality.

4 → **Workshop:** Analysing a cartoon → **S17:** How to work with cartoons

Visit the UN Women website and look at some cartoons which are part of the book *Make way for women!* and were created by members of Cartooning for Peace, a non-profit international network of cartoonists. **Webcode** DSW-73698-16

Group work Each of you picks one of the cartoons and prepares a short presentation about it.
- Introduce the cartoon. (Name the cartoonist and the topic.)
- Describe the cartoon. (Give a detailed account of its pictorial elements and its caption.)
- Analyse the cartoon. (Explain the function of its elements and its message.)
- Evaluate the cartoon. (Do you agree with the message?)

5 Pair work

Partner A: Read the following extracts from an article from the website of the British Library. Describe the situation of women in Shakespeare's time. Then exchange the information with your partner.

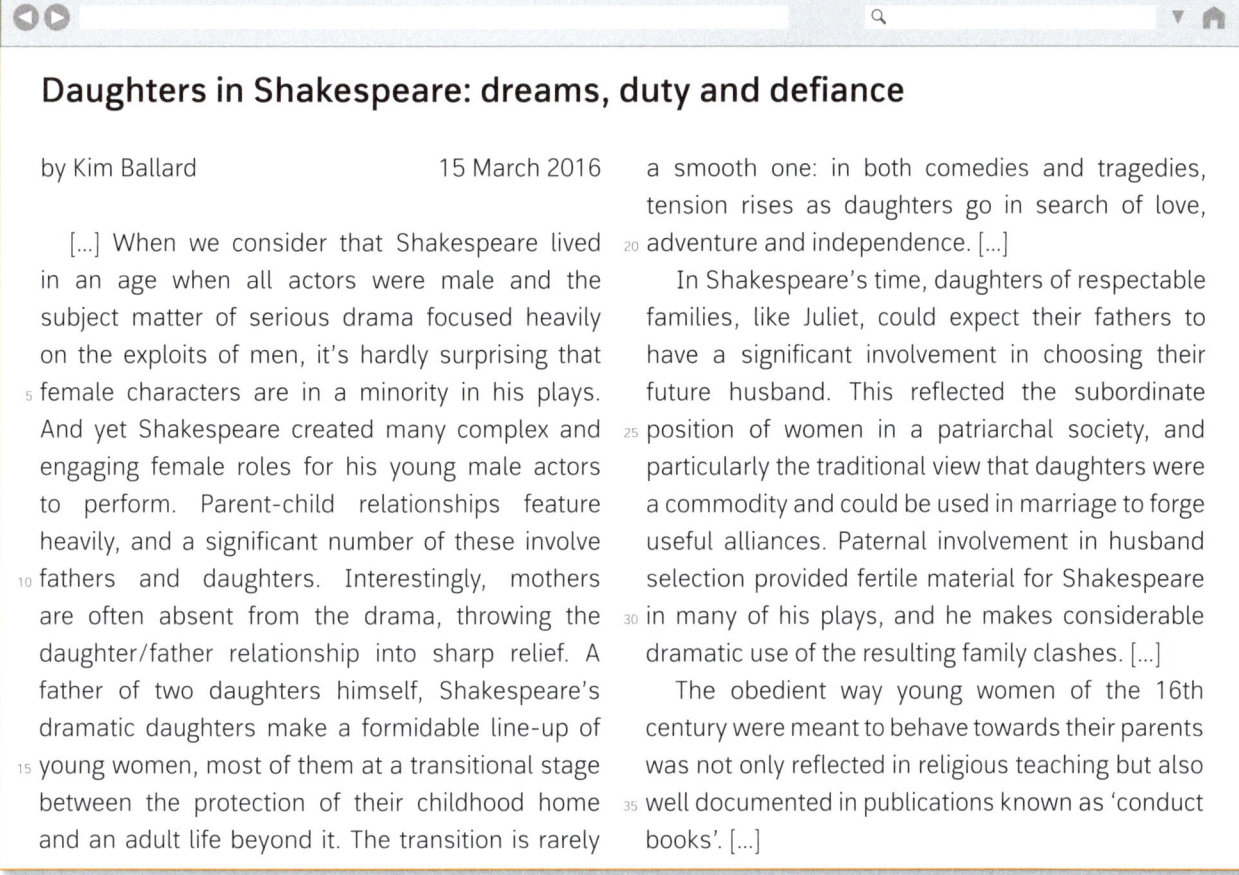

Daughters in Shakespeare: dreams, duty and defiance

by Kim Ballard   15 March 2016

[...] When we consider that Shakespeare lived in an age when all actors were male and the subject matter of serious drama focused heavily on the exploits of men, it's hardly surprising that female characters are in a minority in his plays. And yet Shakespeare created many complex and engaging female roles for his young male actors to perform. Parent-child relationships feature heavily, and a significant number of these involve fathers and daughters. Interestingly, mothers are often absent from the drama, throwing the daughter/father relationship into sharp relief. A father of two daughters himself, Shakespeare's dramatic daughters make a formidable line-up of young women, most of them at a transitional stage between the protection of their childhood home and an adult life beyond it. The transition is rarely a smooth one: in both comedies and tragedies, tension rises as daughters go in search of love, adventure and independence. [...]

In Shakespeare's time, daughters of respectable families, like Juliet, could expect their fathers to have a significant involvement in choosing their future husband. This reflected the subordinate position of women in a patriarchal society, and particularly the traditional view that daughters were a commodity and could be used in marriage to forge useful alliances. Paternal involvement in husband selection provided fertile material for Shakespeare in many of his plays, and he makes considerable dramatic use of the resulting family clashes. [...]

The obedient way young women of the 16th century were meant to behave towards their parents was not only reflected in religious teaching but also well documented in publications known as 'conduct books'. [...]

Partner B: Read the following extracts from an article from the website of the British Library. Outline the practice of playing female roles. Then exchange the information with your partner.

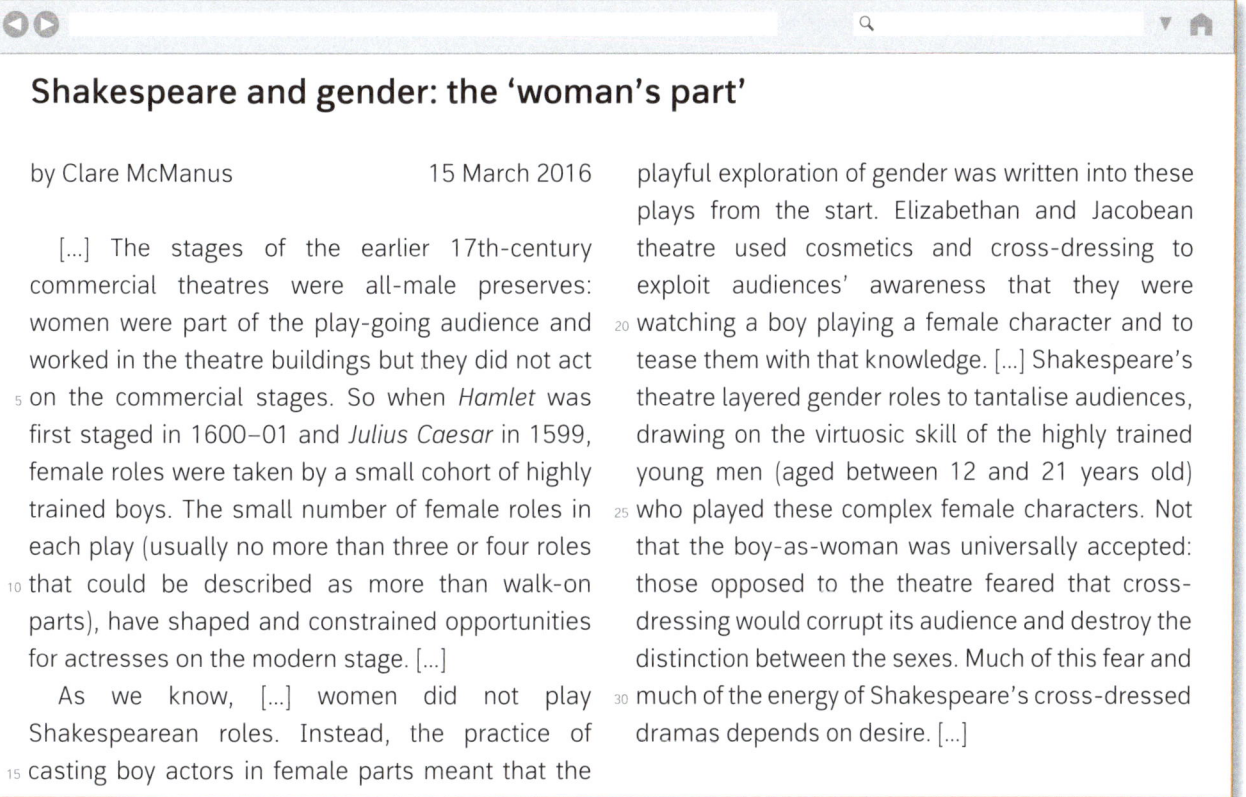

Shakespeare and gender: the 'woman's part'

by Clare McManus   15 March 2016

[...] The stages of the earlier 17th-century commercial theatres were all-male preserves: women were part of the play-going audience and worked in the theatre buildings but they did not act on the commercial stages. So when *Hamlet* was first staged in 1600–01 and *Julius Caesar* in 1599, female roles were taken by a small cohort of highly trained boys. The small number of female roles in each play (usually no more than three or four roles that could be described as more than walk-on parts), have shaped and constrained opportunities for actresses on the modern stage. [...]

As we know, [...] women did not play Shakespearean roles. Instead, the practice of casting boy actors in female parts meant that the playful exploration of gender was written into these plays from the start. Elizabethan and Jacobean theatre used cosmetics and cross-dressing to exploit audiences' awareness that they were watching a boy playing a female character and to tease them with that knowledge. [...] Shakespeare's theatre layered gender roles to tantalise audiences, drawing on the virtuosic skill of the highly trained young men (aged between 12 and 21 years old) who played these complex female characters. Not that the boy-as-woman was universally accepted: those opposed to the theatre feared that cross-dressing would corrupt its audience and destroy the distinction between the sexes. Much of this fear and much of the energy of Shakespeare's cross-dressed dramas depends on desire. [...]

Topic: A Midsummer Night's Dream

GENDER ISSUES IN *A MIDSUMMER NIGHT'S DREAM*

6

a) Read the following quotations from the play. Identify the speaker and the context in which they are said.

1 "Be it so she will not here, before your grace,
Consent to marry with Demetrius,
I beg the ancient privilege of Athens;
As she is mine, I may dispose of her;
Which shall be either to this gentleman
Or to her death, [...]" *(Act I, Scene 1)*

2 "Your wrongs do set a scandal on my sex!
We cannot fight for love, as men may do;
We should be woo'd, and were not made to woo." *(Act II, Scene 1)*

3 "Tarry, rash wanton! Am not I thy lord?" *(Act II, Scene 1)*

4 "But, gentle friend, for love and courtesy
Lie further off, in human modesty;
Such separation as may well be said
Becomes a virtuous bachelor and a maid,
So far be distant, and good night, sweet friend;
[...]" *(Act II, Scene 2)*

5 "Egeus, I will overbear your will; [...]" *(Act IV, Scene 1)*

b) Find adjectives to describe the characters. You can use adjectives from the box on p. 152.
c) Analyse how and to what extent the characters in the play fulfil the roles that are expected from them.

7

In class, discuss if Shakespeare can be considered a critic of gender inequality.

8 Group work

Each group member slips into the shoes of one of the characters from the play in their respective situation.

CHOOSE Write their soliloquy, in which you reflect upon the following questions:
- What is your situation like?
- What do you think about the other character(s) on stage?
- What is expected of you? How do you feel about the situation you are in? Why?
- What would you like to change?
- What are your hopes and dreams?

Then present your soliloquy to your group members. (You can find more information about soliloquies in the box on p. 103.)

OR

Have a discussion on gender roles and expectations.

Copyrights

TEXTQUELLEN

7–14	Charlotte Perkins Gilman: "The Yellow Wallpaper." (Original title: "The Yellow Wall-paper. A Story.") In: *The New England Magazine*, January 1892.
16	Quotes from Charlotte Perkins Gilman: "The Yellow Wallpaper." (Original title: "The Yellow Wall-paper. A Story.") In: *The New England Magazine*, January 1892.
18–19	Kate Chopin: "The Story of an Hour." (Original title: "The Dream of an Hour.") In: *Vogue*, 6 December 1894.
21	Quote from Kate Chopin: "The Story of an Hour." (Original title: "The Dream of an Hour.") In: *Vogue*, 6 December 1894.
22–29	Fay Weldon: "Weekend." In: *Cosmopolitan*, 1978.
33–35	Bernardine Evaristo: "The First Feminists." Holly Fraser (ed.), Amsterdam: WePresent/WeTransfer, 09.04.2020. https://wepresent.wetransfer.com/stories/literally-bernardine-evaristo (05.09.2023)
36–37	Quotes from Bernardine Evaristo: "The First Feminists." Holly Fraser (ed.), Amsterdam: WePresent/WeTransfer, 09.04.2020. https://wepresent.wetransfer.com/stories/literally-bernardine-evaristo (05.09.2023)
37	Quotes from Kate Chopin: "The Story of an Hour." (Original title: "The Dream of an Hour.") In: *Vogue*, 6 December 1894.
37	Quotes from Fay Weldon: "Weekend." In: *Cosmopolitan*, 1978.
37	Quotes from Charlotte Perkins Gilman: "The Yellow Wallpaper." (Original title: "The Yellow Wall-paper. A Story.") In: *The New England Magazine*, January 1892.
39	Infographic: Medical Model	Social Model. Windsor, New South Wales, Australia: EPIC Assist/EPIC Employment Inc. https://epicassistau.b-cdn.net/wp-content/uploads/2021/07/Medical-model-vs-social.png (12.12.2023) (verändert)
40	Paul Sloane: "The Dangers of Conformity." London: BBN Times, 24.07.2023. https://www.bbntimes.com/politics/the-dangers-of-conformity (13.12.2023)
41	Quote by Gloria Steinem: "A gender-equal society …" In: Praneta Jha: "Feminism makes love easier, says Gloria Steinem." In: *Hindustan Times*, 18.01.2014. https://www.hindustantimes.com/india/feminism-makes-love-easier-says-gloria-steinem/story-CMt7gY31ffRlpYcfetbvBL.html (14.12.2023)
43	Quotes from Emmaline Soken-Huberty: "10 Causes of Gender Inequality." Wien: Human Rights Careers. https://www.humanrightscareers.com/issues/causes-gender-inequality/ (14.12.2023) (verändert)
43 f.	„Gemeinsame Doppelnamen reichen nicht!" Ein Kommentar von Tanja Dückers. Köln: Deutschlandfunk Kultur/Deutschlandradio, 03.04.2023. https://www.deutschlandfunkkultur.de/heirat-nachname-meshing-100.html (14.12.2023)
46	Dictionary entry: "behold". In: *Oxford Languages*. Oxford: Oxford University Press 2023.
50–67	Quotes from Imbolo Mbue: *Behold the Dreamers*. New York: Random House (Penguin Random House LLC) 2016.
51	"Bankruptcy of Lehman Brothers." In: *Britannica*. Chicago, IL: Encyclopædia Britannica, Inc. 2023. https://www.britannica.com/event/bankruptcy-of-Lehman-Brothers (07.11.2023)
55 ff.	Aaron Bady: "Has Imbolo Mbue Written the Great American Novel?" New York: *Literary Hub*, 26.10.2016. https://lithub.com/has-imbolo-mbue-written-the-great-american-novel/ (08.11.2023)
57 ff.	Annabelle Hirsch: „So hat Amerika die Einwanderer immer gebraucht." In: *Frankfurter Allgemeine Zeitung*, 11.02.2017. https://www.faz.net/aktuell/feuilleton/buecher/rezensionen/roman-das-getraeumte-land-von-imbolo-mbue-14873429.html (09.11.2023)
60	Quote from James Truslow Adams: *The Epic of America*. Boston: Little, Brown and Company 1931.
60, 63	Quote from the *United States Declaration of Independence*, In Congress, July 4, 1776. Washington, D.C.: The U.S. National Archives and Records Administration 2023. https://www.archives.gov/founding-docs/declaration-transcript (13.11.2023)
60	Quote from Malcolm X (el-Hajj Malik el-Shabazz): "The Ballot or the Bullet." Speech given in Detroit on April 12, 1964. St. Paul, Minnesota: American Public Media 2023. https://americanradioworks.publicradio.org/features/blackspeech/mx.html (13.11.2023)
60	Quote by George Carlin: "The reason they call it the American Dream …" In: Kelly Carlin: "George Carlin: Every American Dreams." Washington, DC: National Portrait Gallery. https://npg.si.edu/blog/george-carlin-every-american-dreams (13.11.2023)
60	Quote from Michelle Obama: Speech at the Democratic National Convention in Charlotte, N.C. on September 4, 2012. Washington, D.C.: National Public Radio (NPR) 2023. https://www.npr.org/2012/09/04/160578836/transcript-michelle-obamas-convention-speech (13.11.2023)
61	Quotes from Martin Luther King Jr.: "I Have a Dream." Speech delivered during the March on Washington for Jobs and Freedom on August 28, 1963. Washington, D.C.: National Public Radio (NPR) 2023. https://www.npr.org/2010/01/18/122701268/i-have-a-dream-speech-in-its-entirety (13.11.2023)
61	Jeannette L. Nolen: "Equality." In: *Britannica*. Chicago, IL: Encyclopædia Britannica, Inc. 2023. https://www.britannica.com/topic/equality-human-rights (13.11.2023)
61 f.	Catherine Hoffmann: „Die Illusion vom amerikanischen Traum." In: *Süddeutsche Zeitung*, 27.01.2017. https://www.sueddeutsche.de/wirtschaft/soziale-gerechtigkeit-die-illusion-vom-amerikanischen-traum-1.3350589 (13.11.2023)
63	Quote from Carmela Ciuraru: "New Books by Imbolo Mbue, Krys Lee, Gonzalo Torné and Lisa McInerney." In: *The New York Times*, 28.08.2016. https://www.nytimes.com/2016/08/29/books/new-books-by-imbolo-mbue-krys-lee-gonzalo-torne-and-lisa-mcinerney.html?_r=0 (13.11.2023)
65 ff.	Andrew Ross Sorkin: "From Trump to Trade, the Financial Crisis Still Resonates 10 Years Later." In: *The New York Times*, 10.09.2018. From The New York Times. © 2024 The New York Times Company. All rights reserved. Used under license. https://www.nytimes.com/2018/09/10/business/dealbook/financial-crisis-trump.html (09.11.2023)
68 f.	Barack Obama: "The American Promise." Address Accepting the Presidential Nomination at the Democratic National Convention in Denver on August 28, 2008. In: Gerhard Peters and John T. Woolley. The American

Copyrights

	Presidency Project. Santa Barbara: University of California, Santa Barbara. https://www.presidency.ucsb.edu/documents/address-accepting-the-presidential-nomination-the-democratic-national-convention-denver (14.11.2023)
70	Brian Duignan: "January 6 U.S. Capitol attack." In: *Britannica*. Chicago, IL: Encyclopædia Britannica, Inc. 2023. https://www.britannica.com/event/January-6-U-S-Capitol-attack (14.11.2023)
70	Quote from Lucia Grave: "America's Trump nightmare has arrived." In: *The Guardian*, 04.05.2016. https://www.theguardian.com/commentisfree/2016/may/03/americas-trump-nightmare-has-arrived (14.11.2023)
74	Jessie Thompson: "Jasmine Lee-Jones interview: I want people to come to the theatre like they watch Netflix." In: *The Standard*, 17.06.2021. © Evening Standard 2024. https://www.standard.co.uk/culture/theatre/jasmine-lee-jones-seven-methods-of-killing-kylie-jenner-royal-court-london-b940966.html (02.04.2022)
75–96	Quotes from Jasmine Lee-Jones: *seven methods of killing kylie jenner*. London/New York/Dublin: Methuen Drama/Bloomsbury Publishing Plc 2021.
78	Quote from Jasmine Lee-Jones: *seven methods of killing kylie jenner*. London: Oberon Books/Bloomsbury Publishing Plc 2019, p. 1.
85 f.	Yvette Brazier: "What is body image?" In: Robin Hough (ed.): *Medical News Today*, 25.05.2023. Brighton: Healthline Media UK Ltd. 2024. https://www.medicalnewstoday.com/articles/249190#definition (07.02.2024)
86	Quote by Jasmine Lee-Jones: "I keep a scrapbook with pictures …" In: Amel Mukhtar: "Meet The 20-Year-Old Playwright Behind The Provocative Drama 'Seven Methods Of Killing Kylie Jenner'." In: *British Vogue*, 04.07.2019. https://www.vogue.co.uk/article/jasmine-lee-jones-seven-methods-of-killing-kylie-jenner-interview (04.04.2022)
88	Kate Wyver: "Seven Methods of Killing Kylie Jenner review – sharp, furious and funny." In: *The Guardian*, 23.06.2021. Copyright Guardian News & Media Ltd 2024. https://www.theguardian.com/stage/2021/jun/23/seven-methods-of-killing-kylie-jenner-review-royal-court (04.04.2022)
88	Natasher Beecher: "seven methods of killing kylie jenner review: 'This is one of the best plays I've ever seen'." In: Sophia A Jackson (ed.): *Afridiziak Theatre News*, 23.06.2021. http://www.afridiziak.com/reviews/seven-methods-of-killing-kylie-jenner/ (04.04.2022)
89	Christopher B. Balme: "Theatre and media." In: *The Cambridge Introduction to Theatre Studies*. Cambridge: Cambridge University Press 2008, p. 195. https://www.cambridge.org/core/books/abs/cambridge-introduction-to-theatre-studies/theatre-and-media/4829F5F357C29C2E9D28407C0818CC6A (29.01.2024)
92 f.	„Anfeindungen gegen Sarah-Lee Heinrich – Medienexpertin: Koordinierte Twitter-Kampagnen als Methode." Tajana Graovac im Gespräch mit Sebastian Wellendorf. Köln: Deutschlandfunk/Deutschlandradio, 13.10.2021. https://www.deutschlandfunk.de/anfeindungen-gegen-sarah-lee-heinrich-medienexpertin.2907.de.html?dram:article_id=504219 (04.04.2022)
94	"Michelle Obama: 'I'm no angry black woman'." London: BBC, 11.01.2012. https://www.bbc.com/news/world-us-canada-16515834 (23.05.2022)
95 f.	Ritu Prasad: "Serena Williams and the trope of the 'angry black woman'." London: BBC, 11.09.2018. https://www.bbc.com/news/world-us-canada-45476500 (04.04.2022)
100–154	Extracts from William Shakespeare: *A Midsummer Night's Dream* (ca. 1595/1596).
134	The Bible: 1 Corinthians 2 – New International Version (NIV). Palmer Lake, CO: Biblica 2011–2023. https://www.biblica.com/bible/niv/1-corinthians/2/ (09.03.2023)
145	Roger Ebert: "William Shakespeare's A Midsummer Night's Dream." Ebert Digital LLC, 14.05.1999. https://www.rogerebert.com/reviews/william-shakespeares-a-midsummer-nights-dream-1999 (10.02.2023)
147	Gene Brown: "Difference Between Conformity and Individuality." In: *Difference Between*, 17.09.2021. http://www.differencebetween.net/miscellaneous/difference-between-conformity-and-individuality/ (31.01.2024)
148 f.	Renee Goyeneche: "Want To Fit In Or Stand Out? The Conformity Paradox." In: *Forbes*, 02.06.2022. https://www.forbes.com/sites/womensmedia/2022/06/02/want-to-fit-in-or-stand-out-the-conformity-paradox/ (05.02.2024)
153	Kim Ballard: "Daughters in Shakespeare: dreams, duty and defiance." London: British Library Board, 15.03.2016. https://www.bl.uk/shakespeare/articles/daughters-in-shakespeare-dreams-duty-and-defiance (13.02.2023)
153	Clare McManus: "Shakespeare and gender: the 'woman's part'." London: British Library Board, 15.03.2016. https://www.bl.uk/shakespeare/articles/shakespeare-and-gender-the-womans-part (13.02.2023)

BILDQUELLEN

|Alamy Stock Photo, Abingdon/Oxfordshire: LWM/Art 6.1; travellinglight Titel. |Alamy Stock Photo (RMB), Abingdon/Oxfordshire: GL Archive 151.1; public domain sourced / access rights from The Picture Art Collection 107.1. |Alpen-Kühne, Svenja, Hatten: 93.1. |Andertoons, Schaumburg: 146.2. |CartoonStock.com, Bath: Cordell, Tim 39.2; Jones, Taylor 70.2; Madden, Chris 146.1; Nease, Steve 72.2; Obradovic, Slobodan 89.1; Talimonov, Alexei 89.2; Weyant, Christopher 70.1. |fotolia.com, New York: Föger, Reinhold 42.1. |Imago Editorial, Berlin: Everett Collection/Cercone, Dee 75.1; ZUMA Press/Sheehan, Beowulf 62.1. |iStockphoto.com, Calgary: PeterSnow 41.1; vichinterlang 69.1. |mauritius images GmbH, Mittenwald: Alamy Stock Photos / SOPA Images 74.1. |Penguin Random House LLC, New York: 46.1. |Pew Research Center, Washington: 38.1. |Picture-Alliance GmbH, Frankfurt a.M.: dpa/Nietfeld, Kay 92.2. |Royal Shakespeare Company, Warwickshire: Photo by Angus McBean © RSC 121.1; Photo by Ellie Kurttz © RSC 121.3; Photo by John Haynes © RSC 121.2. |Shutterstock.com, New York: 4 PM production 55.2; Andrey_Popov 65.1; Coman, Lucian 32.1; etorres 45.1; Everett Collection 73.1; fizkes 38.5; Frog, Jack 43.1; Gordic, Dragana 38.2; Kang, Hyejin 38.4; lev radin 69.4, 72.3; mikeledray 69.2; Pressmaster 55.1; Rudy, George 38.3; Stocksnapper 98.1; Sykes, Steve 69.3; Tverdokhlib 70.3; Wong, Debby 94.1. |Shutterstock.com (RM), New York: 20th Century Fox/Kobal 143.2; Mario Tursi/20th Century Fox/Kobal 143.1, 143.3, 143.4, 143.5, 143.6, 145.1; Muir, Alastair 97.1. |stock.adobe.com, Dublin: DigiClack 52.2, 52.3; fotohansel 39.1, 48.1, 48.2, 52.1; goldpix 92.1; karandaev 47.2; madiwaso 80.1, 80.2; olinchuk 49.1, 49.2; Smileus 42.2; TripleP Studio 47.1. |Wiener Staatsoper, Wien: Michael Pöhn 97.2, 97.3, 97.4. |Zyglis, Adam, Buffalo: 72.1.